Educating Across Borders

MARÍA TERESA DE LA PIEDRA,
BLANCA ARAUJO, AND
ALBERTO ESQUINCA
Foreword by Concha Delgado Gaitan

Educating
Across Borders

The Case of a Dual Language Program
on the U.S.-Mexico Border

THE UNIVERSITY OF
ARIZONA PRESS
TUCSON

The University of Arizona Press
www.uapress.arizona.edu

ISBN-13: 978-0-8165-3847-8 (paper)

Cover design by Lisa Force
Cover photo by Samat K. Jain

Publication of this book made possible in part by funding from the University of Texas at El Paso
Department of Teacher Education, and by the proceeds of a permanent endowment created with the
assistance of a Challenge Grant from the National Endowment for the Humanities, a federal agency.

Library of Congress Cataloging-in-Publication Data are available at the Library of Congress.

Printed in the United States of America
♾ This paper meets the requirements of ANSI/NISO Z39.48-1992 (Permanence of Paper).

Contents

Foreword

DAILY NEWS REPORTS about immigrants crossing the U.S.-Mexico border project an image of a narrow territory between the two countries, leaving most people ignorant about the lives of the people that live on both sides of that strip of land called the border.

Gloria Anzaldúa writes that "To live in the Borderlands means you / are neither *hispana india negra española* / *ni gabacha, eres mestiza, mulata*, half-breed / caught in the crossfire between camps / while carrying all five races on your back / not knowing which side to turn to, run from . . . To survive the Borderlands / you must live *sin fronteras* / be a crossroads."* The *transfronterizx* construct, in this book, illustrates how the languages and ethnicities merge through daily interactions across the U.S.-Mexico border.

Borders are created and defined by those who stand to benefit most by the demarcations. A case in point is the immigration debate, which divides us by political and legal borders. These challenging and engaging times also provoke us to cross the barriers of culture and consciousness. We assume positions as "us" and "the other" while we find comfort in the fact that voiceless communities transact and experience their value.

---

* Anzaldúa, Gloria. 1999. *Borderlands / La Frontera: The New Mestiza*. San Francisco: Aunte Lute, 194–95.

Transfronterizx stories of students, teachers, and school leaders in the Border Elementary School (BES) bring to light insightful issues of daily life on the border. The authors utilize dual language practices and funds of knowledge tools to theorize on the linguistic portrait created by border-crossing.

The uniqueness of this book is that the linguistic and cultural transfronterizx community commonly known as the border exists against the backdrop of a mostly bilingual militarized El Paso border. Nearly twenty thousand agents patrol the seven hundred miles of the border by air surveillance and other electronics. And yet life moves along day after day. Every morning one can awaken to traffic reports on the three main bridges that connect El Paso with Ciudad Juárez. Businesspeople cross these bridges; they are engaged in international commerce. Thousands of transfronterizx students also cross every morning; among them are students such as Gabriela and her classmates.

During a fifth grade history assignment, the teacher gave the class roles to play depicting a period of history known as the Great Famine. Gabriela and her team brought their home practices to school. Students included a remote control during the multimodal role-play so that they could forward, rewind, pause, and repeat small segments in their presentation. This part of their performance was based on their home practice of reading Mexican newspaper comics at home. The digital transfronterizx literacies were accompanied by a discourse of words and idioms in Spanish with accents in English, which they learned from the English television program *Dora the Explorer*.

By constructing new discourse norms in a shared space in this specific historical point in time, we learn the importance of the language of transfronterizx students as well as the relationship between the children and their teachers.

Educating Across Borders is reminiscent of Ana Celia Zentella's ethnography of the social and linguistic realities of New York Rican students and their mastery of their bilingualism and multidialectal repertoire. These linguistic abilities enable them to navigate their family networks and their antagonistic cultural environment outside the home.

I worked closely with de la Piedra, Araujo, and Esquinca at the University of Texas, El Paso, in their early careers. During that period, I became aware of their strong commitment and scholarship applied to issues in the schools. They were equally dedicated to the communities that are home to the families of the transfronterizx students. Throughout the book, we follow the authors' hearts into the dual language worlds that transfronterizx students embrace. Not only are the authors theoretically engaged with the concept of transfronterizx, but they are also embedded in the communities of the young people whose stories help us to understand the linguistic dynamics of the students who reside in the U.S.-Mexico region that most people know as "the border."

Concha Delgado Gaitan

Acknowledgments

WE FEEL TRULY GRATEFUL for the opportunity to write this book about the language and literacy practices on the U.S.-Mexico border from this beautiful desert we call home.

We would like to thank the teachers and leaders of Border Elementary School (BES), who welcomed us with openness, interest, and *cariño*. Ms. Ornelas, in particular, was not only an inspiring participant in our study, but a colleague who thought with us about language, knowledge, and learning. *A los chicos de 4to, 5to, y 6to grado del programa dual, mil gracias por darnos sus sonrisas, su calidez, y su tiempo.* It was humbling to learn about your lives and your resilience.

We wish to thank Concha Delgado Gaitan for her friendship and mentorship. She worked with the three of us when we started as assistant professors at the University of Texas at El Paso. Her *consejo* helped us grow as Latinx scholars. It is a great honor to have her words as the foreword to our work.

We would like to thank colleagues who have read parts of this book as members of our writing group and colleagues: Erika Mein, Aurolyn Luykx, Zulma Méndez, Amy Bach, and Katherine Mortimer. We are also grateful to our students: Mayra Ortiz Galarza, Diana Camberos, and Betina Valdez. *También agradecemos a Ricardo Vásquez por ayudarnos con la edición del texto en español.* Finally, we are grateful to the blind reviewers for valuable insights that allowed us to improve our work.

Gracias a mis co-autores, colegas y amigos, Blanca y Alberto, con quienes hemos compartido los últimos ocho años en este proyecto colectivo, y los últimos dos de intenso trabajo de escritura. Blanquita, tu cariño y disposición fueron muy importantes en este proceso, y Alberto, tus comentarios y preguntas nos ayudaron a pensar los datos desde distintas perspectivas.

A mis padres, Teresa Schroth y Alberto de la Piedra, gracias por su apoyo y amor constante. ¡Gracias por creer en mí y apoyar mi sueño de ser antropóloga aun cuando muchos me trataban de convencer de dejarlo! Gracias por su paciencia y enseñanzas, siempre.

A mi esposa Verónica Gallegos, gracias por tu compañía y por leer varios borradores de este y otros proyectos. Gracias por entender mis ausencias para terminar este primer libro y siempre estar dispuesta a acompañarme para descansar después de largas horas de trabajo.

A mis dos chiquitos, que ya no lo son más, Nicolás Hernández y Lucía Hernández, gracias por su paciencia y comprensión cuando los dejé de lado por "el tenure" y, recientemente, por "el libro." A Nicolás, gracias por editar el libro, porque todavía necesito ayuda con el inglés y tú lo escribes con mucha facilidad. A Lucía, gracias por hacerme tecitos cuando no me sentía bien pero igual tenía que trabajar.

I am genuinely grateful to be surrounded by generous friends, family, and colleagues.

—*María Teresa (Mayte) de la Piedra*

My extreme gratitude to all the students and teachers at BES who welcomed us in their school.

To all my friends and *colegas* who provided feedback and insight.

A mi familia, en especial en memoria de mi papá, quien también fue transfronterizo.

—*Blanca Araujo*

A los que cambian muros por puentes
   A los estudiantes que cruzan todo tipo de puentes para llegar a estudiar
   A las maestras que crean puentes de entendimiento para sus estudiantes
   A todos las amigas y amigos que alguna vez me acompañaron en el cruce
   A mi madre, que me enseñó a leer (en) el Puente Libre

                                                    —Alberto Esquinca

Educating Across Borders

Introduction

THIS BOOK FOCUSES ON a three-year ethnographic study of *transfronterizx* (border-crossing) students* conducted by a team of researchers in a dual language (DL) program at Border Elementary School (BES) on the U.S.-Mexico border. We are glad we can share the students', teachers', and administrators' stories as transfronterizxs and analyze how these educational agents experienced daily border-crossings and life on the border in general. The ethnography conducted responds to a broad question: "What tools do transnational students use to navigate U.S. schools?" This inquiry brings new insight into our specific research interests. In this book, we center on language practices, as well as the particular kinds of knowledge that transfronterizx students used as learning resources to navigate the DL program at BES. This school was located just a few minutes from the river that forms the border between the United States and Mexico. This river is called the

---

*The term *transfronterizo* has been previously used by academics (Relaño Pastor 2007; Zentella 2009) and the media, such as BBC (Sparrow 2015), the *Chronicle* (Viren 2007), and NPR (McGee 2015). Recently, Tatyana Kleyn has used the term in her work with returnees to Mexico (Kleyn 2015; Donnellon et al. 2016). We use the gender-neutral term *transfronterizx*. However, students did not call themselves transfronterizxs; they identified as Mexican.

Rio Grande in the United States and known as the Río Bravo in Mexico. Transfronterizx students enrolled in BES could, and often did, walk just a few blocks and cross the bridge between these two nations.

The two-thousand-mile line that divides the United States and Mexico is the place where the Global North and South meet. El Paso and Ciudad Juárez are considered sister cities by virtue of the social, cultural, economic, and ecological interdependence tying both cities. In total, there are about 2.5 million residents in the Ciudad Juárez / El Paso border region. Ciudad Juárez, Chihuahua, is currently considered one of the five most dangerous and militarized cities in Mexico. Furthermore, Ciudad Juárez was considered the most dangerous city in the world in 2008 because of the high levels of murders related to organized crime and femicide. Ironically, the city of El Paso—with close to one million inhabitants—is considered one of the safest and least violent cities in the United States. All this occurred in the context of the drug war between cartels that skyrocketed between 2008 and 2015. El Paso has its share of the militarization of the border, with twenty thousand patrol agents, frequent arrests and deportation of "undocumented immigrants," and electronic and air surveillance practices (Heyman 2015). El Muro de la Vergüenza (the Wall of Shame), spanning seven hundred miles, is part of the growing surveillance practices deployed to stop Mexican nationals from crossing this border.

Context influences not only the research we conduct but also who we are as researchers. Our context is particular. We live on the U.S. side of this border, in "el otro lado." Nonetheless, we see, breathe, and listen to Ciudad Juárez. We see Juárez from our office windows and our backyards. We smell the Mexican food when we walk our streets, in our homes and restaurants. Stores smell of Fabuloso while the clothes of our students smell like Suavitel. We hear and speak the Spanish language every day in a great variety of contexts, including, of course, the *corridos* (Mexican folk ballads), *rancheras* (Mexican folk songs), and *baladas* (ballads) that fill the air and our hearts in stores, in cars, and on the streets. The violence that occurred during the last decade touched us in many ways, as did the transfronterizx students in these pages. This context colors our ethnographic work.

The border holds special places in our hearts and lives. The three authors are transfronterizxs in different ways; our positionalities explain our interests in the topic of transfronterizx education, our ways of approaching the research, and the ways the research participants related to us. In many ways, we were insiders and shared many of the experiences of the transfronterizx students, like our bilingualism and biliteracy, our experiences as members of a minoritized group, and our experience of immigration (de la Piedra and Esquinca) and belonging to a working-class family (Araujo). However, we were also outsiders, who tried to learn from these experiences. Our privileges as college professors who had an office in *el otro lado* (the other side), who moved comfortably in the English-dominated world of academia and the university, and who had the privilege of deciding if and when we wanted to cross the border, describe some of the crucial differences between our transfronterizx experience and that of the research participants.

When we started our fieldwork in 2009, we set out to understand the lives of transfronterizx students who were immigrating by the thousands in the unique linguistic and cultural landscape of the border.[†] We observed the flows of students and the different ways schools met these students, sometimes with welcoming *abrazos* (hugs), but mostly with misunderstanding, discrimination, and frustration. Thus, we decided to focus on a school that had sizable numbers of transfronterizxs, that was close to one of the crossing points ("el puente," or "the bridge"), and that offered DL education. We wondered if the DL program would be a learning context where transfronterizx students could use their language and funds of knowledge for academic purposes.

Previous studies document that transnational students and their experiences are mostly invisible in U.S. schools (Cline and Necochea 2006; Conteh and Riasat 2014; Gallo and Link 2015; Mangual, Suh, and Byrnes 2015), as well as in schools in other countries, in particular in Mexican schools (Franco 2014; Hamann, Zúñiga, and García 2008; Leco 2006; Sánchez and Zúñiga 2010; Zúñiga 2013). Although our research focuses on one kind

---

[†]A flow of Mexican families went in the opposite direction from most of the country's experience at that time to El Paso, Texas, when one million Mexicans returned from the United States to Mexico from 2009 to 2014. See the documentary *Una vida, dos países, or Children and Youth (Back) in Mexico* (Donnellon et al. 2016) at http://www.unavidathefilm.com.

of transnational experience, the transnational experience on the El Paso–Ciudad Juárez border, we draw from the prior literature of transnationalism and education, which provides background about the lives and schooling of transnationals in general. The students in this ethnographic study navigate two countries, two languages, and two homes on a weekly and sometimes daily basis. By focusing on *transfronterizxs*, we highlight the intensity of the border-crossings that take place along the geographical and cultural border that both unites and divides the United States and Mexico.

An invisible line that exists on a map with tangible implications for the lives that take place around it, *la frontera* (the border) is a fascinating context in which to research issues related to Spanish-English biliteracy and multilingualism. The transfronterizx experience allows us to highlight the complexities of language, literacy, and identity on the border, while complicating binaries such as global and local, micro and macro, and sending and host community. In this way, we expand the enterprise initiated by scholars of transnationalism and education (Hamann, Zuñiga, and García 2008; Orellana et al. 2001; Sánchez 2007). This ethnography contributes to this emerging and timely research literature by documenting and analyzing the practices that transfronterizx students engage in which are a result of the relationships they keep on both sides of the border, through their intense daily contacts. The transfronterizx experience itself questions binaries, as transfronterizxs' lives themselves are in constant movement, back and forth.

The DL program at the research site allowed exciting and productive border-crossings concerning knowledge, language, and literacy practices. Thus, with this book we also contribute to the field of DL education. In general, researchers have demonstrated higher academic and linguistic gains for emergent bilinguals who attend one- and two-way immersion programs rather than other program models, such as the transitional bilingual education model or English-only (Lindholm-Leary and Genesee 2014; Thomas and Collier 2002). This is true for both native English speakers and native speakers of another language. In particular, research shows that two-way immersion programs provide a context where students have the opportunity to learn each other's languages and literacy practices while building positive intergroup social relationships (Christian 1994; de Jong and Howard 2009).

Nevertheless, there are also critical perspectives on DL programs which caution us that they may also serve to reinforce the privileges of native English speakers (Valdés 1997), as well as those who enjoy white racial privilege and wealth (Valdez, Freire, and Delavan 2016). These programs might also, paradoxically, foment negative perceptions of minority languages (Durán and Palmer 2013). Thus, DL programs may also be a space of reproduction of privilege for the already privileged and of discrimination for emergent bilinguals.[‡] For example, in her article about dual immersion programs, Valdés (1997) offers us a cautionary perspective on the low quality of native language instruction, the inequalities of English and Spanish speakers in these programs, and the reproduction of power relationships between the two languages and those who speak them. In particular, Valdés refers to the unequal power relations among the two main groups of students in the DL immersion program she studied: middle-class Euro-American students and low-income Mexican origin students. However, we argue that the program we studied—which included both one-way and two-way DL programs—is not one that reproduces the privilege of Anglo-Americans, the middle class, or English speakers.[§] In this program, almost 100 percent of students were Mexican or Mexican-Americans, and the community served low-income families. Thus, the DL program described here includes "the disempowered socioeconomic groups" (Hossain and Pratt 2008, 69) within the Spanish-speaker language group in the United States. Besides, the majority of English-dominant students were Mexican-American students raised in homes where adult family members spoke Spanish or both languages.

More recently, some studies have provided details on the productive uses of language, literacy, and cultural practices in DL programs (de Jong 2016;

[‡]We use the term "emergent bilingual" (García 2009) rather than other terms, such as "English Language Learners" or "English Learners," to avoid defining emergent bilinguals solely by their relationship to English.

[§]Dual language programs vary by the languages spoken and the amount of instructional time in each language. One-way DL programs serve language minority students while two-way DL programs combine students who are learning English and students who are learning another language. The program we studied was a 90–10 DL model, rather than a 50–50 DL model, where students start in the lower grades with 90 percent of instructional time in the non-English language.

Henderson and Palmer 2015; Poza 2016; Sayer 2013). These studies question the "ideal" model of DL programs as spaces where two languages are equally distributed over time and where the program population is characterized by an equally "ideal" distribution of the target population of fifty-fifty. These studies question these ideals by documenting the actual bilingual proficiencies and hybrid language practices in the classrooms. Findings of the research presented in this book contribute to the literature on hybridity since it questions artificially created and neat language distributions, and it documents the language and literacy practices of transfronterizxs, a constantly mobile population that crosses national (and other) borders. In a world dominated by monoglossic notions that privilege English over any different language, as well as ethnocentrism that privileges mainstream practices over practices of minoritized groups, documenting rich transfronterizx language and literacy practices is crucial to counter entrenched deficit perspectives about transfronterizx and other transnational students. This study contributes to developing a theory to understand the physical and metaphorical border-crossings of linguistic and ethnic minoritized students in U.S. schools.

We base our analyses on extensive ethnographic research, during which we collected data through participant observation in classrooms and other school settings, focus group interviews with transfronterizx students, and individual interviews with teachers, administrators, and staff members. Thus, first and foremost, this book is informed by the voices of the transfronterizx students that talked to us and shared their views and experiences, as well as the voices of the teachers (Ms. Ornelas, in particular) and administrators. Our perspectives as transfronterizxs and residents of this border also inform this book, as well as our experiences as teacher educators and researchers of language and literacy practices in Mexican immigrant communities.

Chapter 1 introduces relevant literature and critical concepts for understanding the transfronterizx experience. We draw on research on immigration and education, transnationalism, and transnational students to situate the broader context of transfronterizxs in schools. Also, we discuss theoretical constructs that allow us to understand transfronterizxs, such as simultaneity (Levitt and Glick Schiller 2004), border thinking/gnosis (Mignolo 2000), and border theory (Anzaldúa 1999; Vila 2000). In this chapter, we start to develop the most significant theoretical frameworks we used to make sense of the findings of this ethnography.

Chapter 2 continues the discussion of relevant literature and theoretical frameworks. Here we discuss concepts key to understanding the transfronterizx experience with language, literacy, and identity in academic settings. We introduce sociocultural perspectives on language and literacy studies, including the New Literacy Studies (Barton and Hamilton 2005; Gee 2000; Kalman and Street 2013; Street 1984), the notions of recontextualization and translanguaging practices (García 2009), and research in DL programs.

Chapter 3 introduces the researchers and the research setting. It starts with the introduction of the researchers and our positionalities as primary instruments of this ethnography. Then we introduce the El Paso–Ciudad Juárez border as the context of this study, as well as crucial information about the social, cultural, and linguistic context. We also include descriptions of the school, the DL program, and the participants.

In chapter 4, we present an in-depth description of the transfronterizx experiences and stories. The U.S.-Mexico border region is a unique context in which different cultures and languages blend. Transfronterizxs' lives take place in two countries and two languages. Maintaining constant contact with both sides of the border influences the experiences and identities of transfronterizxs. The purpose of this chapter is to present the stories of the transfronterizx experience in the school community: principals, teachers, and families. Through these narratives, we analyze the discourses that construct the transfronterizx experience and context in which the practices discussed in the subsequent chapters will be situated.

Chapter 5 addresses the transfronterizx literacies. Research on transnational literacies has focused on youth who live in one country and communicate using digital literacies across national boundaries. This chapter describes the literacies that these transfronterizx youth acquire as border-crossers. Our focus is on the print and digital literacies learned outside of the classroom and how the students are using these in academic settings.

Chapter 6 continues with the topic of transfronterizx literacies; however, in this section, we emphasize how students used transfronterizx literacies for academic purposes, particularly in the language arts classroom. We illustrate how transfronterizx texts and experiences are used for academic purposes, in particular in the context of learning narrative writing. We present the case of one transfronterizx teacher who successfully facilitated literacies crossing many borders. Drawing on the continua of biliteracy model and the New Literacy Studies perspective, we show the recontextualization of texts and practices. These processes help us understand biliteracy development in this border area, which is both global and local.

Chapter 7 analyzes meaning-making practices in a fourth grade two-way dual language classroom. We show how emergent bilingual learners and their teacher participate in activities that mediate understanding of science content knowledge. The teacher creates a borderland space in which the full repertoire of students' languages, including translanguaging, is recognized and validated. We illustrate how the teacher guides students to use strategies and meaning-making tools in both languages to construct meanings of the science content. We also demonstrate how she scaffolds students' language development, develops students' higher-order thinking, and involves all students in constructing understanding.

Among the tools recent immigrant students used to navigate U.S. schools, we found multimodal literacies in two languages, Spanish and English. In chapter 8, drawing from literature on multimodality (Dicks et al. 2011; Gutiérrez et al. 2011) and recent research on translanguaging practices (García 2009), we analyze multimodal literacy events in this DL program that serves transfronterizxs. In this context, one immigrant teacher's ideas about how to best teach literacy to emergent bilinguals and immigrant students aided her in creating an authentic learning environment. We contend that the everyday construction of "safe learning spaces" in DL classrooms through multimodal and translanguaging practices become possibilities for social change. These findings contribute to the growing conversation on how multimodal literacies challenge traditional views of literacy as isolated skills and construct safe spaces for learning.

Chapter 9 discusses how young transfronterizx students bring their funds of knowledge (González, Moll, and Amanti 2005) to the classroom and use them in relevant ways to understand the content. We argue that developing awareness of how students use transfronterizx knowledge in schools can provide teachers and researchers of students in other contexts with a better, more complex understanding of the resources students bring to school to recognize ways in which to capitalize on these mobile resources for relevant educational experiences. In this chapter, we also reflect on the community cultural wealth (Yosso 2005) of transfronterizx students.

Finally, we address the conclusions and implications for pedagogical practice. Results of this research challenge traditional views of language and literacy as isolated skills and allow us to theorize the transfronterizx experience in academic settings. We will summarize findings presented throughout the book. This chapter will also have the objective of synthesizing main findings concerning pedagogical practices with emergent bilinguals.

1

Theoretical Frameworks to Understand the Transfronterizx Experience

THE PURPOSE OF THIS CHAPTER is to examine relevant literature and concepts to understand the transfronterizx experience with a particular emphasis on language, literacy, and identity in academic settings. The critical perspective of community cultural wealth (Yosso 2005) serves as the broader theoretical framework that includes the diverse forms of capital that students bring with them to school. Community cultural wealth is our starting point, as we believe the transfronterizx practices we describe here are part of the rich repertoires of practice that students have at their disposal to act in the diverse contexts they traverse. In order to analyze language use and literacies among transfronterizxs, we review literature on transnationalism and transnational students (Hamann, Zuñiga, and García 2008; Orellana et al. 2001; Sánchez 2007), border theory, border thinking, and border epistemologies (Anzaldúa 1999; Mignolo 2000; Vila 2000). These complementary bodies of literature provided the background for the study and the theoretical constructs that allowed us to analyze the unique, fluid, and complex experiences of transfronterizxs in a DL immersion program. This chapter and the next will briefly introduce related literature and theoretical frameworks; in subsequent chapters we will continue the description of these frameworks as they pertain to each topic developed in the respective chapter.

Community Cultural Wealth and Transfronterizx Capital

Community cultural wealth refers to the unique forms of cultural capital, resources, and assets of students of color (Villalpando and Solórzano 2005). Yosso (2005) defines community cultural wealth as the array of knowledge, skills, abilities, and contacts possessed by marginalized groups that usually are not recognized and acknowledged in schools. This perspective critiques deficit thinking and deficit structures that disadvantage communities and people of color (Contreras 2009; Jain 2010; Oropeza, Varghese, and Kanno 2010; Pérez Huber 2009; Rincón 2009; Yosso 2005). There are six categories of capital within the community cultural wealth framework. The different categories of capital utilized by communities of color to survive and resist oppression are navigational, social, resistant, linguistic, aspirational, and familial.

Navigational capital is the ability to make it through social situations or move through "institutions not created with communities of color in mind" (Yosso 2005, 80). Examples include navigating through hostile universities or other institutional structures permeated by racism, such as judicial systems, healthcare facilities, and the job market. This form of capital acknowledges individual agency even within constraining situations. Social capital comprises the networks, community resources, and people that can provide support to navigate through institutions. Social capital is also utilized to get employment, health care, immigration assistance, and education. We saw both forms of capital in our study when families relied on each other to get jobs and housing.

Resistant capital is the resistance to subordination by people of color. It includes legacies of communities that have resisted racism, capitalism, and other forms of subordination and forms of oppression. Resistant capital comprises various types of oppositional behavior, challenging the status quo, and transforming oppressive structures.

Linguistic capital is the "intellectual and social skills attained through communicating in more than one language and/or style" (Yosso 2005, 78). Linguistic capital values the communication and language skills that students of color bring to school. It includes storytelling, *cuentos* (stories), *dichos* (sayings), and the ability to communicate through art, music, and poetry. Linguistic capital also includes drawing on different language registers and styles and translating for parents. In this study, students were using linguistic capital in many ways, such as translating poetry from Spanish into English and writing music lyrics.

Aspirational capital is the "ability to maintain hopes and dreams for the future even in the face of barriers. This includes high aspirations of families for their children, resiliency through dreaming of possibilities beyond present conditions, and the nurturing of a culture of possibility" (Yosso 2005, 77). Aspirational capital is encouragement to do all the things that some members of the family and community never had the opportunity to do. In the case of the transfronterizx students, families did whatever was necessary for them to be safe and to continue in school.

Familial capital is knowledge nurtured among *familia* (family). This form of capital includes a deep commitment and healthy connection to a community and to the extended family which may consist of *abuelos* (grandparents), amigos (friends), *tíos* (aunts and uncles), *primos* (cousins), and compadres.*
In this study, these networks developed in both nations, Mexico and the United States. Familial capital can be fostered through many social events, settings, and models, such as caring, coping, and providing. Familial capital includes family lessons that help shape one emotionally and give moral guidance (Yosso 2006). Familial capital is being committed and maintaining healthy connections to the community. This commitment allows people to realize that they are not alone in situations. During our study, we experienced families sending their children to live in El Paso with relatives to keep them safe from the violence in Juárez. Families in El Paso were making sure the children were safe and had a place to stay. These acts demonstrate how extended families were committed to children being and feeling safe. As presented in chapter 4, transfronterizx children also committed to helping parents to "arreglar" (arrange or fix) their immigration status.

These forms of capital build on one another as cultural wealth, are strongly related, and overlap. Through an analysis of the data, it was evident that the participants in our study demonstrated the use of several forms of

---

* Although there is no exact translation, the term "compadres" in this context refers to close friends—almost family—who are bonded by a child's baptism.

capital in their experiences with language, literacy, and school. When these kinds of capital were related to crossing borders, both physical as well as metaphorical borders, we called it transfronterizx capital.

Transnationalism and Transnational Practices from Below

The term transnationalism has been used in different fields, with particular emphasis on the flows of capital, goods, services, and labor that transcends national boundaries. Literature about the economics of labor migration, remittances, transnational corporations, and international trade emphasizes the cross-border flows of capital and goods. Transnationalism also implies the movement of people across national borders. "Transnationalism involves individuals, their networks of social relations, their communities, and broader institutionalized structures such as local and national governments" (Portes, Guarnizo, and Landolt 1999, 220).

Research on transnationalism initially focused on international enterprises, systems, organizations, and associations; however, studies paid less attention to the private sphere (Sánchez and Machado-Casas 2009) of transnationalism and its everyday practices, which are also manifestations of globalization. Transnational practices are defined as "the political, economic, social, and cultural processes occurring beyond the borders of a particular state, including actors that are not states but that are influenced by the policies and institutional arrangements associated with states" (Levitt 2001, 202). These everyday transnational practices "from below" (Smith and Guarnizo 1998)—including language and literacy practices such as the ones described here—were a response to the global institutional contexts of transnationalism imposed by governmental policies and "dependent capitalism fostered on weaker countries" (Portes, Guarnizo, and Landolt 1999, 220).

Transnational practices "from below" are both local and global, in that they are local responses to political and economic policies with global impacts beyond the local community. Practices from below are tied to social relationships and issues of power and become important tools to survive and resist oppression. Portes, Guarnizo, and Landolt (1999) noted the need to engage in research that understood the reaction of everyday transnationals to these policies and their larger geopolitical, economic, and social contexts: "These activities commonly developed in reaction to governmental policies and to the condition of dependent capitalism fostered on weaker countries, as immigrants and their families sought to circumvent the permanent subordination to which these conditions condemn them" (220). In other words, everyday transnational practices from below are a response to global institutional contexts of transnationalism, which place transnationals in a situation of subordination. Transnationals develop these practices "from below" as survival mechanisms and as a response to situations of marginalization experienced from below. Thus, we posit that transnational practices are part of transnationals' community cultural wealth (Yosso 2005) that is the "array of knowledge, skills, abilities, and contacts possessed and utilized by Communities of Color to survive and resist macro and micro . . . forms of oppression" (Yosso 2005, 77).

The technological advancement in communication and transport technologies of the last decades made transnational practices "from below" (Smith and Guarnizo 1998) or "grassroots" transnationalism possible. These technologies have not only made communications across borders constant and fluid but also have brought new practices tied to these intense communications. In 1999, Portes, Guarnizo, and Landolt described "the ready availability of air transport, long-distance telephone, facsimile communication, and electronic mail" as providing the "technological basis for the emergence of transnationalism on a mass scale" (223). Technologies are space- and time-compressing (Harvey 1990); thus, they are necessary conditions for transnationalism (Portes, Guarnizo, and Landolt 1999). Today, the space- and time-compressing circumstances are even more evident with newer technologies that include chat rooms, games, Skype, and instant messaging. Then the world experiences an even larger transnationalism phenomenon.

Individuals and their social networks and communities have appropriated these tools and engaged in a wide variety of learning activities both in and out of school contexts. Thus, these actions may or may not be institutionalized, but they all involve learning and language use. In this book, we focus on the language and literacy learning tied to transnational activities "from below"—that is, activities that are organized by individual transnational persons. We focus on the movement of people, their practices, "and more abstract items, such as information, advice, care, love, and systems of power" (Sánchez and Machado-Casas 2009) across nations. To understand these practices, like Portes, Guarnizo, and Landolt (1999), we "delimit the concept of transnationalism to occupations and activities that require regular and sustained social contacts over time across national borders for their implementation" (219). Within these activities, language, literacy, and educational practices—the focus of this book—have been understudied (Sánchez and Machado-Casas 2009).

Simultaneity

Within the field of immigration, a close look at the literature of immigrant children during the last decades of the twentieth century reveals a notion of immigrants and immigrant families that saw a linear process in their trajectory, from the "country of origin" to the "host country." This notion assumed that immigrant families moved to the United States and settled, ignoring that most maintained frequent contacts with their countries of origin. During the last couple of decades, there has been a "transnational turn" (Lam and Warriner 2012) in immigration research, which considers these complex lives of immigrants. We follow Henry Trueba's distinction between the concepts of immigrant and transnational:

> Conceptually, the main difference between an immigrant and a transnational person is that the immigrant does not have frequent and intensive contact with his original culture and consequently can eventually lose his home language and culture and assimilate to the mainstream society. A transnational person cannot afford to lose his language and culture because his contact with the home culture is frequent and intensive . . . [and] goes back and forth between the country of origin or residence and another country. (Trueba 2004, 40)

Ethnographic studies with immigrant families offered a critique of these limited views, revealing, for instance, that transnational practices have become a regular part of life (Orellana et al. 2001). These practices are acquired and moved through transnational social networks. Furthermore, "networks are both a medium and an outcome of social practices 'from below' by which transnational migrants, individually and collectively, maintain meaningful social relations that cut across territorial boundaries, link several localities in more than one country, and extend meaningful social action across geographical space" (Smith 1994, 20). Thus, transnational networks and transnational social practices are an intricate part of the daily lives of immigrants. Furthermore, many of these families live in "a state of 'betweenness,' orchestrating their lives transnationally and bifocally" (Smith 1994, 20). Even though we draw from an important body of literature that proposes the term "immigrant" for this literature review, we will use the term "transnational" to include the diverse kinds of migrants who still have contacts, relationships, practices, and other types of interactions with people, businesses, institutions, and places across national boundaries.

In general terms, transnationals are persons who live in and belong to two or more countries at the same time. In their work on simultaneity, Levitt and Glick Schiller (2004) define that notion as living life "that incorporates daily activities, routines, and institutions located both in a destination country and transnationally" (1003). This idea allows for broader analytic lenses that enable capturing the complex realities of transnationals, which are "often embedded in multilayered, multi-sited, transnational social fields, encompassing those who move and those who stay behind" (Levitt and Glick Schiller 2004, 1003). We draw on the concept of simultaneity to understand how transfronterizxs are embedded in transnational social fields which function to mobilize knowledge and texts across national boundaries. We adopt Levitt and Glick Schiller's (2004) proposal that to understand the transnational experience it is important to capture "the experience of living simultaneously within and beyond the boundaries of a nation-state" (Levitt and Glick Schiller 2004, 1006). Participants of the present study crossed many borders both physically and metaphorically. The youth described here are transnational "in that they have moved bodily across national borders while maintaining and cultivating practices tied—in varying degrees—to their home countries" (Hornberger 2007, 325). However, because they live on the border between two countries, transfronterizxs have a unique experience of crossing borders, as will be developed in the following sections.

Transnational Students

Definitions

As the notion of superdiversity (Vertovec 2007) suggests, at this moment in history we witness "a tremendous increase in the categories of migrant" (Blommaert and Rampton 2016, 21). Because of the heterogeneity of the transnational experiences, there are several distinct definitions of transnational education and transnational students in the literature. A significant number of studies focus on transnational students in higher education (Soong 2015; Robertson 2013; Wallace 2016; Wilkins and Urbanovic 2014). This literature examines the education-migration nexus and its complexities, focusing mostly on students who have lived their whole lives in one country and travel to another country to attend higher education, most of the time as young adults or adults. For example, Poyago-Theotoky and Tampieri (2016) define transnational education as the education offered by an institution for students from different countries. Transnational students in higher education are also called international students. Most of these students are privileged in several senses. The fact that they can study abroad says that most have had high levels of education in their countries of origin, as well as the economic means to leave their countries and arrive in the country where they attend college. This is significantly different from the transfronterizx students who participated in this study. The students in our study are not elite international students but are refugees fleeing economic and violent insecurity.

Researchers also focus on transnational students and their experiences in K–12 U.S. or other nations' public school settings. These are also a heterogeneous group of students with a diversity of backgrounds. In general, transnational students are those students who have affiliations in schools in two countries and build cultural roots in both contexts (Franco 2014; Sánchez and Zúñiga 2010; Vázquez and Hernández 2014; Zúñiga, Hamann, and Sánchez 2008).

Transnational students lead lives immersed in two different countries. These students are immigrants themselves or have one or two immigrant parents, and as a family, they remain connected to both their new country of settlement and their country of origin. Transnational students have experiences, perceptions, and social relationships that span two nations and may be entirely different from those of the "traditional" immigrant. In fact, many transnational students may forego some of the normal life experiences of immigrants and live comfortably for years between two countries and two cultures. Some transnational students, however, do not differ markedly from immigrant students and may gradually adopt life patterns associated with being immigrants. (Sánchez 2008, 857)

Within the umbrella term of transnationals, scholars have used several terms to capture these experiences, such as transmigrant, binationals, *retornos* (returns), or *migrantes retornados* (returned migrants), and transfronterizxs. The multiplicity of terms reflects the diversity among transnationals. For example, transnational students may be students attending school in the United States and who visit their country of origin for short periods of time, such as during the summer (Sánchez 2007). Other students have attended U.S. schools but returned to live in their country of origin—in this case, Mexico—due to repatriation or economic reasons (Hamann, Zuñiga, and García 2008; Jacobo-Suárez 2017; Sánchez and Zúñiga 2010; Zúñiga 2013). These students are called "retornos" or "retornados" (returned migrants) (Petrón 2009).[†] The term "transmigrant students" has been used to describe migrant students who are in one country temporarily only as part of their journey to another country. These students generally do not have long-term lives in any of the places they inhabit, frequently following their parents in their journey searching for work opportunities (Bantman-Masum 2015; Gnam 2013; Prickett, Negi, and Gómez 2012). Literature includes "emotional transnationalism" (Wolf 2002), a term used to describe students who may have never set foot in another country; however, their everyday lives incorporate values, goods, and practices from that country. Undocumented students in the United States may also be considered part of the group that experiences emotional transnationalism. Researchers have also paid atten-

---

[†] Although infrequently studied, this is a significant population. Recent calculations estimate that more than half a million "U.S.-born children of Mexican immigrants moved to Mexico" from 2010 to 2016 (Borjian, Muñoz de Cote, van Dijk, and Houde 2016, 42).

tion to the unique lives of indigenous transnationals (Machado-Casas 2009; Stephen 2007). Referring to the U.S.-Mexico border, Monty (2015) used the term "transnational students" to identify Mexican students who live on the border and study in the United States but go back to Mexico for diverse reasons during the semester. de la Piedra and Araujo (2012a) initially referred to transnationals on the border as cross-border transnationals; however, in later publications, they used the term transfronterizxs. Although diverse, in general terms "transnational students lead lives immersed in two different countries . . . [and] have experiences, perceptions, and social relationships that span two nations" (Sánchez 2008, 857). The literature shows that transnational migration principally impacts economically disadvantaged students who attend U.S. schools, and who deserve an educational system that understands and values them.

Transfronterizx Students

Within the umbrella concept of transnational students, we locate transfronterizxs (Relaño Pastor 2007; Zentella 2009), who deserve a particular term because of the unique experiences of transnationalism that occur on the border between the United States and Mexico. Transfronterizxs are border-crossers who live and study on both sides of the U.S.-Mexico border, often crossing on a daily or weekly basis. They may have spent years going back and forth between both countries (Zentella 2009). The concept of transfronterizx students is different from transnational students in that the contacts between two countries and across borders are more intense and engaged in an embodied experience. In other words, transfronterizxs physically cross the bridge between two countries.

In the U.S. Southwest, this back-and-forth movement has characterized the communication and population movement since the Mesoamerican Age (Vélez-Ibáñez 1996). These contacts take place often, sometimes the same day or the same week, and entail back-and-forth movement from one country to another. After the space- and time-compressing technologies, a second necessary condition, according to Portes, Guarnizo, and Landolt (1999), for transnationalism is the creation of networks across space. We posit that transfronterizxs are in a better position than other transnationals to initiate cross-border activities because of the closeness between the United States and Mexico. Because of the geographical location, most transfronterizxs have a "dense network of communications" (Portes, Guarnizo, and Landolt 1999, 224) across the border. Transfronterizxs "are from acá y allá [from here and from there], actively transcending borders and fronteras" (Relaño Pastor 2007, 275). In the case of transnationals who do not live on the border, it seems that the greater the access "to space- and time-compressing technology, the greater the frequency and scope of this sort of [transnational] activity. Immigrant communities with greater average economic resources and human capital (educational and professional skills) should register higher levels of transnationalism because of their superior access to the infrastructure that makes these activities possible" (Portes, Guarnizo, and Landolt 1999, 224). However, because of transfronterizxs' unique geopolitical situation, unlike other transnationals, they do not need high economic capital to engage in transnational activities, as they may cross the bridge by walking or driving. Granted, compared to other fronterizxs who do not have the privilege of crossing the border (Lugo 2008), transfronterizxs do have the opportunity of mobility across the national border, as well as the privilege of having U.S. citizenship or permanent U.S. residence (Bejarano 2010). Some transfronterizxs belong to middle-class or privileged families, but most of the participants of this study were members of working-class families and experienced marginalization from U.S. mainstream culture.

The binational context of transfronterizxs' lives is not the only element that makes their transnational practices unique. The border is a marginalized and complicated context on both sides of the border, and students learn to navigate this complicated context. "In El Paso, the unemployment rates are twice the state and national average, and per capita income is two times lower than the national average" (Moya and Lusk 2009, 49). Although attractive for labor possibilities and a growing city, Ciudad Juárez was hit with violence, militarization, and a history of colonial relationships with the United States. Thus, the marginalized space of the border characterized by coloniality (Cervantes-Soon and Carrillo 2016) colors the transfronterizxs' transnational experience. Transfronterizxs experience daily surveillance where boundary reinforcers (Bejarano 2010, 392)—that is, checkpoint border patrol agents, teachers, students, administrators, and school staff—"judge, assess, surveil, and 'inspect' them as 'aliens' or who have 'illegally' crossed" (Bejarano 2010, 392) into U.S. or school territory.

Literature on border theory (Anzaldúa 1999; Vila 2000) and Mignolo's ideas of border thinking (2000) add to the definition of transnationalism to explain this experience on the border "where colonial difference is embodied and experienced in the literal demarcation and crossing of international boundaries" (Cervantes-Soon and Carrillo 2016, 282). "'Borders' are not only geographic but also political, subjective (e.g., cultural) and epistemic and, contrary to frontiers, the very concept of 'border' implies the existence of people, languages, religions, and knowledge on both sides linked through relations established by coloniality of power" (Mignolo and Tlostanova 2006, 208). Transfronterizxs experience the border as a tangible national border as well as borders that are less tangible, such as linguistic, ethnic, and school-community boundaries.

Border thinking (Anzaldúa 1999; Michaelsen and Shershow 2007; Mignolo 2000; Mignolo and Tlostanova 2006; Vázquez 2011) is the notion that our epistemological stances must have an embodied component. Transfronter-izxs' experiences with education are embodied. Border thinking also means using nondominant knowledge and languages to break through the limits of colonially instantiated educational practices. "Border thinking brings to the foreground different kinds of theoretical actors and principles of knowledge that displace European modernity . . . and empower those who have been epistemically disempowered by the theo- and ego-politics of knowledge" (Mignolo and Tlostanova 2006, 206–207). In the context of the education field, border thinking is a way to move beyond the epistemological stances of mainstream learning organization and theories. Furthermore, "epistemology is woven into language and, above all, into alphabetically written languages. And languages are not something human beings *have*, but they are part of what human beings *are*. As such, languages are embedded in the body and in the memories (geo-historically located) of each person" (Mignolo and Tlostanova 2006, 207). Transfronterizxs' border thinking supported them to use their language—characterized by translanguaging and recontextualizing—to narrate alternative narratives or counterstories (Yosso 2006).

The border's marginalized location is also evident in the narratives about it. Outsiders conceptualize the border as a transitional space (Heyman 2013); like its name in Spanish, "El Paso" is narrated as a place of temporary residence. From a mainstream outsider's perspective, "the only relevant persons are transitory crossers who are deemed subject to official examination and enforcement" (Heyman 2013, 62). Recently, U.S. Attorney General Jeff Sessions came to our city and used words used to describe war zones when talking about the U.S.-Mexico border.[‡] These negative and damaging perceptions of our border perpetuate the coloniality and asymmetrical relations of power. These narratives impact daily social interactions and support the creation of exclusion. This dehumanizing perspective on the border and the stories presented in this book depict very different images of borderland residents and everyday lives. Instead of outsiders' simplistic views of the border, border views tend to depict subtleties, complexities, and gray areas in the daily transnational practices of borderlanders (Heyman and Symons 2012).

Gloria Anzaldúa (1999, 25) defines the borderland as an open wound "where the third world grates against the first and bleeds" and where the life force of two worlds merges "to form a third country—a border culture." Thus, transfronterizxs live in "the space between two worlds" (Anzaldúa 1999, 237), which is in itself a space of change or a "third space" (Moje et al. 2004). From this space, transfronterizxs use their experiences and resources to navigate their diverse worlds. We will see in the following chapters that "the fluidity of languages and cultural milieus in which [transfronterizxs] are involved every day highlight the influence of border-crossing experiences in the construction of their identity" (Relaño Pastor 2007, 264).

Thus, the transfronterizx everyday experience is colored by the fluid, contradictory, and marginalized context of the border, where people are in a state of *nepantla* (in-between) living within and among multiple worlds (Anzaldúa 1999). The practices we analyze in this book are a product of this fluidity and also of the contradictions and subordination of the transfronterizx context. These "third spaces" (Moje et al. 2004) or "epistemic borderlands" (Cervantes-Soon and Carrillo 2016) "where the colonial/modern

[‡]See Borunda's article, "U.S. Attorney General Calls Border 'Ground Zero,'" published in *El Paso Times* (Borunda 2017).

global design intersects with local histories" (Cervantes-Soon and Carrillo 2016, 285) are genuinely spaces of possibility for education of transfronterizx and other transnational students.

Relevant Literature on Transnational Students in the United States and Mexico

Demographic trends today show the importance of transnationalism in U.S. schools. Latinxs are the largest "minority" group, comprising 17.6 percent of the total U.S. population (Flores 2017) and 25.4 percent of the public school students (Geiger 2017). While 11 percent of Latinx students are foreign-born, 52 percent of U.S.-born Latinx children are "second generation" or children of immigrants (Fry and Passel 2009), and 70 percent of Latinx students speak a language other than English at home (Fry and Gonzales 2008). It is estimated that by the year 2030, 40 percent of U.S. public school students will have come from homes where the first language is not English (Howard, Levine, and Moss 2014). These numbers underscore the significant presence of both the Latinx population in U.S. schools and the transnational realities in these households. Concerning Mexican nationals, in 2011 nearly 12 million lived in the United States, and 6.3 million U.S.-born children had at least one parent born in Mexico.

As transnationalism becomes more common in today's globalized world and increasing flows of students find their way across borders, educators are struggling to understand how to meet the needs of transnational students. These students are often framed as a problem to be solved, and as lacking resources to contribute, very much like the deficit thinking perspective described by Valencia (1997). Teachers are unprepared to work with them, starting with a lack of information about what transnational students know (Cline and Necochea 2006; Gallo and Link 2015). As a result of this situation, transnational students' particular needs are seldom reflected in the curriculum (Boske and McCormack 2011; Conteh and Riasat 2014; Knight and Oesterreich 2011; Stewart 2014). Mainstream teachers often do not acknowledge the cultural and linguistic assets transnational students bring with them to the school context, and policy makers blame students themselves for low literacy and academic performances, rather than a lack of policy that includes them (Mangual, Suh, and Byrnes 2015).

Researchers have presented evidence that U.S. schools do not always construct environments conducive to the academic success of transnational students. Researchers show that Latinxs are less likely to participate in advanced level courses and Gifted and Talented programs (Ford 2010). Dramatic dropout rates for Latinx students (Noguera 2012), in particular foreign-born (National Center for Education Statistics 2010; Romo and Pérez 2012), overrepresentation in special education (Noguera 2012), and lower academic achievement rates of emergent bilinguals as compared to non-emergent bilinguals (Fry 2008) show that schools are not addressing these students' needs or their assets. Ethnic segregation (Reardon et al. 2012) and complex relationships between U.S. schools and Spanish-speaking parents (Cavanagh, Vigil, and García 2014; Delgado-Gaitan 1990; Díez-Palomar and Civil 2007; Stromquist 2012; Valdés 1997) have been documented. In some schools nonwhite students often are ignored, resulting in what Hall (2016) called "bleaching syndrome," in which students change their behaviors and language patterns. Jasis (2013), for example, reported segregation of Latinx students and no academic guidance. This literature shows a complex and adverse set of circumstances that contribute to the limited opportunities of quality education for linguistic minorities in the United States.

Even though we are aware of the benefits of multilingualism, societies and educational systems are not doing enough to maintain transnational students' languages. We know that the majority of immigrant families in the United States lose their native language by the third or even second generation (Rumbaut 2009). Subtractive schooling (Valenzuela 1999), school practices that not only ignore but devalue the cultural and language practices of transnational students, have been amply demonstrated by a good number of studies that document disappointing results. Researchers have documented discriminatory practices against Spanish native speakers (Cortéz and Jáuregui 2004; Petrón and Greybeck 2014; Whiteside 2006) and linguistic segregation (Gifford and Valdés 2006) in U.S. schools. For example, Conteh and Riasat (2014) show that mainstream teachers believed that using two languages is not beneficial, but on the contrary could purportedly "confuse" and "block" transnational students' academic progress. All in all, there is still much to do to support the actual enactment of language policies that promote multilingualism and multiculturalism (Torrente 2013), as well as more inclusive relationships with transnational students and their parents (Durand 2010).

In the Mexican school system, things are not much better for transnational students (Franco 2014; Hamann, Zúñiga, and García 2008; Hamann, Zúñiga, and Sánchez 2006; Sánchez and Zúñiga 2010; Zúñiga 2013). Despite Mexican federal programs specifically meant to help transnational students, the few studies that explore transnationals' schooling experiences paint a bleak picture of Mexican schools' preparedness to receive transnational students and their families.[5] For many of these students, the transition is a complicated process that sometimes jeopardizes their educational success. Mexican classrooms face serious economic hardships, including lack of resources, materials, and even teachers (Franco 2014). Besides, these students are invisible or face discrimination by their teachers, classmates, and even from the educational system. Transnational students in Mexico may be children of Mexican immigrants, but they have seldom lived in Mexico for long periods of time. While their last names and physical characteristics may initially allow them to blend in with their classmates (Hamann, Zúñiga, and García 2008; Sánchez and Zúñiga 2010; Zúñiga 2013), soon after the initial impressions, mainstream Mexican students perceive and treat their transnational peers as different (Zúñiga and Hamann 2008). Transnational students were perceived as problematic, rebels, disobedient, or even potential *narcos* (drug dealers), who tended to establish dysfunctional relationships due to their experience in their "dislocated families" (Zúñiga, Hamann, and Sánchez 2008). Teachers and school authorities in Mexico often ignore students' educational biographies. For example, Zúñiga (2013) describes the story of a transnational student who had been classified by a U.S. school as "gifted and talented." However, she was labeled as "problemática" (problematic student) in a Mexican school due to her ways of "doing" school: she actively participated in class discussions and often questioned her teachers' knowledge. Thus, Mexican teachers interpreted transnational students' behaviors from

---

[5]PROBEM (Programa Binacional de Educación Migrante) and EBSF (Educación Básica Sin Fronteras) are two examples of these national programs.

their idealized views of the "good student," ignoring not only the students' life experiences and funds of knowledge but also their actual abilities and skills developed and recognized in other contexts.

Like the U.S. situation, mainstream teachers in Mexico are not prepared to understand transnational students' linguistic backgrounds. Although Mexican nationals highly valued English, the transnational students' use of English was considered a disloyalty to their country and culture. In Hamann, Zuñiga, and García's (2008) study of teachers' perceptions of transnational students, a prevailing belief among teachers was that no special support was needed because students could speak Spanish, thus they could incorporate and assimilate to the school context with no support from the teacher or peers. Furthermore, some teachers did not allow English spoken in their classes, which could lead to these transnational students' English language loss (Franco 2014; Hamann, Zúñiga, and Sánchez 2006; Vázquez and Hernández 2014). Furthermore, it is easier for transnational students to use Spanish in U.S. schools than English in Mexican schools (Zúñiga and Hamann 2008). Paradoxically, transnational students were not allowed to use their Spanish in U.S. schools, and when they went back to Mexico, they were prohibited from using English in the Mexican school. Students experienced these contradicting messages about language in their everyday practices in academic settings in both countries. This situation may have terrible consequences for students' academic identities, their language and biliteracy development, and their academic success.

In sum, from this literature review about transnational students' schooling in both the United States and Mexico, we conclude that many transnational students face a complex trajectory in their education compounded by the limited opportunities of relevant education for linguistic minorities in both countries. There is still much to do to support inclusive instructional practices and relationships with and for transnational students, their families, and their communities. The transfronterizx everyday experience documented and analyzed in this book—colored by the fluid, contradictory, and marginalized context of the border—shows how these students use their experiences and resources to navigate their complex worlds. From the perspective of the historically subalternized borderlands (Cervantes-Soon and Carrillo 2016), we analyze the language and literacy practices which are part of the repertoire of transfronterizx community cultural wealth (Yosso 2005). Practices analyzed in this book show the integration of linguistic, navigational, resistant, familial, social, and aspirational capitals (Yosso 2002) of transfronterizxs. The DL program, as well as the teachers' and school leaders' understandings of the transfronterizxs' lives and funds of knowledge, contributed to the creation of "third spaces" (Moje et al. 2004) or "epistemic borderlands" (Cervantes-Soon and Carrillo 2016), as will be presented through the examples offered in this book.

2

Sociocultural Perspectives on Learning in Dual Language Settings

THE PREVIOUS CHAPTER INTRODUCED relevant literature on transnational students, border epistemologies, and community cultural wealth that we drew on to define the concept of transfronterizx students and transfronterizx capital. In this chapter, we further develop our theoretical framework by complementing the literatures on transnationalism, border epistemologies, and community cultural wealth with sociocultural perspectives on language, literacy, and learning (Barton and Hamilton 2005; Gutiérrez et al. 2011; Kalman 2008; Rockwell 2018; Rogoff, Goodman Turkanis, and Bartlett 2001; Street 1984; Wertsch 1991). We will refer back to chapter 1, as the literature on language and literacy practices intersects with the research and theory revised in that particular section. Within these large bodies of knowledge, we focus specifically on literature about biliteracy (Hornberger and Link 2012), mobile literacies and recontextualization (Barton and Hamilton 2005; Bernstein 1996; Kell 2000), and translanguaging practices (García 2009). In this chapter, we also review the literature on DL programs, with a particular emphasis on language use and literacy practices. Research on DL classrooms provides the background to understand the school context where students were encouraged to use their transfronterizx practices.

We draw on sociocultural and ideological models of language and literacy practices. Ideological models of literacy, as explained by Street (1984,

1993) help to understand literacy (and orality) in its social contexts, taking into account the discourses, symbolic representations, and complex historical, social, and cultural processes around literacy. Sociocultural perspectives on language and literacy emphasize the need to approach literacy in the moment of interaction. "Situations are rarely static or uniform, they are actively created, sustained, negotiated, resisted, and transformed moment-by-moment through ongoing *work*" (Gee 2000, 190). Thus, rather than focus on language systems themselves, scholarship in the field of language and literacy education focuses on "languages as emergent from contexts of interaction" (Pennycook 2010, 18). More recently, from a sociocultural perspective, ecological models of language and bilingual practices shed light on the environment where these practices occur and inform "on the complex interrelationships among the different factors within this environment" (Gort and Sembiante 2015, 9). These perspectives emphasize that language and literacy are not discrete objects; rather they are diverse, multiple, fluid, complex, and dynamic. "Such ecological models acknowledge that bilinguals' language practices are dynamic, malleable, and influenced by naturalistic opportunities in the environment that tap into their potential to develop and use multiple languages, language varieties, and literacies" (Gort and Sembiante 2015, 9).

In the last decade, scholars have proposed a good number of concepts to try to capture this multiplicity of language realities, such as translanguaging (García 2009), polylanguaging (Jørgensen 2008), translingualism (Canagarajah 2013), and metrolingualism (Pennycook and Otsuji 2015). All these terms represent a new turn in language and literacy scholarship, which not only defines language as a social practice but also assumes that language diversity is not the "unexpected," but rather the "expected" (Pennycook 2010). This trend of scholarship cautions us to be aware of the discourses that normalize monolingualism, language separation ideologies, and artificial linguistic boundaries, which ecological realities question every day. Recent scholarship in the field has proposed alternative narratives to those dominant narratives. Tied to these counterstories on linguistic realities, scholarship on transnationalism also questions artificial cultural, identitarian, subject matter, time, and geographic boundaries. "Migration makes communicative resources such as language varieties and scripts globally mobile, and this affects neighborhoods in very different corners of the world" (Blommaert and Rampton 2016, 23). The notion of superdiversity (Vertovec 2007) relates to these counterstories, as "superdiversity is characterized by a tremendous increase in the categories of migrant" (Blommaert and Rampton 2016, 21).

In these anti-essentialist perspectives about language and literacy, the notions of repertoires of practice or language repertoires account for the flexibility of use of resources in a wide variety and moving array of contexts. "This dispenses with a priori assumptions about the links between origins, upbringing, proficiency, and types of language, and it refers to individuals' very variable (and often rather fragmentary) grasp of a plurality of differentially shared styles, registers, and genres, which are picked up (and maybe partially forgotten) within biographical trajectories that develop in actual histories and topographies" (Blommaert and Rampton 2016, 26). It is in this new moment of the field of language and literacies that we locate our study. Data presented here on the repertoires of language and literacy practices of transfronterizxs speaks to superdiversity, as transfronterizxs offer particular ways to be in the spectrum of transnationalism, and their complex and mobile language and literacy practices—as will be shown in the next chapters—are tied to their mobile trajectories across national borders. Moving away from essentialist perspectives that may see Latinx/Mexican immigrants or transnationals as one homogenous linguistic group, we propose that transfronterizxs' everyday practices question the artificial identitarian, linguistic, geographic, and national boundaries created by institutions, such as the U.S. Immigration and Customs Enforcement (ICE), the Texas Education Agency (TEA), and local school districts, to name a few. These everyday practices include language and literacy repertoires.

Literature on Transnational Literacy Practices

The "transnational turn" in immigration research reviewed in chapter 1 has also influenced the field of language and literacy studies (Lam and Warriner 2012). Studies of transnationals explore the flows of knowledge and practices that occur in transnational contexts (Lam and Warriner 2012). We use the concept of *transnational literacies* as defined by Jiménez, Smith, and Teague as "the written language practices of people who are involved in activities that span national boundaries" (2009, 17). Recent studies stress the link between transnational literacy practices and new digital communication technologies (Alvermann et al. 2006; Lam and Rosario-Ramos 2009; Lam and Warriner 2012; Mclean 2010; Stewart 2014), similar to the research findings presented in chapter 1. Transnational young people engage in digital literacies to read across a variety of symbol systems when they use the Internet for instant messaging (Lam 2009; Lam and Rosario-Ramos 2009) or send emails to kin and friends transnationally (de la Piedra 2010, 2011). Thus, outside the context of the school, youth read and create a variety of multimodal texts. Usually, these texts represent the youth's purposes and motivations, "engaging their subjective experiences in ways that school texts do not" (Moje et al. 2008, 111). A few studies have also noted that students draw on their textual resources "derived from their transnational fields of activity in approaching" (Lam and Warriner 2012, 210) literacy in school (Ajayi 2016; de la Piedra 2011; Skerrett 2015).

Researchers also emphasize the multiplicity of language, language varieties, and registers used in these transnational interactions. Among transnational students and their families, translanguaging practices—that is, the "multiple discursive practices in which bilinguals engage in order to make sense of their bilingual world" (García 2009, 45)—are used every day in and outside the context of the school. For example, Purcell-Gates (2013) documented the biliterate practices of immigrant farm workers and their families, who spoke Spanish at home with the purpose of maintaining the Spanish language for communication with their families in Mexico, while also using English in everyday literacy events. Scholars have long stressed the importance of promoting biliteracy practices at home, as well as inside the classrooms (Durand 2010; Purcell-Gates 2013; Gallo et al. 2014; Martín-Beltrán 2014; Stewart 2014), with the purpose of developing both languages in flexible ways. Lam and Rosario-Ramos (2009) present a study in which transnational students employ the Internet and more than one language to communicate, seek information, and develop relationships in their countries with people who speak their native languages. For these students, digital media is used as a mediator to participate in different linguistic communities in which they make social links. Thus, language and literacy practices are resources that transnationals have available to them in order to preserve transnational identities, connections, and relationships—that is, transnational social capital as part of their community cultural wealth.

Transnational literacy practices are not limited to speaking or writing. Richardson Bruna (2007) documented informal literacy practices of Mexican transnationals in a U.S. school, such as tagging, branding, and shouting out. These informal practices were used by Mexican students to honor their country and state of origin; they wrote the name of their state of origin in benches or the whiteboard, used clothes referring to Mexico, and shouted "vocal tributes" to their land. Religious literacy practices are among transnational practices. Transnational families read and wrote sacred text in Spanish, such as religious literacies on candleholders, calendars, and church buildings (Jiménez, Smith, and Teague 2009; Purcell-Gates 2013; Smith and Murillo 2012; Stewart 2014). Other studies have emphasized transnational students' skills as literacy mediators (de la Piedra and Romo 2003) or translators for their communities (Orellana 2009; Stewart 2014). Stewart (2014) analyzes the case of a bilingual student whose rich biliteracy practices gained him recognition as a translator in church, in a recovery group, and as a poet.

These studies have one thing in common. For the most part, precious and valuable transnational practices are not recognized at school. In an assimilationist context where the Spanish language is not valued, biliteracy practices are essential for transnational students to preserve not only their communities' language (Díaz and Bussert-Webb 2013; de la Piedra 2011) but also their social practices and identities. Language practices are linked to students' identities (Andrews 2013), and if perceived as a resource, they are powerful tools for learning. Bilingual identities are tied to students' funds of knowledge and language knowledge. However, the pervasive ideology of "English-only" can shape students' schooling experiences and identities. Some students perceive English as more important and valuable than Spanish, for example, aligning with the negative perceptions that mainstream teachers have about transnationals' native languages (Andrews 2013; Díaz and Bussert-Webb 2013; Farruggio 2010; Relaño Pastor 2008).

In addition, researchers also document the spontaneous uses of transnational practices—with no recognition by teachers and schools—or the explicit and organized instructional practices that include transnational assets of the students for learning. Thus, in these studies, students utilize their transnational literacies to position themselves academically (Hornberger 2007). These scholars talk about the creation of a "third space" (Moje et al. 2004, 41). Moje and colleagues define third space as the

> integration of knowledges and Discourses drawn from different spaces the construction of "third space" that merges the "first space" of people's home, community, and peer networks with the "second space" of the Discourses they encounter in more formalized institutions such as work, school, or church. . . . What is critical to our position is the sense that these spaces can be reconstructed to form a third, different or alternative, space of knowledges and Discourses. (41)

For example, Martín-Beltrán (2014) argues that there is a "third space" in the translanguaging practices of bilingual students with different fluency levels. Others have also documented similar practices where students translanguage in order to help each other to mediate learning (Olmedo 2003). Thus, findings of selected studies by scholars in the field suggest that pedagogical approaches in the U.S. classroom that facilitate transnational students' engagement with transnational literacy practices already exist. These pedagogical practices usually include encouraging students to use textual resources and knowledge that traverse boundaries, guiding students to investigate the ways texts function in their communities, recognizing when students use diverse frames to interpret texts, and engaging with texts in personal and experiential levels (Creese and Blackledge 2010; Dworin 2006, Gutiérrez, Morales, and Martínez 2009; Medina 2010).

We have contributed to the discussion of transnational literacies outside and inside schools, proposing the term transfronterizx literacies:

> Transfronterizo literacies are the multiple ways in which youth communicate across national borders in and around print. They are intimately related to everyday life on the border and transfronterizos' fluid and multiple border identities. These include the events where youth physically or virtually moved texts across national borders. These literacies vary in terms of purposes, content, media, and identity work. (de la Piedra and Araujo 2012b, 709)

The types of transnational literacies presented here have unique character-istics because students' literacies are intimately related to their experiences as border-crossers. We found a set of practices that transfronterizx engaged in when finding ways to navigate U.S. classrooms.

New Literacy Studies, Literacy Practices, and Context

In this section, we address essential concepts that originated from the New Literacy Studies (NLS) framework, such as literacy events and literacy prac-tices, as well as the relationship between these concepts and context. We draw on the theoretical and methodological framework of the New Lit-eracy Studies, the *ideological model of literacy* (Baynham 1993; Gee 2000; Kalman 1996, 1999; Kalman and Street 2009; Street 1984; Zavala, Murcia, and Ames 2004), which approaches language and literacy from a critical and ideological perspective. It avoids the polarization of orality-literacy and technical-cultural aspects of literacy. From this perspective, literacy is a social phenomenon, "inextricably linked to cultural and power structures in society" (Street 1993, 7). In other words, "reading, writing, and meaning are always situated within specific social practices within specific Discourses" (Gee 2000, 189). According to this model, the social uses of literacy relate in diverse ways to the ideologies of literacy and the cultural values of its users. An assumption of this paradigm, then, is that literacy is not one, but *multi-ple* and *local*. Furthermore, there are dominant and subordinate literacies, according to how they are socially valorized.

The notion of *multiple literacies* implies that there is not just one kind of literacy based on technical skills. On the contrary, literacies vary according to the context and society in which they are embedded (Street 1984). The notion of *local literacies* accounts for the literacy practices that are related to local identities (Street 1994). For example, literacy is performed and val-ued very differently in a school classroom in the United States, where essay and literary texts in English are highly valued and tied to "good" students' identities, from literacy in a rural Quechua community in the Peruvian Andes, where religious biliteracy and communal literacies linked to local government and Andean rituals are most valued. Context, then, is crucial to the interpretation of language and literacy practices. In turn, language and literacy practices are inextricably connected to, even constitutive of social meanings, discourses, or social narratives. These literacy practices that occur in everyday interaction influence, in turn, the ways we think about ourselves and our ways of being in the world, as well as dominant discourses and our counterstories.

A fundamental concept that allows the researcher to "see" the social character of literacy is *literacy practices* (Street 1993). Street builds upon the notion of "literacy event" developed by Heath (1982) to define this notion. *Literacy event* is "any occasion in which a piece of writing is integral to the nature of participants' interactions and their interpretive processes" (Heath 1982). Literacy events also include talk around the written text, multimodal forms of communication, and the social rules of the interaction (Baynham 1993). Street adds to this definition, arguing that literacy practices are "a broader concept, pitched at a higher level of abstraction and referring to both behavior and conceptualizations relating to the use of reading and/or writing. 'Literacy practices' incorporate not only 'literacy events' as empirical occasions to which literacy is integral, but also 'folk models' of those events and the ideological preconceptions that underpin them" (Street 1993, 12). An example, and relevant to this study, is the deficit thinking perspective on the Spanish language, the hegemony of English that spreads monolinguistic language ideologies, as well as the simplistic views of bilinguals as the sum of two monolinguals. These are part of the folk models or discourses that are enacted in everyday practice and that influence language teaching and learning. In turn, these theories are co-constructed in everyday interaction, through teaching activities, teachers' and students' messages, and attitudes toward languages. Thus, "people's understanding of [language and] literacy is an important aspect of their learning" (Barton and Hamilton 2000, 14) because these direct their actions.

Using the notion of literacy practices, we were able to approach literacies, taking into account the micro and macro contexts in which practices are embedded. The NLS model accounts for both a broader societal context—power and cultural structures and broader discourses of school districts and state educational agencies—and the moment-to-moment, negotiated, interactional context of literacy. The children in this study participated in the fast and interconnected world of superdiversity (Vertovec 2007).

"Transnational literacies can be seen as literacy practices that reflect the intersection of local and global contexts" (Hornberger and Link 2012, 264). Transfronterizx language and literacy practices developed within mobile multilingual repertoires "across local and translocal spaces" (Blommaert 2010, 9). Drawing on Blommaert and Rampton's (2011) discussions of language, literacy, and superdiversity, "rather than working with homogeneity, stability and boundedness as the starting assumptions, mobility, mixing, political dynamics and historical embedding are now central concerns in the study of languages, language groups and communication" (3). In Hornberger and Link's words, this represents

> a further paradigmatic shift from a sociolinguistics of variation to a sociolinguistics of mobility befitting today's increasingly globalized world and mobile linguistic resources, and he draws on long-standing conceptual tools such as sociolinguistic scales, indexicality, and polycentricity to help us think about language in this new sociolinguistics. In this paradigm, contexts of biliteracy can be understood as scaled spatiotemporal complexes, indexically ordered and polycentric, in which multilingualism and literacies develop within mobile multilingual repertoires in spaces that are simultaneously translocal and global. (Hornberger and Link 2012, 265)

Thus this paradigm shift in the study of language is tied to the paradigm shift of superdiversity introduced in chapter 1. These changes emphasize the importance of understanding the continuum and intersections rather than the duality of micro/macro, global/local contexts of language and literacy practices in superdiversity. Because of the mobility of the transfronterizxs' lives, it was mainly important to pay attention to aspects of the context to understand language and literacy practices.

Biliteracy, Translanguaging, and Multimodality

Because of the superdiversity and globalization phenomena described above, language and literacy researchers have grown interested in biliteracy (Hornberger 2003) and multilingual literacies (Martin-Jones 2000); that is, "in the

growing significance of two 'multi' dimensions of 'literacies' in the plural—
the multilingual and the multimodal" (Cope and Kalantzis 2009, 2). Scholars
add to the definition of literacy practices to include multiple languages, as
well as a wide variety of means of communication, such as sound, image,
video, and body movements. Responding to a "linguistic view of literacy and
a linear view of reading" (Jewitt 2005, 330), multiliteracies and multimodality
literature (Dyson 2003; Gee 2008; Kress 2000; Rowsell, Prinsloo, and Zhang
2012) proposes a broader view of literacy that includes multiple modes of
communication and is rooted in social interaction. Similarly, literature that
addresses polylingual and polycultural learning ecologies (Gutiérrez et al.
2011) proposes a social organization of learning for emergent bilinguals that
privileges hybrid literacy practices and translanguaging.

Research on biliteracy and multiliteracy focuses on the intersections of
the fields of bilingual education and literacy studies. For example, Hornberger's *continua of biliteracy* addresses the complexities of teaching and
educational research, accounting for the enormous variation of what we
mean by "being biliterate." This framework helped us make sense of the
transfronterizx's literacy practices because, far from organizing dichotomist
schemes (for example, L1 and L2, monolingual and bilingual individuals,
or oral and literate communities), it accounts for "continua [that] are inter-
related dimensions of one highly complex whole" (Hornberger 2003, 5).
Transfronterizx students developed biliteracy along the continua of their
Spanish and English languages, the continua of the contexts of language use
on the border and across national borders, and the continua of a wide variety
of topics that reflected their experiences as transfronterizx. Research in the
last decade has reframed biliteracy (Escamilla et al. 2013) to reflect more and
more the continua introduced by Hornberger's continua of biliteracy model,
and thus has moved away from a simple definition of biliteracy as reading
and writing in two languages.

We also draw on literature that goes beyond the notion of language as
bounded systems to capture the multiplicity of language realities, such
as translanguaging (García 2009). Translanguaging defines language as a
social practice and assumes that language diversity is the "expected" (Pennycook 2010). According to García, translanguaging refers to the "multiple
discursive practices in which bilinguals engage in order to make sense of

their bilingual world" (García 2009, 45). These practices include not only linguistic knowledge but also "cultural knowledge that comes to bear upon language use" (47). Bilingual communities (including school communities) must translanguage in order to construct meaning. We posit that the notion of translanguaging is compatible with the borderland epistemology of transfronterizxs described in chapter 1. Translanguaging is an approach to bilingualism centered in practice and which questions the idealized notion of a balanced bilingual. Transfronterizxs and their practices question notions of nationality, home cultures, home languages, and cultural practices. They question the socially constructed neat divisions of language users. As scholars have recently argued for the case of emergent bilinguals (García 2009; Palmer 2011; Valdés 2003), transfronterizx language and literacy practices question the idealized notions of "a balanced bilingual," who may keep two languages separate as if this were the only and "true" bilingual (Valdés 2003). Questioning these idealized notions is part of a counterstorytelling that confronts deficit perspectives.

A translanguaging framework proposes that bilingualism and biliteracy are resources that can and should be utilized by educators in classroom settings (García, Ibarra Johnson, and Seltzer 2017). For example, Martín-Beltrán (2014) recognizes that bilingual students may use translanguaging with different fluency levels in their classroom. Students naturally participated in translanguaging practices while they tried to help each other mediate learning. Traditionally in DL programs, which are highly supported by research as effective programs for emergent bilinguals and other vulnerable populations (Thomas and Collier 2002), there has been a language separation policy. The rationale for this policy has been to try to protect the minoritized language spaces in instruction. However, this policy has been critiqued as artificial or as unfavorable to second language development (Palmer et al. 2014). Recent research has documented dynamic bilingualism (García and Kleifgen 2010) and translanguaging practices as resources that support learning (Canagarajah 2011; Creese and Blackledge 2010; Martínez 2010; Reyes and Vallone 2007). Contrasting English-only approaches defining students merely by their relationship to English or dominant ideologies of linguistic purism that value bilingualism but still have a dual or plural monolingualism perspective (Palmer et al. 2014; Pennycook and Otsuji 2014), translanguaging pedagogies approaches consider the wealth of meaning-making resources that emergent bilingual students already possess. After all, as García points out (2009), translanguaging is how bilinguals and multilinguals communicate, and we know this phenomenon is common across the globe.

Translanguaging includes multiple modes of communication. Language does not operate in isolation from other modalities but is one of many different semiotic resources. Communicative events include semiotic resources such as gesture, image, audio, and oral and written language (Cope and Kalantzis 2000). As Kress suggested more than a decade ago, "it is now no longer possible to understand language and its uses without understanding the effect of all modes of communication that are copresent in any text" (2000, 337). When we talk about text in this book, we refer to textual practices (Arnold and Yapita 2000) broadly defined. In a prior research project about vernacular literacy practices in the Andes, de la Piedra found that alphabetic literacies coexisted and sometimes were integrated to Andean textual practices that required a broader view about language, text, and literacy (de la Piedra 2009). In order to understand these indigenous multimodal literacy practices, which included ritual and body movements, de la Piedra uses Arnold and Yapita's (2000, 13) definition of *textual practices* to describe the kinds of communication practices that include diverse modalities of communication. They analyzed textual practices found in Andean textiles, as well as the rituals and oral texts, such as prayers, *dichos* (sayings), or *consejos* (advice). According to Arnold and Yapita (2000), these multiple forms of texts represent "a collection of textual practices and Andean texts, which complement each other" (13). These indigenous literacy practices remind us that the alphabetic literacy valued at school is just one textual practice among many others that coexist and are integrated with school literacy practices. *Text* has a broad meaning, expanded to textual forms such as pictures, poetry, song, body movement, photographs, graphics, models, videos, video games, computers, and so on. When we talk about text in this book, we refer to textual practices, defined this way. See chapter 8 for additional literature on multimodalities.

This book contributes to this body of research that seeks to show the creative ways in which bi-multilinguals cross different boundaries (that is, linguistic, cultural, or national boundaries) in order to create new possibilities of language use and participation in educational settings. In this book, we illustrate how transfronterizx emergent bilinguals, with the guidance of their teacher, learn to use the full range of meaning-making tools—including translanguaging and multimodality—to mediate understanding in academic settings. The literature reviewed in this section informs our research with transfronterizxs because these perspectives stress the ideological boundaries between languages, which in turn impact the social construction of learning spaces. Understanding the translanguaging practices in this DL program helped us to understand the dynamic nature of transfronterizx everyday practices, which question binaries concerning context, practices, knowledge, and language and literacy practices. Chapters 7 and 8 will analyze translanguaging and multimodality in this DL setting.

Recontextualizing

The construct of *recontextualization* initially proposed by Bernstein (1996) and later used by NLS scholars (Kell 2000, 2011; Barton and Hamilton 2005) to describe literacy practices movement represents "the way a field is changed as it is transferred from its original site to pedagogical practice" (Oughton 2009, 27). A broader definition includes the idea of language as a social practice, very much in line with NLS argument, in which recontextualization is the norm in language use, to move "beyond the notion of 'context' and instead engage with a notion of locality" (Pennycook 2010, 35). Pennycook (2007) also uses the notion of relocalization, the "reenactment of the same in a different context" (590), when analyzing the multiple ways that hip-hop creative language practices are localized. Furthermore, Pennycook (2010) argues that "relocalization allows us to appreciate that to copy, repeat, and reproduce may reflect alternative ways of approaching creativity" (139). The concept is useful to understand the transnational literacy practices described here. It accounts for the fact that "people move texts across contexts" (Barton and Hamilton 2005, 18). People appropriate, borrow, and repeat texts and literacy practice creatively (Kalman 2005; Pennycook 2007). In other words, literacies are often hybrid and intersecting because users frequently use "practices learned in one situation in new situations. This means that *boundaries themselves are significant, generative spaces* where resources may be combined in new ways or for new purposes" (Barton and Hamilton 2005, 18, emphasis is ours) because "cultural forms move, change, and are reused to fashion new identities" (Pennycook 2010, 35).

Transfronterizxs are members of multiple worlds and act within diverse textually mediated social worlds (Barton and Hamilton 2005). Literacy practices are not isolated skills; instead they are "inextricably connected to identity work" (Gee 2000, 412) and intertwined with everyday experiences in this border region. As argued by the New London Group (2000), "people are simultaneously members of multiple lifeworlds, so their identities have multiple layers that are in complex relation to each other" (17). Participants of this study crossed many borders both physically and metaphorically. Thus, the appropriation of language and literacies across the border and settings that we observed, even though it may look like repetition of these practices, "always produces something new, so that when we repeat an idea, a word, a phrase, or an event, it is always renewed" (Pennycook 2007, 585). For example, during math instruction in the United States, we could observe students using the division operation process and representation that they had learned in Mexico. Even though the mathematical representation and the mental computation may look like a repetition of the division operation used in Mexico, the fact that it was performed in the United States *renewed* this practice. The teachers and classmates may not understand why the students wrote the numbers in different places than the expected places on a worksheet. Students may be asked to "show their work" by explicitly writing their operations, while back in Mexico mental computations were valued. Thus, when students reenacted or recontextualized their math practices, these were transformed by the context and the participants during the activity, as well as the meanings attributed to them. Because they have experiences that are particular to transfronterizxs, their literacy practices become recontextualized in specific ways and take on new meanings based on their lives on the border.

As explained before, literacy practices include ideologies or discourses about social groups, languages, or identities. Ideologies could take different forms also, such as linguistic and cultural assimilation, English monolingualism, or language purism. However, we contend there is also the possibility that an ideology of bi(multi)lingualism and multiculturalism could play in the gap or space created by the process of recontextualization. We transformed the notion into a verb, recontextualizing, so it will communicate that it is a social practice. In the context of the border and the DL program, like translanguaging, recontextualizing provided the space where mobile multilingual repertoires were used, and everyday practices could question dominant discourses about language and literacy. Transfronterizx students engaged in recontextualizing so frequently that we argue that this practice was part of the repertoires of practice that helped transfronterizxs to navigate U.S. schools. Chapters 5 and 6 will further develop this notion and offer examples of recontextualizing.

Dual Language as a Potential Relevant Context for Transfronterizx Students

In this book, our purpose is to contribute to the effort to inform researchers and educators of dynamic bilingual strategies to promote bilingualism, biliteracy, and biculturalism. Literature shows that teachers need support so that they can effectively identify and use the wide variety of student resources, knowledge, and skills available. When teachers use these resources they amplify, rather than limit, students' experiences in the classroom. Herein lies the importance of documenting these rich practices. The DL program at the research site allowed exciting and productive border-crossings regarding knowledge, language, and literacy practices. Thus, with this study we also contribute to the field of DL education.

Researchers have demonstrated greater academic and linguistic gains for emergent bilinguals who attend one- and two-way immersion programs rather than other program models, such as transitional bilingual education or English-only programs (Lindholm-Leary and Genesee 2014; Thomas and Collier 2002). This is true for both native English speakers and native speakers of other languages. In particular, research shows that two-way immersion programs provide a context where students have the opportunity to learn each other's languages and literacy practices while building positive intergroup social relationships (Christian 1994; de Jong and Howard 2009). DL programs have also provided opportunities to close the achievement gaps for emergent bilinguals (Thomas and Collier 2002). They positively influence academic achievement, language proficiency, school attendance, and student motivation (Thomas and Collier 2002; Lindholm-Leary 2001). However, there are also critical perspectives on DL programs which caution that these programs may also serve to reinforce the privileges of native English speakers (Palmer 2011; Valdés 1997). Thus, DL programs may also be a space of reproduction of privilege for the already privileged and of discrimination for non-English speakers—in particular from low-income families—that is, the already marginalized. The case presented here is not one of these latter programs, as almost 100 percent of students were Mexican or Mexican-Americans, and the community served low-income families.

As introduced above, language separation is one of the key features of these programs (Collier and Thomas 2004; Gómez, Freeman, and Freeman 2005). The reasoning behind the strict separation of language policies in dual language is to protect minority languages, which otherwise will be ignored or downplayed for the use of English (Palmer et al. 2014). Programs designate a space for the language of instruction: a physical space, a time, a teacher, or a subject (Adelman-Reyes and Kleyn 2010). Indeed, there is a real need to protect nondominant languages such as Spanish. Today we still find schools that prohibit students from using their home languages, including schools in El Paso, Texas. Studies also underscore this need. For example, work by Freeman (1998) and Potowski (2007) in dual language settings showed that Spanish was used less than educators and administrators expected, due to a variety of reasons related to the lack of materials in the nondominant language, standardized testing requirements, and nonacademic course offerings in English only. That is, there were discrepancies between the schools' language planning and goals toward the equality of Spanish and English and the actual interactions (Potowski 2007). We agree that DL programs should protect the nondominant languages' spaces in order to support—in this case—Spanish language proficiency. However, we also contend that strict language separation policies tend to overlook local varieties of English and/ or Spanish. From a language separation perspective, ideally, students learn the so-called standard variety of the two languages. This feature shows already an ideology that values one variety (that is, "standard Spanish") over others (the variety of Spanish on the border).

Language separation has been found to be artificial because it does not reflect the everyday use of languages by bilinguals in the real world. Cummins (2008) critiques the "two solitudes assumption" and García (2009) warns us about the conception of bilingualism as the sum of two monolinguals. The critique of the ideologies and practice of monolingualism comes from the observation of real practices of bilinguals outside and inside academic settings (Canagarajah 2011; Creese and Blackledge 2010; Gort and Sembiante 2015; Martínez 2010; Reyes and Vallone 2007). These latter studies provide details on the rich uses of language, literacy, and cultural practices in DL programs. Thus, a translanguaging pedagogy is based on real, authentic communicative practices in bilingual and multilingual communities rather than on enforced monoglossic ideals.

By documenting the actual bilingual proficiencies and hybrid language practices in the classrooms, these studies question the "ideal" model of DL programs as spaces where two languages are equally distributed over time and where the program population is characterized by an equally "ideal" distribution of the target population of fifty-fifty (Henderson and Palmer 2015; de Jong 2016; Sayer 2013; Poza 2016). According to Gort and Sembiante (2015), translanguaging in the classroom is "better understood as the dynamic multiple languages and language varieties" (9). In DL programs, everyday engagement with complex bilingual practices benefits students' cognitive and academic development (Martínez 2010). Gort's (2008) study of bilingual peer interactions across Spanish/English-integrated language contexts shows how naturally occurring interactions in two-way immersion programs facilitate bilingual/biliteracy development and sociocultural interaction. The study presents how children become more bilingual, biliterate, and bicultural by developing dual language and cultural knowledge with peers from different backgrounds. In a more recent study (Gort and Sembiante 2015), teachers' translanguaging practices of code-switching, translation, bilingual recasting, and brokering that drew on children's linguistic and cultural knowledge supported experimentation with new language forms, and integrated various language varieties while recognizing, validating, and expressing their shared bilingual identities.

DL programs should protect the status of the nondominant language and organize instructional spaces for this language in order to maintain its value, but not at the expense of local ways of using language. For example, code-switching was presented in earlier research on dual language settings as "evidence of the leakage from mainstream U.S. discourse (in which English is the language of wider communication and therefore attributed more prestige than Spanish) into the . . . educational discourse" (Freeman 1998, 196). Although code-switching in a particular situation may be evidence of "leakage," our data has shown that code-switching is undoubtedly part of the repertoires of the language of bilinguals on our *frontera*. Thus, we agree with recent scholarship on translanguaging that language separation is not only artificial but may also marginalize most bilinguals' practices in the world. In the current study, as well as previous ones conducted on the U.S.-Mexico border (de la Piedra 2010, 2011; Esquinca 2011, 2012a, 2012b; Esquinca et al. 2017; Mein and Esquinca 2017), we have witnessed a flexible use of languages despite of separation of language policies. These and other studies cited in this section have shown how programs may protect the status of the nondominant language while also acknowledging the dynamic models of bilingualism.*

Findings of our study contribute to the current literature presented in this chapter, which questions artificially created neat language distributions by documenting the language and literacy practices on the borderlands. Transfronterizxs are in constant movement across national (and other kinds of) borders. In a world dominated by monoglossic ideas that privilege English over other languages, as well as ethnocentrism that privileges mainstream practices over practices of minoritized groups, documenting rich transfronterizx language and literacy practices, as well as other community cultural wealth/capitals available to them, is crucial in order to counter entrenched deficit perspectives about transfronterizx and other transnational students.

---

*See García, Ibarra Johnson, and Seltzer (2017) for a recent book with examples of how to implement dynamic models of bilingualism in the classroom.

This study contributes to developing a theory in order to understand the physical and metaphorical border-crossings of linguistically and ethnically minoritized students in U.S. schools. In the next chapters, we will see how teachers co-constructed and enacted flexible language pedagogies that supported recent immigrants' participation in literacy activities and academic discourse. Similar to teachers analyzed by Gort and Sembiante (2015), teachers and administrators of this DL program crossed language boundaries in strategic and flexible ways.

3

Conducting Research on the U.S.-Mexico Border

IN THIS SECTION WE FOCUS on the researchers' positionalities and our study's setting. We will first introduce the researchers and our positionalities, followed by a brief description of the U.S.-Mexico border. We will then describe the elementary school where we conducted the ethnography along with the participants and the DL classroom. We discuss the research data collection and analysis processes in the appendix.

Researchers and Positionalities

Positionality is an essential component of the research process. A researcher's personal experience and acknowledgment of who they are as an individual and as a member of various groups and social positions play a vital role in the research. Our positionality as researchers shapes the research in many ways. According to Bourke (2014), "positionality represents a space in which objectivism and subjectivism meet" (3). He states that positionality is to strive to remain objective while being aware of our subjectivities. He also suggests that not only do we have to be mindful of the influence our positionality has on the research process, but we also have to be up front in communicating our positionality with our participants. Milner (2007) also points out that "when researchers are not mindful of the enormous role of their own and others' racialized positionality and cultural ways of knowing, the results can be dangerous to communities and individuals of color" (388). We, the three authors of this study, live on the U.S.-Mexico border and consider ourselves transfronterizxs, although we have very different experiences of the U.S.-Mexico border. We present our positionality statements, written in the first-person singular, below.

de la Piedra Positionality Statement

I am a Peruvian educational anthropologist and consider myself a transnational person; even though I chose El Paso as my home, I have close connections with two other nations, Peru and Mexico. Looking at my life's trajectory, I see some connections with transfronterizxs, as I too have moved back and forth between countries, and I also have experienced being an emergent bilingual. I was born in Lima, Peru, where I belonged to a middle-class family until I was twenty-four years old. As a young adult, I migrated to the United States, where I worked as a housekeeper and nanny. This experience allowed me to improve my English oral language skills and support my family. Furthermore, it allowed me to experience firsthand how U.S. mainstream society views emergent bilinguals and Latinas. I was also the mother of Nicolás, an immigrant Spanish-speaking student enrolled in an elementary school. During those years, I felt discriminated against, undervalued, stereotyped, and invisible. While cleaning the house, friends of the homeowner ignored that I was there or if they talked to me, they slowed down their speech or raised their voices, all while I was enrolling in graduate school. I brought these experiences with me in my work in Mexican immigrant communities, as well as with indigenous Quechua communities in Cuzco, Peru. I moved to El Paso in 2004 after spending four years in Cuzco working in intercultural bilingual education. The last time, I moved back to the United States with my two children, Nicolás, who at the time was eleven, and Lucía, who at the time was four years old. The proximity to Ciudad Juárez was an incentive to decide to move back to the United States. I wanted my children to be close to Latin America, and living on this border has allowed us to cross to Ciudad Juárez on a weekly or monthly basis. We go to Ciudad Juárez to visit my wife's family, go to the movies, see the doctor, and shop or have dinner. My children are bilingual and biliterate, and they move comfortably between the United States, Mexico, and Peru.

Araujo Positionality Statement

I was born in El Paso, Texas, and consider myself a Chicana. Both my parents were born in the state of Chihuahua, Mexico, my father in Parral, and my mother in Ciudad Juárez. My parents lived in Ciudad Juárez when my mother was pregnant with me. When her water broke, she legally crossed the Mexican border to El Paso so that I could be born a U.S. citizen. This was not unusual in those days. I was born in El Paso's Segundo Barrio and lived in Juárez my first year of life, so I can say that I was a transfronterizx even in the womb!

I grew up on a pecan farm in a rural working-class environment. My father was a transfronterizx. During my first years of life, he would cross the international bridge to work in a nearby pecan orchard. He would carpool with other workers every day, traveling to New Mexico to work and back home to Juárez at the day's end. Eventually, my family ended up moving to New Mexico, but as a child, I spent almost every summer in Ciudad Juárez with my grandmother and continued to cross the border back and forth on weekends. I have vivid memories of going to the *mercado* (market) in the mornings to buy chorizo. I also remember my mother telling us stories of growing up in Juárez as she would take us to the different places she frequented as a child. When my grandmother moved to the United States, my family continued to travel back and forth to Juárez on weekends. We would go grocery shopping, go to the dentists and doctors, and get haircuts. My father still had family in Juárez so we would visit them as well. As an adult, I continued visits to Juárez. I particularly liked to accompany my father every other weekend so that he could get a haircut with Don Pedrito. We frequently traveled until the violence in the city got dangerous.

I was also a public schoolteacher for seven years prior to my work at the university. I had worked in a bilingual classroom with recent immigrant students to the United States, including several transfronterizx students. Every school year I would have at least seven students who were transfronterizxs. I recall the students sharing stories with me about their holidays or weekends in Mexico. I could relate to my students and understood their experiences as transfronterizxs.

Esquinca Positionality Statement

I was born in Ciudad Juárez, Chihuahua, to parents who had migrated from working-class homes in the rural provinces to attend the Universidad Nacional Autónoma de México (UNAM), the free, national university in the nation's capital. Because my parents realized that by sending me to private Mexican schools I would have a distorted view of the world, I attended grades one through nine in Juárez public schools in which classrooms had no less than thirty students. When I graduated from *secundaria* (grades seven through nine), my parents and I decided that I would go to school in El Paso, as my sisters did. As a Mexican citizen we understood that choices were limited, so I persuaded my parents to send me to a private school, as they had done for my sisters. During my childhood and early adolescence, I had devoured English storybooks and my older siblings' ESL books and encyclopedias that were around the house, watched a lot of *Sesame Street* and *Electric Company*, and translated English pop lyrics as a hobby, so I could carry on a conversation in English. However, I was held back one year, and in that year I experienced cultural shock—school prayer, strict behavior codes, an all-male school, and an English-only environment. I also experienced the in-betweenness of border life: most of the Juárez kids were oblivious to their class privileges, most of the El Paso kids refused to speak Spanish to me, and it seemed that everyone was homophobic. When the time came to choose a college, I chose the University of Texas at El Paso (UTEP), in part because it offered a program for affordable tuition for Mexican citizens. By the time I was twenty-five, after a decades-long wait for U.S. residency application approval, I was able to move to El Paso. After about twelve years of going back and forth, I left Juárez and moved to the United States permanently.

Our positionalities as insiders of this U.S.-Mexico community helped us to develop rapport with the teachers and students in the DL program; however, we also were constantly aware of and reflected on our privileged positions as university professors and how these outsiders' positionalities might impact our research. Sofia Villenas (1996) specifies that "researchers can be insiders and outsiders to a particular community of research participants in different levels and different times" (722). Because our study was done with transfronterizx students, we were aware of what it meant to live in the border and to be "de allá y de acá" ("from there and from here") (Relaño Pastor 2007, 275). We are also bilingual and biliterate, as most of our participants were emerging to be. This insider status gave us an advantage such as having cultural understanding, knowing the language, and being knowledgeable of the popular culture of the times, such as the current *telenovelas* and popular songs such as *narcocorridos* (drug ballads). We were also aware that our experiences were different from those of the participants in the study, keeping in mind Delgado-Gaitan's (1993) words, "sharing the same ethnic background as the participants does not make the researcher more knowledgeable about the meanings of the participant's feelings, values, and practices based on influences such as assumed cultural knowledge" (391). Although we all had experience in U.S. schools, because we were not teachers in this school we were somewhat outsiders to the school community. We were also well aware of our privileged class positions since we all had obtained a PhD and worked at the university.

The U.S.-Mexico Border: El Paso–Ciudad Juárez

The U.S.-Mexico border is 1,989 miles long and encompasses four U.S. states and six Mexican states. The four U.S. states are Texas, New Mexico, Arizona, and California. The six Mexican states are Tamaulipas, Nuevo León, Coahuila, Chihuahua, Sonora, and Baja California (Lorey 1999). The border crosses a variety of terrains from deserts to urban areas and is characterized by two major rivers, the Rio Grande (known in Mexico as Río Bravo) and the Colorado River (Staudt, Fuentes, and Monárrez Fragoso 2010). The U.S.-Mexico border is the most frequently crossed international boundary in the world. It has forty-five U.S.-Mexico border-crossings and 330 ports of entry. There are six border-crossings or bridges in the El Paso / Juárez, Mexico, area.

More than 3.6 million passenger vehicles and 300 thousand commercial vehicles cross into Juárez from El Paso, Texas, every year (Staudt, Fuentes, and Monárrez Fragoso 2010).

The Paso del Norte region is a large metropolitan region with more than two million people. The region is a tri-state, binational area and is considered the second most crucial trade point on the border (City of El Paso 2016). People from El Paso travel to Juárez to visit the dentist, eat and drink, go to the nightclubs, or just hang out at the Mercado Juárez. People from Juárez travel to El Paso to go shopping, visit family, or attend school.

El Paso is the fourth largest city in Texas. El Paso has a population of approximately 780 thousand people and borders its sister city on the Mexican side, Ciudad Juárez. It is the third fastest growing metropolis in the United States (Valencia 2015). El Paso is located in the western tip of Texas next to New Mexico and Chihuahua, Mexico. Sixty-nine percent of the population of El Paso is Hispanic (City of El Paso 2016). El Paso is home to several military bases, including Fort Bliss. It is also home to the University of Texas at El Paso. The Franklin Mountains are the backdrop to a city that is warm and sunny.

Ciudad Juárez, once known as Paso del Norte, has an estimated population of 1.4 million. Ciudad Juárez, located in the Chihuahuan Desert, is south of El Paso, Texas, and lies on the Rio Grande. Juárez connects to El Paso by bridges. Juárez is home to Universidad Autónoma de Ciudad Juárez (UACJ) and Instituto Tecnológico de Ciudad Juárez, as well as branches of the Universidad Autónoma de Chihuahua (UACH) and the Instituto Tecnológico y de Estudios Superiores de Monterrey (ITESM). With more than three hundred maquiladoras, Juárez is a major industrial center. With migrants from Mexico's interior moving to Juárez to work in the *maquilas* (short for maquiladoras, or factories) the population has more than doubled since the 1960s.

Juárez gained worldwide notoriety when its streets became the frontlines of the Mexican drug war. Since the government of President Calderón declared war on the drug cartels in late 2006, estimates are that more than one hundred thousand people have died in the Mexican drug war. Juárez was particularly affected by the drug war, likely due to its geographic locale. As battling drug cartels disputed control of a city that is the gateway to the expansive U.S. market, violence surged. The Juárez population decreased as a mass exodus was reported—with many taking refuge in El Paso. Many sought asylum as cartels began to extort money from everyday Juarenses, leading many successful businesses to close (Schmidt and Spector 2015). In 2009, the Mexican Army arrived in Juárez as the government attempted to regain control of the city, but the violence did not subside. Ciudad Juárez became the most dangerous city in the world, reaching an average of eight to twenty homicides a day. Estimates are that between 2008 and 2011, ten thousand Juárez families were directly affected and that thirty thousand children were orphaned (Martínez-Montoya and Garza-Almanza 2013). Many victims died for being in the wrong place at the wrong time (Rosen and Martínez 2015), innocent victims who were killed in public areas. Many Juárez families lost family members, including Alberto Esquinca. In subsequent years, after a truce was negotiated, violence declined. Today, the streets are safer, and tourism is returning to the city. In 2016, Pope Francis visited the city and, on the banks of the Río Bravo, declared:

> The human tragedy that is forced migration is a global phenomenon today. This crisis which can be measured in numbers and statistics, we want instead to measure with names, stories, families. They are the brothers and sisters of those expelled by poverty and violence, by drug trafficking and criminal organizations. Being faced with so many legal vacuums, they get caught up in a web that ensnares and always destroys the poorest. Not only do they suffer poverty but they must also endure all these forms of violence. Injustice is radicalized in the young; they are "cannon fodder," persecuted and threatened when they try to flee the spiral of violence and the hell of drugs. And what can we say about the many women whose lives have been unjustly robbed?

The U.S.-Mexico border region is a distinctive place in which different cultures and languages blend. The U.S.-Mexico border is not one entity but several entities with multiple meanings and in constant change (Duarte-Herrera 2001). After the Mexican-American War, the political line divided a bounded region. "Such bifurcation created an important contradiction: first it split the region into two separate ecologies when they are one; and second, it created two nations glued by nineteenth-century industrial capitalism and its present post-industrial version in the twenty-first century" (Vélez-Ibáñez

2017, 12). Water resources, air pollution, health, and economic transactions cannot be understood as divided by the political line.

Recently, the construct "transborder or transfronterizx region" reflects the complexities of the interactive dynamics in the region (Aguilar Barajas et al. 2014), accounting for cross-border economic and social associations, and long-held practices, such as students crossing the borderline to attend school or the university. Vélez-Ibáñez (2017) states that "phenomenologically very different circumstances exist in the border than from all other areas of either country, which is expressed by important interdependent but asymmetrical realities" (35). On the same lines, Vila (2005) stresses that the border consists of several borders, each with very different identity constructions: "The border is not really one, but multiple, in the sense that not only do different people construct distinct borders and disparate identities around those borders, but those different borders acquire a distinct weight in relation to the different subject positions and the different narratives within that people decide to identify with" (233). Vila further states that "sharing certain aspects of a culture does not necessarily mean sharing a common identity" and "that people who seem culturally very similar consider themselves very different" (2003, 331).

The border is not only distinct from other places in the United States but is also highly marginalized. Asymmetry and inequality taint the relationships, networks, and practices that occur in the region. Marginalization against and on the border occurs at many different levels and due to distinct aspects, such as geography, ethnicity, language, and socioeconomic levels. At the national and state levels, the border is many times ignored by policy- and lawmakers. The voices of border residents are often silenced by national narratives that dominate the public discussion:

> The U.S. border with Mexico is the subject of considerable media attention and policy concern. In general, this discussion contains national-level views of the border and does not take advantage of the knowledge, experience, and values of border region residents. National-level views of the border vary, but often prioritize rigid and inaccurate notions of national security threat over realities of community well-being, democratic participation, and economic development in the region. (Heyman 2013, 61)

The border is conceptualized as a transitional space (Heyman 2013); like its name in Spanish, "El Paso" is narrated as a place of temporary residence. Furthermore "the only relevant persons are transitory crossers who are deemed subject to official examination and enforcement" (Heyman 2013, 62). Furthermore, the history of Spanish colonization and later U.S. colonization, also called "dual colonialism" (Lugo 2008) impacted this region. This is a dehumanizing perspective on the border, and stories presented in this book depict a very different image of borderland residents. Instead of outsiders' simplistic views of the border, border views tend to depict subtleties, complexities, and gray areas in the everyday transnational practices of borderlanders (Heyman and Symons 2012).

Although El Paso is typically seen as living in peaceful coexistence with its sister city, Ciudad Juárez (Vila 2000), there is also ongoing tension present between distinctive voices of people on both sides of a border where different races, classes, ethnicities, genders, cultures, languages, and sexualities coexist. The border has great power asymmetry existing not only to separate but also to define otherness. While Mexican-Americans experience discrimination based on language and class in Mexico (Petrón 2003; Zúñiga 2013), Mexicans experience discrimination and subordination in the United States (Jasis 2013). Mexican immigrants many times arrive with a lack of knowledge of how systems function in the United States, which contributes to exploitation and cheap labor. A constant challenge to the Spanish language is also present (Duarte-Herrera 2001).

The border is fluid and full of contradictions where people are in a state of *nepantla* (in-between) living within and among multiple worlds (Anzaldúa 1999). The practices we analyze in this book are a product of this fluidity and also of the contradictions described above. Transfronterizxs live this state of *nepantla* and use their experiences and resources to navigate their diverse worlds. "The fluidity of languages and cultural milieus in which [transfronterizxs] are involved everyday highlight the influence of border-crossing experiences in the construction of their identity" (Relaño Pastor 2007, 264). Our book will highlight narratives and practices that reveal borderlanders' states of *nepantla* as they navigate two countries, two languages, and two homes on a weekly and sometimes daily basis.

The Community and the School District

Our ethnographic research took place in the community of Canales. Canales is on the outskirts of El Paso and is considered by some to be the oldest town in Texas. Once an agricultural community, it is now a sprawling area that borders the Rio Grande and Mexico. The town got its beginnings in 1680 after the Pueblo Revolt in New Mexico. The Tigua indigenous people occupied the area since 1682. They were farmers who raised corn, wheat, grapes, cattle, and horses. They also traded baskets, pottery, and rope. Canales became part of the United States in 1848. In 1955, Canales was incorporated into the city of El Paso, and it is about twenty minutes by car from downtown El Paso (Hamilton 2010).

At one time the Canales Independent School District (CISD) was a rural education district with only one high school and a few elementary schools. CISD is now the third largest school district in El Paso. It currently serves more than 42,500 students on sixty-two campuses that spread throughout the city. CISD is the third largest employer in El Paso. The students attending the district are 93 percent Hispanic and 80 percent economically disadvantaged. The teachers in CISD are predominantly Hispanic as well, at 81 percent.

CISD has received praise for being a leader in bilingual and DL education. CISD provides several programs to develop full academic literacy in more than one language. The district also has two designated international schools. These schools offer students the opportunity to develop academic skills in English and Spanish and be able to acquire a third language. The school district's commitment to bilingual and DL education is evident in its vision statement that states that students will graduate fluent in two or more languages. This support for DL education and bilingualism was one of the reasons we selected this district as our research site.

The School

Border Elementary School (BES) opened in the 1900s. BES is one of the oldest schools in the district and was once the heart of the community. It was the center for social activities such as dances, plays, nondenominational church services, fire department fundraisers, football games, Boy Scout meetings, bazaars, and enchilada suppers. Political rallies were held at the school, along with dances for soldiers from Fort Bliss, and it also served as an air raid shelter. In 1939 the school taught the students who had come from Mexico in Spanish even though it was against district policy. This was one of the first schools to offer bilingual instruction in CISD.

At the time of the study, BES enrolled six hundred students, 99 percent of which were of Mexican origin; 96 percent received free or reduced lunch, and about half of the students were labeled as "limited English proficient." We selected this school because (1) half of its students attend a well-established DL immersion program; (2) it is located near a port of entry from Ciudad Juárez, Mexico, to El Paso, Texas; (3) it has a significant number of transfronterizx students; and (4) the administrators and teachers expressed an interest in collaborating in this study.

The community has seen a rapid increase in growth. Businesses opened up along the main street bordering the school premises. Now BES is surrounded by fast-food restaurants and chain stores. You can see the border of Mexico near the school, and the traffic going back and forth between countries has increased in recent years. Apartment complexes have now taken over what were once small homes that had chickens, cows, and goats. The *acequias* (irrigation ditches) have survived but are enclosed by streets and highways.

Ethnography in the Dual Language Classroom

DL programs are additive bilingual programs that build on and expand students' language repertoires. DL is an umbrella term to distinguish enrichment programs from subtractive types of bilingual education (such as transitional bilingual education) that emphasize the dominant language acquisition with little attention to the nondominant language maintenance or development. BES offered both one-way and two-way DL programs as well as English-only instruction. The DL programs used both Spanish and English as languages for instruction from kindergarten through sixth grade. The primary goal of both programs is for all students to become fully bilingual and biliterate, as opposed to subtractive approaches to English language learning.

DL programs vary in their implementation. In this school, there were two DL programs as separate strands within the school. The program comprised both one-way and two-way dual language strands. The one-way strand enrolled students proficient in Spanish, including recent immigrants. Thus in these classrooms "only one language group is being schooled through their two languages" (Collier and Thomas 2004, 2). The two-way strand included students who were Spanish speakers born in Mexico and the United States, Mexican origin English speakers, and students who were growing up bilingually. Thus, the population that this two-way DL program served did not resemble the models of two-way DL programs where a balanced number of native English speakers and native speakers of a minority language learn together in their two languages. Nevertheless, in spite of the differences of language proficiency of students in both one-way and two-way DL programs, the basic principles of these programs were "the same—a minimum of six years of bilingual instruction . . . , separation of the two languages of instruction, focus on the core academic curriculum rather than a watered-down version, high cognitive demand of grade-level lessons, and collaborative learning in engaging and challenging academic content across the curriculum" (Collier and Thomas 2004, 2–3).

The DL program used in the district is a 90–10 model, starting first grade with 90 percent of instruction in Spanish and 10 percent in English. The percentages vary gradually, increasing the English instruction by 10 percent in each grade. The study took place in two two-way dual language bilingual classrooms (fourth and sixth grades) and one one-way dual language bilingual classroom (fifth grade). Two teachers taught students in each classroom: one instructed in Spanish and concentrated on language arts and social studies, the other taught math and science in English.

Our participants were emergent bilinguals enrolled in a DL classroom. During the first year of the study, 2009–2010, we recruited fifty-one participants in fifth (Ms. Ornelas's and Ms. Arredondo's two-way and one-way DL classes) and sixth (Ms. Monarrez's and Ms. Ramos's two-way and one-way DL classes) grade DL programs. In 2010–2011, we followed students who had been in fifth grade in the first year of the study into sixth grade (with

Ms. Ornelas's and Ms. Arredondo's class) and added three additional participants that year who were newcomers to the school. During the last year and a half of the study (2011–2012), we decided to focus on Ms. Ornelas's fourth grade two-way DL class. That year, thirteen new fourth graders consented to participate. A total of sixty-seven students in the DL program agreed to participate in the study.

In the participating classrooms, approximately 50 percent of the students who signed the consent form were transfronterizx students who went back and forth to Juárez on weekends and school breaks. Students had different levels of bilingualism, but Spanish was the dominant language among them. Most students reported using both Spanish and English. When asked which their preferred language was, the majority said that Spanish was their first language, and fewer reported that English was their first language. Most students used Spanish as much as possible—including in the content areas which were taught in English.

Many of the students in this study were separated from their families, mostly because of the families' mixed immigration status. Among them was Leticia, who lived with her mother and her brother while five other siblings still lived in Juárez, one of whom could not cross the border because he did not have a passport. Amanda's parents and six siblings remained in Juárez while she lived with her aunt in El Paso. Javier left his mother and a brother behind while he stayed with his grandmother, and Raul was also separated from his parents and at the time of the study lived with his sister and a cousin. Despite this separation, students still returned to Juárez regularly. Their narratives as transnational and border citizens reveal their agency in confronting violence that close family members had suffered, crimes that they witnessed, the sadness of leaving part of their family behind, the struggle to understand a new educational system, and confronting racism and discrimination in this new educational context (Araujo and de la Piedra 2013). The participants in our study were all between the ages of nine and twelve. As a result of their transfronterizx experiences, the students demonstrated particular characteristics such as resilience, maturity, critical awareness, solidarity, and strength.

In addition to the students' stories, we include the stories and words of DL teachers, school leaders, and other school personnel, as well as parents.

These stories revealed that many adults in our study were also transfronter-izxs and some grew up in the local community. All of them were bilingual and of Mexican origin. In chapter 4 we will further describe the participants. Subsequent chapters will address the following themes that emerged from our study: literacies crossing borders (or recontextualization of literacies), translanguaging, transfronterizx funds of knowledge, making connections, and use of language and literacy during content area instruction.

4

Stories of Transfronterizx Experience

AS PART OF OUR ETHNOGRAPHIC work at BES, we conducted extensive interviews with administrators, teachers, and students. In this chapter, we present a selection of the narratives they told us. With the focus of this book on students and teachers in a DL program at BES, we seek to understand the classroom literacy practices by contextualizing them within a broader system of values and ideologies that are expressed in narrative form.

The stories participants shared are more than the mere recollection of events that took place; they are, in fact, expressions of the prevailing values and ideologies in circulation at the school during that time. These stories are part of the cultural toolkit (Bruner 1991), translatable knowledge or wisdom that can be passed down or transmitted across generations. Such knowledge contains a narrator's point of view and experience, and, perhaps most importantly, acts of meaning-making as actors drew on experience to construct life lessons. From a sociocultural perspective, these stories are cultural artifacts that mediate social experiences. Narratives represent the collaborative activity of multiple actors, and they rely on each other to interpret their collective and shared experiences.

The narratives we present here are representations of the collective transfronterizx experiences shared by the BES community. Through our narrative analysis, we seek to capture "the experience of living simultaneously within and beyond the boundaries of a nation-state" (Levitt and Glick Schiller 2004, 1006). Drawing on personal interviews with administrators and teachers at BES, we use a sociolinguistic approach (Gee 2011; Ochs and Capps 1996) to analyze educators' narratives. The narrative approach helps us to understand how the administrators and educators at BES understood themselves, their stories, and who they were in relation to the students in their care. These stories revealed something important about the environment at BES during the time of the study. Educators drew on values of care and empathy for transfronterizx, which translated into pedagogical practices in the DL classroom.

Stories are a tool to make sense of and interpret realities. Bruner wrote that narratives are "able to shape what is real, what must be real" (2010, 45), meaning that stories help us to understand reality and construct a coherent account of our lived experiences. For this ethnography, we documented the complexities of the contexts of language and literacy learning of transfronterizx students. Teachers and administrators narrated the pressures they felt by dominant anti-immigrant discourses and English-only proponents' narratives. In many ways, teachers and administrators countered those deficit discourses and the practices related to them.

In this chapter, we also present selected narratives of transfronterizx students that illustrate their lives on the border. Thus this chapter will serve as the background to understand the language, literacy practices, and funds of knowledge presented in the following chapters. Also, we will analyze educators' stories to identify the ideologies reflecting a position of advocacy and caring toward their transfronterizx students in order to later in the book trace these ideologies to practices we saw in DL classrooms.

Transfronterizx Students' Narratives

Transfronterizx students' lives span national boundaries; the U.S.-Mexico border serves as a point of separation as well as a juncture. Their lives occurred between two countries, with some events taking place only *del lado mexicano* (on the Mexican side) and others taking place *del otro lado* (on the other side or on the U.S. side). Children and their families go to Ciudad

Juárez and participate in meaningful social rituals with their families every week. For instance, one Friday afternoon Brenda shared a busy weekend agenda her family had planned:

> Y luego pues hoy, vamos a ir a la feria de una iglesia y mañana vamos a ir a una quinceañera y el domingo se me hace que vamos a ir a una alberca.

> (And well, today, we're going to go to a fair at a church and tomorrow we'll go to a quinceañera [special celebration of a girl's fifteenth birthday], and on Sunday, I think we're going to a swimming pool.)

Brenda's weekend in Ciudad Juárez looks like many others we heard about with students crossing the border in order to engage in these social rituals with family and friends. Other students, such as Vanessa, moved periodically between both countries, meaning that she highlighted the extended periods of time (years) she spent on both sides:

> Porque primero en pre-kínder estaba en Juárez y luego me vine para acá. Y luego me repitieron pre-kinder y luego me fui para Juárez. Y luego me vine para acá [en Kínder], y luego me dieron primero, segundo y luego me vine para acá [esta escuela] y luego segundo, tercero y luego otra vez para acá y tercero y luego acá también cuarto y quinto.

> (Because first in prekindergarten I was in Juárez and then I came here [to El Paso]. And then I repeated prekindergarten, and then I went back to Juárez. And then I came back here. And then they placed me in first, and second and then came here [to Border Elementary School] and later, second, and third and then again over here and third and also fourth and fifth here.)

The case of Vanessa illustrates the in-betweenness of students' lives. Due to varying circumstances, students would come and go, some for extended periods. Vanessa told us that the reason she moved back and forth so much was "es que a mi mamá le quitaron su pasaporte y duró cinco años allá y me tuvieron que cuidar mis abuelitos acá" ("they took away my mother's passport and she spent five years over there, so my grandparents had to take care of me here"). During the time when Vanessa's mother was not able to cross to El Paso, Vanessa visited her mother every weekend.

Family separations were common among the transfronterizx students we worked with. As in Vanessa's case, one reason for the separation of families was that some families had members who did not have documents to be able to cross to the United States. Amanda, who disclosed that she was a U.S. citizen, saw herself as a key person who would bring the rest of her family to the United States. Amanda added that because of her citizenship status, her family had hopes that she would help them enter the United States as residents:

> Están esperando para que yo cumpla veintiuno para poderles arreglar y que nos vengamos, nos vengamos para acá.

> (They're waiting for me to turn twenty-one so I can fix their papers and that we'll come over, come over here.)

Amanda's words reveal her aspirational and familial capitals, as she accepts her commitment and role in having high aspirations for her family and being able to "*arreglar*" (arrange, regulate, or fix) their immigration status, even in difficult current conditions. Her words also show her life to be in an "in-between" state. Even though she lives in the United States with a relative, her parents and some of her siblings cannot cross the border. Another reason for family separations during the time of our study was the escalation of violence in Juárez. Concerned for their children's safety, parents sent their children to El Paso to live with relatives, thus separating the family. When parents made these decisions, they evidently drew on their aspirational, familial, and social capitals, as illustrated by Vanessa's family story.

The Case of Isabel and María

Many of the families we met had been transformed by their movement back and forth across the border. Their experiences included crossing *el puente* (the international bridge) every day or every week, suffering because of family separation, waiting for immigration papers, fleeing the surge of violence in Ciudad Juárez, living with relatives of their extended families for periods of time, and adapting to schooling in El Paso. One of the most notable cases we saw was that of Isabel and her family because it illustrates the sometimes remarkable transfronterizx family experiences in the BES community. Isabel was nineteen years old at the time of the study; she happened to be her sister's legal guardian. María, Isabel's biological younger sister, was a student at BES.

Me llamo Isabel Rendón, tengo diez y nueve años, tengo once años viviendo en Estados Unidos. Siempre he vivido con mi abuela, pero mi mamá toda la vida ha estado al pendiente o sea nunca me ha dejado. Estoy criada al modo de mi abuela, pero mi mamá nunca me dejó. Siempre estaba constante porque ella no puede vivir aquí todavía. Primero vine a los ocho años, fui a Socorro a la escuela, fue cuando vivía con mi mamá que estaba embarazada de María. Vivíamos en Socorro pero no la hizo y se regresó a Juárez. Me dijo tú no eres un mueble para estarte moviendo. Mi abuela la ayudó, ella es residente y la ayudó y pues ya. Aquí vivo, aquí vive mi abuela, vive mi primo, vivo yo y pues María ahorita.

(My name is Isabel Rendon, I am nineteen years old, I have been living in the United States for eleven years. I have always lived with my grandmother, but my mom has always made sure I am taken care of; she has never left me. She is still constant because she can't live here yet. I first came when I was eight years old; I went to Socorro to school, it was when I lived with my mother that she was pregnant with María. We lived in Socorro but she did not make it, and she went back to Juárez. She told me I was not a piece of furniture to be moving around so much. My grandmother helped her; she is a resident, so she helped her. I live here, my grandmother lives here, my cousin lives here, I live here, and, well, María lives here now also.)

Isabel and María's mother had been waiting for her residency for nineteen years; thus Isabel and María spent most of their short lives crossing *el puente* since their grandmother was a U.S. citizen who provided an apartment in the projects for the children to use in El Paso.

Diez y nueve años y el viernes ya, pues ya se los íban a dar (la residencia) pero perdieron los papeles, los de ahí. Y ahora fue otra vez y le dijeron sí. Ya me habló "mi hija, ya me voy con ustedes, llorando." Hemos sufrido mucho las tres . . . las cuatro, mi abuela, mi mamá y yo e Isabel.

(Nineteen years on Friday already, and, well, they were going to give us the residency, but they lost the papers, the people from immigration. And now we went again, and they said yes. She called me "daughter, I am going with you all, crying." The three of us have suffered, the four, my grandmother, my mother, me, and Isabel.)

Isabel happily stated that they would be "ahora sí unidas" (finally united). Isabel works a minimum wage job or gets food stamps, and her mother sends whatever she can monthly to help support both daughters. Isabel grew up also crossing the border, sometimes every day, occasionally every week.

Sí, yo estaba en la escuela aquí y pues me venía caminando hasta la escuela y luego en la tarde otra vez para Juárez, y así. No quería dejar de ver a mi mamá pero a ella [María] sí se me hace que se le va a hacer difícil y venirnos a las cinco de la mañana y luego irnos hasta BES y luego regresarnos a Juárez y pues ahorita ya no están las cosas como para estar así en Juárez. Juárez está muy feo. Y luego también me la traje porque . . . nos venimos más bien yo y ella porque balacearon enfrente de mi casa. Pues duré desde los ocho hasta los diez y seis viviendo aquí, iba a Juárez pero nada más los fines de semana con mi mamá. Entonces cumplí diez y seis años y entré en la edad de la rebeldía, mi abuela ya no podía conmigo "te regreso a tu lepa" y pues . . . pasó todo así verdad, pues todos entramos a esa edad. Entonces pasaba todos los días, iba y venía, iba y venía y se me hacía fantástico porque yo amaba a Juárez. Y a mi mamá y siempre estaba en Juárez con mis amigos y mi mamá, iba y venía todos los días, duré así hasta los . . . de diez y seis hasta los diez y siete, un año, haciendo todo un año, dos años haciendo todo eso.

(Yes, I was in school here, and I would come walking to school and then in the afternoon back to Juárez, and like that. I did not want to stop seeing my mother but for her [María], I think it will be difficult and to come over at five in the morning and then go to BES and then go back to Juárez, and, well, now things aren't right in Juárez. Juárez is really ugly. And I also brought her . . . we came, her and me because there was a shooting in front of our house. I spent since I was eight years old until I was sixteen here in El Paso, I would go to Juárez but only on weekends with my mother. Then I turned sixteen, and I came into the age of rebellion, my grandmother could not put up with me, "I send back your brat" . . . everything happened like that, and we all came to that age of rebellion, and I would spend every day, coming and going, coming and going, and I thought it was fantastic because I loved Juárez . . . And my mom, I was always in Juárez with my friends and my mother, coming and going every day, I spend it like that until I was sixteen, seventeen, a year, an entire year, two years doing that . . .)

Family separation was hard for both girls and their mother. However, Isabel narrated this part of her story as a reality of their transfronterizx lives, something that was part of the process of getting the residency papers and that the family needed to endure. The girls narrated their act of crossing the bridge to see their mother as the activity they did to reunite as a family. "Mi mamá, cada vez que se me ocurre voy a verla y la niña nada más ve que es viernes [me dice] 'mami, vámonos!'" ("My mom, every time I can, I go and see her, and the girl sees when it is Friday [she says to me,] 'Let's go, Mom!'") At the beginning María was sad to have left Juárez and moved to El Paso; however, for both Isabel and María, these crossings were part of their responsibility toward their family to stay in El Paso, for their mother's sake. María and Isabel considered that staying in El Paso would facilitate the process of their mother's migration:

Sí, pobrecita ha sufrido mucho, ella ha sufrido mucho y todos lo estamos viendo. Pero ella está constante de que estamos ayudando a mi mamá, o sea ella . . . dice "es que yo quiero que mi mamá venga" y ya estando yo aquí ya se le hacen las cosas más fácil.

(Yes, poor girl, she has suffered so much, she has suffered so much, and we are all living it. But she is sure that we are helping Mom, in other words, . . . she says that she wants Mom to come over and once she is here things will be much easier.)

Several of the participants of this study were in a similar situation where they felt—at least at the beginning—forced to live on both sides of the border. "The decision of some families to move some or all of their members to El Paso was not an easy one. As a result, many suffered when far from other family members. Children did not like their school in El Paso as much as their schools in Juárez. Many times moving required great efforts from relatives" (Araujo and de la Piedra 2013, 271). These are some of the hardships that transfronterizx students confront in their everyday lives.

Stories of Border Elementary Educators

While it might seem that transnational movements defined mainly students, actually BES educators shared many of the same border-crossing experiences. In this section, we present educators' stories because stories usually contain narrators' expressions of values, beliefs, and moral or life lessons. Thus, the purpose of our analysis of narratives is to elucidate the values or life lessons narrators espoused and understand the prevailing ideologies which in turn help us to understand practices in DL classrooms.

"I Was Like You So Many Years Ago": Expressions of Empathy and Solidarity

Two of the administrators at Border Elementary that we interviewed were Assistant Principal Prieto and Principal Sevilla, both Latino males. Both had grown up in similar circumstances as BES students; Mr. Prieto had actually attended BES and Mr. Sevilla was a transfronterizx himself. Toward the beginning of the interview, Mr. Prieto started off telling us about how he started working at BES and finished up the story making a point about solidarity.*

> When I got hired, I thought . . . it would have been a good thing if I had known about bilingual ed. services. That is one thing—I see what we have here—I

---

* Selected wording is bolded for readers.

see the great things we have here. They remind me when I was a kid. I was thinking of the possibilities and the great things that the students will have, and the teachers. I hope that they impact the work that I make for them or that we grow with each other. It's positive because **I want them to know "I was like you so many years ago."**

Mr. Prieto's narrative is set at the time of his initial hiring at BES, when he realized that the school had many assets and that he could develop ways to help students (such as through knowledge of bilingual education services). By the end of the narrative, as he winds down the story, he reflects on the ways he is similar to his students.

Similarly, Principal Sevilla, who was familiar with the focus of this research project and the research team, volunteered his own story of being a border-crosser. Like Mr. Prieto, he told a story that expressed values of solidarity with students.

> I grew up on both sides of the border. I really lived in Juárez for most of my life, but for some reason my parents wanted us to go to school here. They brought us with the nuns to this side of the border [El Paso], so it was a daily commute back and forth driving the kids to school. And then, of course, I started school in Juárez starting kindergarten and first grade. It was really a blessing . . . So that's how I started my school experience here. But then it becomes a matter of identity. I identified with people on both sides of the border. **I guess it's a concept of being a border person. I could be in Juárez with all my Mexican friends, and on this side, [I could] be with all my El Paso friends. I fit in with both groups**.

In this narrative, Principal Sevilla told us how he studied on both sides of the border and commuted between Juárez and El Paso and how this trans-fronterizx experience formed his identity. A "border person" fits in on both sides of the border. As he ended his story, he alluded to his interpersonal links; having friends on both sides of the border made him a border person. Through this story, Mr. Sevilla signaled to us that he also understood his students, particularly the transfronterizx ones. Like many of the students at his school, he belongs on both sides of the border.

One of our focal teachers, Ms. Ornelas, also shared a story similar to those of Mr. Sevilla and Mr. Prieto. She told us how, as a young middle school student, she experienced the same things her newcomer students were facing:

Yo empecé mis estudios en México, como le estaba comentando el otro día. Comencé yo, yo viví mucho tiempo en Mazatlán, Sinaloa, que está cerca del Océano Pacífico y ahí crecí hasta los doce años y estudié allá mi mi kínder, primaria y parte de la secundaria. Pero cuando ya iba a ingresar al octavo grado, mi familia y yo nos venimos para acá para El Paso y fue aquí cuando entré a *middle school* y luego ya a la *high school*. Luego ya después empecé mis estudios universitarios aquí en [la universidad]. Ahí acabé, entonces pues tengo esas dos experiencias, tanto en México como aquí en Estados Unidos. Y claro que eso me ayudó mucho a mí porque puedo ver las diferencias en el sistema educativo en los dos países y creo que pues me ha ayudado mucho para entender a mis estudiantes. También porque, muchos de mis estudiantes han experimentado lo mismo que yo.

(I started my studies in Mexico as I mentioned the other day. I started, I lived in Mazatlán, Sinaloa, for a long time which is close to the Pacific Ocean and I grew up there until I was twelve years old, and I studied kinder, elementary, and part of middle school, but when I was going to start eighth grade, my family and I moved to El Paso, and it was here that I went to middle school and then high school. Then I started my university studies here. I finished, and then, well, I have those two experiences, both in Mexico and here in the United States, and that helped me see the differences in the educational system of both countries, and I think that has helped me understand my students also because many of my students have experienced the same things.)

As she wrapped up the story, Ms. Ornelas traced the clear connection to how her experiences as a newcomer transnational student helped her better understand her students.

Together, these educator narratives suggest that at BES transnational experiences are not unique to students. In fact, border-crossing experiences and identities may have bonded educators and students. Educators like Principal Sevilla and Ms. Ornelas communicated their values of solidarity and empathy with students.

Facing a Border Crisis Together

Values of solidarity and empathy presented in the previous section were crucial to face challenges together. During the times of high violence in Ciudad Juárez, the BES leadership came together to support students who were fleeing the violence in their hometown. Mr. Prieto told the story of how the situation affected the school, which he deftly connects to the value of acceptance.

> Starting here last year we had a lot of students coming here from Mexico, and the reason they are leaving Juárez—you know what is going on with the cartel and killings . . . we have and [had] registrations last year we have a lot, we have at least eleven in a year, in one grade level, so we look at it, and we are like "Okay we have to help out these students, we are not going to close our doors." And one thing Mr. Sevilla stressed was: We are not going to make it difficult for them; we're just going to accept them and, you know, we have to do that.

Mr. Prieto wrapped up his story by invoking the values of acceptance and belonging shown in the previous section. While many educators at BES shared the same values, Principal Sevilla told us the story of how accepting students had become a point of contention on campus. In response to the complaint that borders should be maintained by identifying markers of national identity such as foreign license plates, Mr. Sevilla alluded to the responsibilities and ethics of the profession.

> Sometimes, people come to me, some of our teachers even say: "Well have you seen the parking lot? We have a lot of cars, and a lot of them have Juárez license plates, right? We pay taxes." I said "Okay, let me ask you. When you became a teacher in your mind, did you say 'I'm going to become a teacher of U.S. citizens only? Or Chinese people only? Or everyone except Mexican people?' Well we become teachers—and I think we all are teachers [here in this table]—we become teachers because we want to teach, so we have to love

the profession first and then you don't care. You only need a job, a classroom, and people to go in and teach. That's why we become teachers."

Not incidentally, being a lifelong border-crosser, Mr. Sevilla knows that many students live their lives on both sides of the border. They can be U.S. citizens and live in El Paso but have an extended family on both sides of the border who can pitch in with raising children and take them to school in the mornings. A Mexican license plate just means that a car was registered in Mexico, not that a child who was riding the car is not entitled to an education. As Mr. Sevilla notes, in his view, the values that guide teachers are not tied to discriminating on the basis of national origin.

From Theory to Practice, or "nos podemos entender"

In this book, we show, among other things, how transfronterizx students were able to draw on their transnational funds of knowledge to learn at BES. A key consideration is the role of educators in empowering students to use those funds of knowledge. Thus it is important to stress that the values and ideologies expressed in these narratives are reflective of what we understood to be a prevailing ethos at BES. Namely, that transfronterizx students are an integral part of the BES community and that their funds of knowledge are recognized and valued.

We repeatedly heard the message of how these values helped teachers to best work with transfronterizx students. Our focal teacher, Ms. Ornelas, enacted the values of inclusion and acceptance to learn. At one point, Ms. O noted that, through shared languages and experiences, she and her students created a "natural" learning community.

Por ejemplo, lo veo yo con las materias que yo enseño, sí necesitamos mucho hacer conexiones con su vida diaria porque en matemáticas tenemos que estar aplicándolo a la vida real, en ciencias igual. Ahora hablando de cultura y eso pues, es muy natural para nosotros hacerlo. En realidad yo creo que hasta inconscientemente lo hacemos porque pues compartimos las mismas costumbres, nuestro, como se dice? *background*, sí pues es igual. Es muy parecido. Yo creo que eso nos ha ayudado también a nosotros para formar un grupo un poco más sólido, más unido porque podemos nosotros compartir las mismas costumbres, las mismas experiencias. Creo que nos podemos entender, tanto yo como a mis niños y ellos a mí, nos entendemos mucho mejor por eso que compartimos, que tenemos en común. Pero yo creo que lo hacemos inconscientemente, no lo hacemos tan conscientes, yo creo que ya es algo natural que se da.

(For example, I can see it with the subjects I teach, we need to make connections with their daily lives because in mathematics we need to apply it to the real world, same with science. Now talking about culture and all that, well it is very natural for us to do so. In reality I believe that we even do it unconsciously because we share the same customs, our, how do you say it? Our background is the same, very similar. I believe that it has helped us also to form a more solid group, more united because we can share our same customs, same experiences. I believe we can understand each other, I my kids, and them me, we understand each other much better because of what we share, what we have in common. I believe that we do so unconsciously. I believe we don't do it consciously I think it is something natural that happens.)

In another part of her interview, Ms. Ornelas told us how the values of acceptance and inclusion made a difference in learning. She made the case that, because she and her students shared customs, experiences, and languages, she was able to create a learning community of transnational learners, again suggesting that this knowledge made her a good teacher.

I go back and forth, not as often [as I used to], right? But I do at least once a year or something like that; and many of my colleagues are the same. So that's what makes this school very unique. You don't see that in many schools, I think. Most of us are always talking about it and how that makes us a group of teachers that know—or at least we try to—understand our students better and we use that to help them learn. And I think that has become a very strong tool for us to reach them and make that connection and make them feel that they can and it's okay to make mistakes, that they are in a safe place where they are allowed to make those mistakes, where they can say something wrong and nothing is going to happen to them.

As with the other narratives, the end of the story is where we can find the expression of the values. In this case, Ms. O portrays her understanding of students as a tool that allows her to enact the values of acceptance. For instance, she added that acceptance meant that an error is an opportunity to learn and classrooms are safe spaces for learning.

Conclusion

In this chapter, we presented a range of narratives about transfronterizx experiences at BES. Starting with the stories of students' lives, we saw how the border-crossing experience defined their lives. The international boundary divided families. The border is a tangible material experience that organizes the Juárez–El Paso landscape, but it is also an organizing entity that transforms people's time. In this sense, we saw the narratives of students who narrated their life experience based on how much time they spent on each side of the border.

Furthermore, borders are made more tangible for mixed-status families in which only some have documents to cross the border. The case of Isabel and María is a particularly stark reminder of how the border is not just an imaginary line. Instead, it has material effects on the family and, by extension, on the lives of children and their learning experiences. In families torn apart when only some can cross the border, legal arrangements can include a young woman becoming the legal guardian for her young sister. In contrast, families whose members all have documentation can move seamlessly across borders.

This stark social reality is crucial to understand the ideologies that arise to make sense of lived experiences. Stories are born of these experiences, but also simultaneously shape experience (Ochs and Capps 1996). Educators can choose to stand with students and embrace an open-door policy on welcoming students, such as the educators whose voices we highlight here. Educators described here constituted social capital for transfronterizx children and families, acting as cultural brokers and providing support when navigating the U.S. educational institutions. Mr. Sevilla, Mr. Prieto, and Ms. Ornelas all expressed narratives of empathy and openness. They chose to make sense of their transborder experience by highlighting in their minds how they are, in fact, just like their students. In that sense, they expressed an ethic of empathy and care. This ideology, as we will see in the next chapters, was evident in words and actions.

5

Language and Literacies Crossing Borders

Introduction

THE PURPOSE OF THIS CHAPTER is to analyze the transfronterizx literacies of upper-grade transfronterizx elementary students of the Ciudad Juárez–El Paso border.* Literacy practices transcend not only national boundaries but also metaphorical borders between the home, the community, and the school. Here, we focus on diverse literacy practices outside the formal educational context. Later, we emphasize transfronterizx literacies for academic purposes or the literacy practices that youth learned across the border and outside of the context of the school and used for educational purposes in the context of this DL program. Despite the fact that much has been written about immigrant children in U.S. schools, Mexican transnational youths' out-of-school literacy practices have not received the attention they deserve. Youth are engaged in literacies outside the academic context (Alvermann et al. 2006); however, researchers show that most teachers, unlike the educators at BES, do not recognize the out-of-school literacies and funds of

---

* This chapter is derived in part from an article by de la Piedra and Araujo (2012a) published in *Language and Intercultural Communication*, July 27, 2012, available online: http://www.tandfonline.com/doi/full/10.1080/14708477.2012.667416.

knowledge of Latinx students in the classroom. These researchers have called for educators to "listen closely to their transnational immigrant students and recognize the global understandings and experiences they undergo on a daily and cumulative basis" (Sánchez 2007, 513); thus, the importance of documenting literacies crossing borders. The scarcity of literature about transfronterizx linguistic practices (Zentella 2009) and literacy practices is even more critical.

Like the term *transfronterizx*, the literacies presented here emphasize "the continuous linguistic and cultural contact that border youth maintain as part of the multiple daily transactions across both sides of [the border]" (Relaño Pastor 2007, 264). Thus, transnational literacy practices are intimately related to the lives of these youth as transfronterizxs. In coping with the complicated situations presented in previous chapters, such as discrimination, militarization and violence, low socioeconomic realities, and dominant negative narratives about the border and transnationals, the children learned and used strategies that assisted them in surviving their everyday lives; hence the importance of documenting their literacy practices as resources. The border is fluid and full of contradictions where people are in a state of *nepantla* (in-between), living within and among multiple worlds (Anzaldúa 1999). The literacies we analyze here are a product of this fluidity and also of these contradictions. The students' out-of-school experiences took place in two countries and two languages. In this way, the transfronterizx literacy practices we found expand the definition of transnational literacies.

As presented in chapter 2, the sociocultural perspective of the New Literacy Studies (NLS) provides a framework for understanding the "literacy practices of everyday life" (Barton and Hamilton 2005, 14) of transfronterizx youth and how they use them in and out of school, across many borders. We drew on the construct of *recontextualization* (Barton and Hamilton 2005) to analyze literacy practices described here. This term accounts for the fact that "people move texts across contexts" (18). Some of the literacies we found were instances of biliteracy, "in which communication occurs in two (or more) languages in or around writing" (Hornberger 1990, 213), while others were characterized by the use of only one language, primarily Spanish. Recontextualizing literacies is related to border identities that are fluid and multiple. We conceptualize the various ways in which youth communicate across national borders as transfronterizx literacy practices. Transfronterizx literacies vary concerning purposes, media, and identity work, all of which we describe later.

Transfronterizx Literacies in Print: Physically Crossing the Border

We found literacy practices in print in which youth would either read or write texts in Spanish on the Mexican side of the border. Sometimes the students also physically took these texts with them back to the United States. Significant to understanding literacy practices are the activities that the kids engaged in when reading or writing or participating in other modes of communication. During the focus group interviews with students, children stated that there were specific activities that they did mostly in Juárez, which were not necessarily part of their lives in El Paso. Because of their mobility across the national boundary, students participated weekly or even daily in these textually mediated social worlds which were also full of diverse texts (Barton and Hamilton 2005). Pepe and Jonathan, for example, stated that they read the Bible mostly in Spanish and in Juárez. Pepe had a Bible in his home in Juárez and Jonathan went to Juárez on weekends to attend catechism studies. Students also read Mexican magazines and newspapers while in Juárez, particularly the *chistes* (comics section), all in Spanish. For example, Rosa, who had recently moved to El Paso from Juárez, went to visit her grandmother and other family members almost every weekend. At her grandmother's home, she read the newspaper with her cousins, taking turns to read each comic strip.

Olga and Amanda added to Rosa's comment during the same focus group interview that when in Juárez she also read the comics in the same newspaper, *PM*. Olga added that she memorized the *chistes*. The following interaction is an excerpt from that conversation during one focus group when the girls were talking about different activities that they engaged in during their everyday lives in Ciudad Juárez. Olga shared some games they played, and she added that she reads the *PM* newspaper. Olga's comments prompted Rosa and Amanda to share their views and to talk about their literacy practice of reading the newspaper in Ciudad Juárez:

OLGA: Well, we always play tag, freeze tag or sometimes my cousin, a girl, brings a game and we play, and then my cousin . . . in the *PM* we read . . .

MAYTE: What is that?

ALL: A newspaper.

ROSA: Uh-huh, a newspaper. And then my grandma, because in the *PM* there are naked women and all of that, well [I] would take that page and my grandma thought I saw them, but I didn't. You would open the thing, and there were just jokes, and she [my cousin] only wanted to see the jokes.

OLGA: But they're really boring . . .

AMANDA: That's not true.

OLGA: Only some of them . . .

ROSA: Yes, and then we start reading, one at a time and all that.

OLGA: I've learned almost all of them.

These three girls shared the activity of getting together with family in Juárez to read the newspaper comic strips. Amanda, Olga, and Rosa acted within the textually mediated social world of the family in Juárez. As per Olga's words, they engaged in reading comics reasonably regularly. In this case, through reading in Spanish with relatives on the Mexican side of the border, students participated as legitimate members of their family and their community. "Learning them" by memory also shows how children appropriated the discourses they found in the comics. Thus, this literacy practice was "inextricably connected to identity work" (Gee 2000, 412) as transfronterizx children who crossed the border and experienced their everyday lives on the Mexican side, in Spanish, and appropriated the discourses of Mexican popular media. These discourses were used for academic work—as will be presented later in this chapter; children and their discursive practices crossed borders twice: physically they crossed the U.S.-Mexico national border, and metaphorically, these literacy practices crossed the invisible boundaries between home in Juárez and the DL program in the United States.

Another activity which was popular with transfronterizx students was the *luchas* (Mexican wrestling). Jackelyn represented the lives of many transfronterizx children who had family on both sides of the border. In her case, she lived with one parent in each city. With her mother, and her family on her mother's side, she spent Monday through Friday in El Paso, while spending the weekend—starting Friday night—with her dad's side of the family in Juárez. During a focus group interview, when students were sharing their literacy practices, Jackelyn frankly and candidly stated that she rarely read anything outside of school except reading about *luchas* in a specialized magazine. This transfronterizx literacy practice was connected with her experience as a border resident because she watched and read about *luchas* on both sides of the border. *Las luchas* is a prevalent and entrenched Mexican tradition that many of the participants shared with family and friends in Ciudad Juárez. In her words below, Jackelyn described the different literacy practices that involve her love for *luchas*:

> Sometimes I start watching the *lucha* videos on the computer [at the library], I get pictures so I can put them up in my room. Pictures of several things, like of "peace" . . . And of the wrestlers, Miss, . . . On Mondays, I watch the *luchas* with my cousins from here [El Paso], and on Fridays, I watch them with my dad and my cousins from Juárez.

Jackelyn's example shows an everyday activity that crossed borders throughout the week and entailed various multimodal literacies. Watching *luchas* on TV was part of what she did, and she engaged in this activity with different people on both sides of the border. But Jackelyn also read about *luchadores* (wrestlers) in a specialized magazine and on the Internet while she looked for pictures of her favorite *luchadores*. Learning about the *luchas* was related to identity work as a transfronterizx who lives her life with her mother and mother's relatives in El Paso but with her dad and dad's side of the family in Ciudad Juárez on the weekend. She moved across national borders and cultivated practices that were related to Mexico, but she did it on both sides of the border, as part of her transfronterizx identity and way of life.

While in Juárez, the participants not only read material in Spanish but also produced their own written texts. Elsa liked to write poems and had a *poemario* (a notebook where she wrote her poems), mostly about love and friendship. Elsa learned this literacy practice when she visited her cousin, who lived in Juárez. The girl regularly updated her notebook by copying new poems from her cousin. Elsa's notebook was not only an artifact she kept; she shared these poems with her friends in El Paso. We once observed

Elsa and her closest friends gathered around her notebook, reading each poem and commenting whether they had heard or read it before or which one was their favorite. In this way, Elsa recontextualized (Barton and Hamilton 2005) her *poemario*, a practice initially developed in Juárez, and used it with schoolmates in the United States, most of them also transfronterizxs. This example shows Elsa recontextualizing a literacy practice by crossing the borders of community—school and Mexico—into the United States. Elsa used her linguistic capital as a resource for bonding with her new classmates and to navigate her world on the U.S. side of the border. We contend that these practices are part of the transfronterizx's "border thinking" (Mignolo 2000) because they allowed students to navigate the U.S. school through establishing affectionate relationships with their classmates.

Music played a significant part in the students' everyday lives. They listened to music using different media and recorded the lyrics on paper, computers, or other digital devices. Girls kept notebooks similar to Elsa's *poemario* with song lyrics in both Spanish and English. Some of these lyrics were written while in Mexico. One boy, Jonathan, also kept a notebook with written song lyrics. Although Jonathan did not want to show us the notebook, teachers and classmates had read it and described it to us. The notebook contained songs in both languages and included a variety of genres such as hip-hop radio hits, Mexican *rancheras*, and other music popular in the northern region of Mexico. Jonathan also wrote *narcocorridos*, ballads that tell stories about drug trafficking. The narcocorrido musical genre is a mass product and expression of the *narco-cultura* that "exalts traffickers as the new heroes of Mexican youth. This musical genre is specially accompanied by a specific kind of band called tambora or banda, typical of the state of Sinaloa, where the narcocorridistas celebrate the deeds of the fearless narcos who engage in 'adventures' with the Mexican police, the United States Drug Enforcement Agency (DEA), or the United States Border Patrol" (Holguín Mendoza 2011, 417). During the focus group, Jonathan sang a couple of songs. One of them was "El Águila Blanca" by Los Tucanes de Tijuana. The following were Jonathan's words when he sang this *narcocorrido*:

Judiciales a la vista claven todos relajados si preguntan yo contesto ustedes son mis empleados. Si hay algo no se asusten, estamos apalabrados . . .

[whistles] . . . Acabé de ver reten, los agentes preguntaron "¿a qué se dedican compas?" "Trabajamos de empresarios." "Tienen finta de mañosos bájense pa' revisarlos." Le hallaron un papel y una bolsita manchada. Les preguntaron ¿qué es esto?, contestaron de volada, ya con esto descubrieron que la troca iba cargada.

Officers on view, hide everything, everyone be relaxed, if they ask questions, I'll respond you're all my employees. If something happens, don't get scared, we have an agreement . . . [whistles] . . . When we got to the checkpoint, the agents asked: "What do you do?" "Pal, we work as businessmen." "You look suspicious, get out so we can check you." They found a piece of paper and a stained bag on him. They asked them what this was, they answered right away, and that's how they discovered that the truck was loaded [continues singing the song].

Liking, performing, using, and singing these songs in everyday practice are inextricably related to Jonathan's identity as a transfronterizx boy and his border-crossing activities. He learned *narcocorridos* while he visited Juárez: "Well, I would listen to it; every time I went to Juárez I would hear it." Jonathan, as all our transfronterizx participants, was knowledgeable about drug-trafficking operations and traffickers' relationships with some corrupt Mexican authorities. When asked about the song, Jonathan explained that policemen stopped narco-traffickers, who "called the people who sent them, and they knew the police officers, and they let them go." Children had access to various representations of the narco in mass media, music, films, tele-novelas, and fashion which often exalt death and violence. Transfronterizx literacies related to these depictions of violence were intimately associated with the identity work performed by youth living on the Juárez–El Paso border. In 2015, *narcocorridos* were prohibited in public events in Ciudad Juárez; other Mexican cities have promoted similar policies to avoid the promotion of violence and death. However, the easy access to *narcocorridos* through social media and the Internet has made these policy changes ineffectual.

This transnational literacy practice was intimately related to the lives of many youth, particularly boys, who were growing up in this border area. We have further developed the theme of violence affecting the students elsewhere (Araujo and de la Piedra 2013). For this chapter, it is essential to understand that the identities of many transfronterizx boys were shaped in a context where violence related to drug trafficking was commonplace. From 2008 to 2011, there were ten thousand violent murders in Juárez. Of these, 95 percent were men; many of them were youth (Cruz Sierra 2014). We knew of several boys of different ages who had expressed to their teachers in BES their wish to become *sicarios* (hitmen) when they grew up. This expression reinforced the implied or wished-for movement from people fleeing the drug violence to becoming part of it as hitmen. It also pointed to the influence that the students' border-crossing experiences played in the construction of their identities as transfronterizxs. For research that has studied the phenomenon of the border and transfronterizx youth, violent social practices, and masculine subjectivities, see the work of Cruz Sierra (2014) and Valenzuela Arce (2009).

It is important to stress that students were not only attracted by these images presented in the *narcocorridos*, but they were also terrified of the violence that was spreading in Ciudad Juárez. Students communicated their fears and needs for security. Thus, they were critical of the consequences of the narco-violence and the war on drugs by the *federales* (federal police) (Araujo and de la Piedra 2013). Regardless of this ambiguity and the disturbing nature of these multimodal literacy practices, they were part of the linguistic capital of transfronterizxs; that is, they were part of the repertoires of language practices which included "a plurality of differentially shared styles, registers, and genres, which are picked up (and maybe partially forgotten) within biographical trajectories that develop in actual histories and topographies" (Blommaert and Rampton 2016, 26).

Digital Transfronterizx Literacies

Print is only one among many modalities of communication, such as visual images, speech, sounds, and video (Barton and Hamilton 2005). Digital literacies—those that include the use of new communication technologies that allowed for transnational practices from below (Smith and Guarnizo 1998) as defined in chapters 1 and 2—were the most prevalent form of literacy within our focus group interviews and in our observations with the fifth and sixth graders. Digital literacies occurred on both sides of the border and children engaged in these literacies for different tasks such as recreation, and to stay in touch with family and friends in Mexico and the United States. When they participated in these literacies, transfronterizx students were not only reading and writing a wide variety of texts but also establishing affiliations with friends and family on both sides of the border.

Most of the boys and girls reported that they communicated with relatives and friends in Mexico and the United States using digital literacies. At the time of this fieldwork, some had their pages on MySpace and others reported using email accounts and Instant Messenger (IM) to communicate across borders or with friends and family who lived in the same city where they lived. Examples of different situations are detailed in the following paragraphs.

Johnny, Pepe, Mariel, and Amanda used their MySpace and Messenger accounts from their homes in El Paso to stay in touch with family living in Mexican border cities such as Juárez and farther inland cities such as Guerrero, Chihuahua, and Guadalajara. These literacies were mainly in Spanish.

> I chat with my cousins, we play, and then we post who lost on MySpace so that everyone can see it. And then we fight on camera, "that you're the worst cousin, that I don't know what else" and then we make drawings. (Amanda)

Some transfronterizx students had already participated in these transfronterizx practices before moving to the United States, as Rosa's words show: "When I was in Juárez, I would chat with the people from here." These multi-layered, multi-sited practices show the simultaneity (Levitt and Glick Shiller 2004) that characterized transfronterizx's practices.

Some of the students also had relatives in other parts of the United States, in which case they used both Spanish and English. Doris exchanged emails, mostly in English, with a cousin in Houston. Alberto exchanged emails with his cousin in Chicago. Antonela, who had recently changed schools in El Paso, wrote emails in Spanish "with my friends, some from another school, about how they're doing in school." Bertha communicated through MySpace with her brother, who lives in El Paso, but far from where she lives, in both languages. Also, classmates from the DL program wrote to each other using MySpace and email. Thus, social networks across both Mexico and the United States show how children maintained meaningful communications with people across boundaries and multiple localities (Smith 1994).

Students enjoyed reading and interacting with web pages about games, music, videos, and TV programs on the Internet. Five students reported using YouTube to download music. Most used "YouTube Mexico." For example, Pepe and Rosa watched soap operas in Spanish on the Internet: "On YouTube, sometimes the episodes of the novela (soap opera) that I miss, I go watch them there . . ." As the reader can imagine, watching YouTube in Spanish and visiting web pages of their favorite music bands, videos, and TV programs—many of them in Spanish—were ways to maintain their Spanish language and cultural practices.

Students used video cameras from computers, iPods, video game consoles, and cell phones to record themselves, their friends, their siblings, and other relatives. For example, one day Valentina showed us a video on her phone where she and her little brother had recorded a newscast. Amanda reported:

> The other day I made a video of my little cousin biting her fingernails and then her toenails . . . And then I put music on it, and then I uploaded it on YouTube, and then I saw it, and I told her, look at that little girl, who knows what she's doing?

Mariel also took pictures of herself with the family computer, and her sister helped her design her MySpace page using the images. Pedro added, "We make ourselves look deformed, we use effects."

The literacies we analyze here are a product of the fluidity and also of the contradictions argued by contemporary scholarship on the U.S.-Mexico border. Youth were savvy users of particular kinds of technology. In some ways, their practices are similar to those of other teens who do not live on the border. These were also particular to their transfronterizx lives on the border. Specifically, when students chatted or emailed with relatives on any side of the border, they showed their desire to maintain their different linguistic and cultural contacts on both sides. Digital literacies were important ways of accomplishing this. Digital literacies provided students with spaces of communication with friends and relatives living in Juárez even when they did not physically cross the border and were able to communicate with their friends and family in El Paso when they moved to Juárez for the day or weekend. These practices facilitated and also were a result of their transfronterizx lives; they showed students in a "state of 'betweenness,' orchestrating their lives transnationally and bifocally" (Smith 1994, 20). Digital literacies aided transfronterizxs to become involved in a fluid use of two languages and diverse cultural resources on a daily basis. They used biliteracy, both Spanish and English, in these communicative practices. Digital literacies contributed to "the continuous linguistic and cultural contact that border youth maintain as part of the multiple daily transactions across both sides of [the border]" (Relaño Pastor 2007, 264). Thus, they were connected to the students' identity work as transfronterizx members of their communities on both sides of the border.

Interestingly, a few of the students engaged in digital literacies in Juárez more frequently than in El Paso. According to Mariana, "We don't have Internet [in El Paso], but in Juárez we do, and I go to Juárez on the weekends." Mariana, like many others, felt that she had two homes, one in El Paso and the other in Juárez. She had Internet service at her home in Juárez, but in El Paso she went to her aunt's house to access the Internet. These instances showed how the students were "in a state of Nepantla (in-between) living within and among multiple worlds" (Anzaldúa 1999). Some of the students enjoyed access to more resources in Juárez while lacking these services in El Paso. Through their digital literacy practices, students lived and communicated these contradictions.

Transfronterizx Literacies for Academic Purposes

Print and Digital Literacies to Improve English Skills

These students participated in different worlds and this required from them an ample repertoire of literacy practices. They were learning how to navigate the DL program in a U.S. school. We found that they recontextualized their literacy practices within transnational spaces "in order to position themselves as academically . . . successful" (Hornberger 2007, 326). For example, Amanda, a student who had moved from Juárez a few months before our fieldwork, used an online translator to complete her homework in English, especially when looking for unknown vocabulary:

> When I don't understand a word, I translate them on the Internet, and then I understand them. (Do you really do that? Wow, Amanda!) No one sees me . . . [laughs] (How did you think of that?) I don't know, Miss, I put it in Google, and then I hit translator, and that's it, I translate whatever I want to say in Spanish or English, and that's it.

Other girls also reported they used this kind of strategy at home to improve their English. Amanda stated that she learned new vocabulary in English when she used an online translator: "I understand them [the words] better." Rosa added, "Miss, I do see an improvement from the English when I was in Juárez and [the one] here." The resourcefulness of these students came from their experience with digital literacies, mainly to communicate with friends and family on both sides of the border. Students recontextualized these literacies with an academic purpose: to improve their English language skills.

Like many of the students described in the previous chapter, Valeria was a transfronterizx student who exemplified the dynamic recontextualizing of literacies and texts we observed in these classrooms. From Monday through Friday, Valeria lived in El Paso with her mother and siblings. During the weekend, she visited her extended family. When in Juárez, she spent much of her time in her grandmother's house. During a focus group interview, Valeria told us that when visiting her grandmother in Juárez, she copied recipes from her grandmother's *recetario* (recipe book). During our observations and informal conversations with her, we noted a similar literacy practice that Valeria recontextualized, from the context of her grandmother's home in Juárez to her school in El Paso: copying songs in a *cancionero* (songbook) in order to improve her English. Valeria combined her print transfronterizx literacy practice of keeping a *recetario* with her digital literacies in order to keep a *cancionero* in both Spanish and English. On the Internet, she listened to music and looked for pictures and videos of her favorite genre, rock. Valeria believed this practice helped her to learn English: "Because on YouTube,

I play the song that I like and I get the lyrics, and I read it along . . . I start to learn the words [in English]."

According to Valeria's views, this transfronterizx literacy practice—characterized by recontextualizing and translanguaging—helped her to improve her English. Accordingly, this practice helped her to navigate the U.S. school context and was an example of not only the linguistic capital but also the navigational and resistant capital (Yosso 2005) that transfronterizxs had. According to Yosso (2005), navigational capital "acknowledges individual agency within institutional constraints" (80) and "infers the ability to maneuver through institutions not created with Communities of Color in mind" (80), such as schools, and shows students attaining academic success despite the institutional constraints. Resistant capital is "knowledge and skills fostered through oppositional behavior that challenges inequality" (80). During our interview, Valeria reported wanting to improve her English to avoid other students "making fun of her." As did other participants in this study, she experienced discrimination when her peers made fun of her for not speaking English "well." Recontextualizing her literacy practices and texts revealed the student's agency in confronting discrimination in this new educational context. Valeria, like other students, wanted to be "successful" in school, and to do that she needed to learn the language of power. However, the fact that she used her literacies in Spanish, across the border, simultaneously with recontextualizing her literacy practices with the purpose of improving her English demonstrated her desire to belong to her two worlds by creating her own "third space" (Moje et al. 2004). It is clear that from Valeria's perspective, recontextualizing this literacy practice was a navigational tool which allowed her to maneuver through the institutional constraints, as well as the structures of inequality that students found in schools. In the same way that the mothers analyzed by Villenas and Moreno (2001) wanted their daughters to learn, Valeria was learning to "valerse por si misma" (be self-reliant).

Other students communicated similar strategies as part of their community cultural wealth (that is, linguistic, navigational, resistant, and social capital). Improving their English skills was their main motivation for coming up with these strategies. Students wanted to improve their English to avoid other students making fun of them: "But the thing is that they make fun of us because we don't know English," said Amanda. "If we say a word wrong, well, they laugh at us," Olga added. The participants in this study experienced discrimination as transfronterizxs when they were made fun of by their peers for not speaking English. However, these literacies revealed the students' agency in confronting discrimination in this new educational context. As Vila (2005) suggested, the border is multiple in terms of the numerous identities people construct "around those borders, but those different borders acquire a distinct weight in relation to the different subject positions and the different narratives within that people decide to identify with" (233). We saw here students recontextualizing some of the transfronterizx literacy practices they used out of the context of the school in order to improve their English skills at school and position themselves as successful students in the new educational context in the United States. Transfronterizx literacies not only disrupted dominant ideologies of literacy as single and monolingual, but they also allowed students to meaningfully participate on both sides of the border by using their transfronterizx experiences with multiple literacies in both languages. In other words, students used their literacies from *aquí y allá* (here and there) as part of their everyday practices in the DL program, moving texts and practices across borders and creating a third space (Moje et al. 2004) and border thinking (Mignolo 2000).

The Use of Transfronterizx Literacies in a Multimodal Presentation of a Social Studies Theme

As part of their linguistic and navigational capital, students used their print and digital transfronterizx literacies in the classroom when doing academic work. From many events that we observed, we selected the following example as one of the richest regarding the ways students drew from their transfronterizx literacies and knowledge when designing and delivering an academic presentation that would appeal not only to their teacher but their classmates as well.

During an observation of the social studies period in the two-way dual language fifth grade class, fifth grade teacher Ms. Arredondo read the Spanish textbook about the American Colonization with the students.[†] The entire class was conducted in Spanish. They discussed the main ideas of each paragraph as preparation for the following activity, an oral presentation. The teacher assigned one part of the text to each team for role-play. One of the groups, composed of four girls, Ana, Mariel, Gabriela, and Patricia, developed the topic "John Smith y el Tiempo de la Hambruna" (John Smith and the Great Famine). They worked well together, and all participated collaboratively in the planning and rendering of a multimodal play. Multimodality will be further developed in depth in chapter 8; however, it is important to stress here that students drew from their ample repertoires of semiotic practices to make meaning of the social studies topic.

Ana and Mariel dominated the interaction because of their creativity when writing dialogues and including special effects in the role-play. Ana had the idea to include a remote control during the multimodal role-play, simulating playing a DVD. She drew a remote control with labels such as TV, CABLE, VOLUME, CHANNEL, PLAY, REWIND, and FORWARD. Ana planned to use it during role-playing, to forward, rewind, pause, and repeat small parts of the scenes. The girls also included large speech bubbles made out of cardboard, similar to those used in comic strips, in the play. They wrote or drew on these speech bubbles what the characters were thinking while they were speaking. For example, to communicate that the first English settlers were looking for gold instead of wanting to work the land, John Smith said, "Pero esto me hace chin chin" ("But this goes ka-ching, ka-ching"), and while this character talked, he held a speech bubble depicting dollar symbols. The inclusion of the remote control shows youth recontextualizing digital transfronterizx literacies in an academic setting. Similarly, the use of speech bubbles shows transfronterizx youth recontextualizing the literacy practice of reading the comics in a Mexican newspaper (described in the previous section) for academic purposes.

The girls used discourse they learned in Mexican films when writing a script for the role-play to make it more appealing to their audience. For

---

[†]Ms. Arredondo taught language arts and social studies and was the homeroom teacher for the two-way dual language group, while Ms. Ornelas taught math and science and was the homeroom teacher for the one-way dual language group.

example, Ana and Mariel wrote part of their script about how the Powhatan confederacy attacked the English settlers, especially how John Smith was made a prisoner and brought before Powhatan. The following is their narration of the instructions Pocahontas's father gives to a "servant" to look for John Smith:

ANA: "Ve por él y . . ." ("Go, get him, and . . .")

MARIEL: "¡Mátalo como un perro!" ("Kill him like a dog!")

The girls laughed when Mariel said this line. Mariel said, "I know this because my dad buys a lot of those Mexican movies." In the following few moments, the girls negotiated their next lines, clearly using their knowledge of Mexican films. Gabriela suggested the servant answer, "Sí señor, hago lo que Ud. me mande" ("Yes, sir, I will do whatever you ask"), and Mariel suggested something shorter instead: "Sí, señor, ¡a sus órdenes!" ("Yes, sir, at your service!"). Then Ana suggested that Pocahontas's father reply: "Así te vas" ("Just go"), and Mariel completed the scene by telling Ana to write "truena los dedos" ("snaps his fingers") in parenthesis.

The girls continued working enthusiastically. The next line in the script is about John Smith being taken prisoner by the Powhatan. At this point, the girls used their experience on the border and their shared experience of a game they play together at the end of the school day. Each girl suggested different lines: "Me persiguen" ("They're following me"), "¡Ahí viene la migra!" ("Immigration is coming!"), "¡Ah! Me alcanzan" ("Oh, they're catching up with me"), "¡Ah! Me atrapan" ("Oh, they got me"). They decided to use "¡Ahí viene la migra!", a line that Gabriela suggested after recalling a game the kids played when they saw several big trucks arriving at the school.

Drawing from their knowledge of both sides of the border, students also used discourse they learned from TV shows in English (like *Dora the Explorer*), such as words, idioms, and accents when it was fitting. For example, the girls wrote the following dialogue for John Smith: "Wow dude, hogar, dulce hogar. ¡Qué cool! ¡Lo que encontré! ¡¡¡Mucho y mucho dinero (oro)!!! Bling, bling." ("Wow, dude, home sweet home. How cool! What I found! Lots and lots of money (gold)!!! Bling, bling.") The dialogue was to be rendered in Spanish spoken with an English accent.

The students enjoyed organizing and performing this presentation. They captured the interest of their audience, which actively participated and added a few special effects to the play. The teacher ended the presentation congratulating the girls for their work but giving them feedback about the themes they did not cover within their selected topic. They had forgotten, for example, to address the famine. "You missed that little detail," the teacher said. As observers during this assignment we confirmed that while the role-play was spectacular, the knowledge of content was not sufficient to demonstrate mastery.

This event shows that by recontextualizing transfronterizx literacies and knowledge, these students were able to engage their subjective experiences and those of their classmates in ways that school texts alone did not. The students utilized transfronterizx literacies and their everyday experiences on the border to position themselves as academically successful in this DL program, organizing and implementing a presentation that was characterized as a success by both their teacher and their classmates. As introduced in chapter 1, we found several different experiences we could name "border" (Vila 2000). In this case, the four girls demonstrated fluid ways to incorporate literacies and knowledge they learned as transfronterizxs into their academic lives.

Discussion

In sum, students recontextualized both print and digital literacies from one side of the border to the other and from home to school. Through their everyday experiences with family and friends, they acquired literacy knowledge that was firmly related to their identities as transfronterizxs and, at the same time, became a resource in navigating the U.S. educational system and resisting structures of inequality, such as linguistic discrimination and racism. These were part of the transfronterizx students' repertoires of language and literacy practices, as well as their linguistic, navigational, social, and resistant capital.

The DL program and most of the teachers in it enabled this to happen. The freedom to use their native language to contribute to their academic development in a U.S. school made it easier for students to access their rich array of literacy practices, discourses, and knowledge acquired through their participation in multiple border worlds. By using their full repertoire of semiotic resources, including writing the script in Spanish, they were able to bring their transfronterizx literacies to the academic setting. We believe, as did the teacher who framed the girls' presentation as a satisfactory account, that the acquisition of school literacies is facilitated by creating spaces where students can use their literacies. By recontextualizing literacies, students combined their out-of-school transfronterizx resources in new ways and for new academic purposes. In this way, teachers created generative spaces where students could use and connect their transfronterizx digital and print literacies (their ways of knowing) with the purpose of successfully navigating the U.S. educational context.

6

Making Connections

Recontextualizing for Academic Writing

IN THIS CHAPTER WE DISCUSS how young transfronterizx students bring their literacy practices and content to the classroom.* We illustrate how transfronterizx texts are used for academic purposes, in particular in the context of learning narrative writing. We emphasize the role of one transfronterizx teacher who successfully facilitated literacies crossing many borders. Drawing on literature from DL education, the continua of biliteracy model, and the New Literacy Studies (NLS), we show students recontextualizing texts and practices. These processes help us understand biliteracy development in this border area, which is both global and local. We argue that developing awareness of how transfronterizx literacies are used in classrooms can provide teachers and researchers of linguistically minoritized students in other contexts with a better and complex understanding of the resources students bring to school in order to recognize ways in which to capitalize on these mobile resources for relevant educational experiences.

Transfronterizx students bring their linguistic and literacy practices to the classroom, in particular to writing instruction. In the previous chapter,

---

*This chapter is derived in part from an article by de la Piedra and Araujo (2012b) published in *International Journal of Bilingual Education and Bilingualism* on August 23, 2012, available online: http://www.tandfonline.com/doi/abs/10.1080 /13670050.2012.699949.

we explored the transfronterizx literacies of these youth, and we found that transfronterizx students' literacy practices transcend different borders, national borders as well as metaphorical borders between the home, the community, and the school. Thus, students take texts and practices across various borders. Transfronterizx literacy practices afforded students with spaces of communication with friends and relatives living on both sides of the border, creating an interesting back-and-forth movement of texts physically and virtually crossing the U.S.-Mexico boundary. These literacies are a result of an increasingly globalized world characterized by mobile linguistic resources. In this chapter, we will take our construct of transfronterizx literacies and discuss some ways in which we found students using these literacies for academic purposes. Thus, we will look at texts and literacy practices crossing national boundaries, as well as home-school boundaries. In the following examples, we will see that knowledge production was mediated by the teacher's and students' use of language and literacies. The teacher's role in this process, as well as the fact that the recontextualizing occurred in a DL program, was fundamental.

Transfronterizx Literacies and Recontextualizing

Particularly important for our discussion of transfronterizx literacy practices are the aspects of context. Drawing on the work of Blommaert (2010, as cited in Hornberger and Link 2012, 265), Hornberger and Link argue that in today's globalized world we need to understand the contexts of biliteracy as contexts "in which multilingualism and literacies develop within mobile multilingual repertoires in spaces that are simultaneously translocal and global." Thus, the notion of transnational literacy practices is important to understand biliteracy, in particular where we live and work: the U.S.-Mexico border region. (See chapter 1 for a developed definition of transnationalism and transnational literacy practices.)

As presented in chapter 2, we use the notion of recontextualizing in order to describe the mobility of textual practices and texts. Kell (2000), in her research on adult literacy in Africa, showed how common texts used outside of the adult literacy classroom were recontextualized into classroom practices. This process was not uncomplicated; conflicts related to identities and literacy skills arose. Kell looked at letter writing, a practice significant to the everyday lives of unschooled and resourceful adults in South Africa. However, this very same practice was recontextualized problematically into the adult literacy classroom, where adults were characterized as non-knowledgeable and had imposed on them a foreign and impractical way of writing and sending letters. Thus,

> taking a discourse from its original site of effectiveness and moving it to a pedagogic site, a gap or rather a space is created. As the discourse moves from its original site to its new positioning as pedagogic discourse, a transformation takes place. The transformation takes place because every time a discourse moves from one position to another, there is a space in which ideology can play. (Bernstein 1996, 47)

This ideology could take the form of modernism (Kell 2000) or, in the context of elementary classrooms, of linguistic assimilation, or the need of English monolingualism. However, we contend in a DL program there is also the possibility that an ideology of bi(multi)lingualism and multiculturalism could play in the gap or space created by the process of recontextualization. Recontextualization and "a focus on meaning making across contexts enables finely grained study of the relation between literacy, its affordances and issues of power and scale; in the context of intensified mobility and the flows of people, objects and information" (Kell 2011, 606–7).

Because recontextualization is concerned with understanding the movement of discourse across different contexts, including the ideologies and power relations that come with this process, it resonates with the everyday lives of transfronterizxs. Recontextualization helped us to understand better the local realities of children who read and wrote texts on both sides of the border, in Spanish and English, and with diverse purposes concerning their identities as transfronterizxs. Participants in this study frequently cross the Ciudad Juárez–El Paso bridge back and forth; when they do that, they recontextualize linguistic, cultural, and literacy practices.

As we have shown in the previous chapter, children recontextualized print and digital texts from their homes in Juárez to their homes and classrooms in El Paso. Print texts and literacy practices that enabled the elaboration of those texts were related to activities that children performed traditionally in Juárez, such as attending *catecismo* and reading the Bible in Spanish, reading the *chistes* in Spanish from a Mexican newspaper, reading about *luchas* in Spanish in a Mexican magazine, and writing *cancioneros* and *poemarios* in Juárez. They brought these texts and practices to El Paso social networks (for example, their friends at school). We also found digital transfronterizx literacies.

We situate the concept of recontextualization in the context of biliteracy continua. The ideas of recontextualization of literacy practices suggest a concept of "horizontal recontextualisations" (Kell 2011, 609) (that is, home-classroom), but also "global/local concerns suggested recontextualisation along a vertical axis, with the concept of global representing higher scale issues and broader power relations" (Kell 2011, 609).

Recapping our definition in chapter 1, transfronterizx literacies are the multiple ways in which youth communicate across national borders in and around print. They are intimately related to everyday life on the border and transfronterizxs' fluid and multiple border identities. These include the events where youth physically or virtually moved texts across national borders. These literacies vary regarding purposes, content, media, and identity work. "Recognizing, valorizing, and studying these multiple and mobile linguistic resources are part of what Blommaert (2010) refers to as a critical sociolinguistics of globalization that focuses on language-in-motion rather than language-in-place" (Hornberger and Link 2012, 263). We bring to the discussion of transnational literacies the notions of recontextualizing texts, literacy practices, and knowledge. We look at how one teacher consciously models what she calls "making connections," which are "border-crossing strategies" and recontextualizing practices. In addition, we ask ourselves what is globalizing about these literacy practices.

Facilitating the Use of Transfronterizx Biliteracy and Knowledge: Making Connections

As we described in chapter 4, some of the teachers were transnational and transfronterizx themselves. Thus they tended to better understand students who brought these experiences. However, others did not share this background or were less interested in incorporating students' transfronterizx literacies and knowledge in the classrooms, even in the dual language context. As Ms. Ornelas shared, some teachers "have not had the same experiences, understanding, or sensibility to work with this type of students." In this chapter, we share the case of Ms. Ornelas, a teacher who did construct a space for students to recontextualize transfronterizx texts, literacy practices, and knowledge. She articulated that in so doing, she helped students better navigate their U.S. school context.

Ms. Ornelas's teaching style included many of the practices that the bilingual education and English as a Second Language (ESL) literature presents as "best practices" for emergent bilinguals. One of the strategies she used and modeled for her students was "making connections." It was very common to hear her students yell enthusiastically, "Miss, I have a connection!" They made connections to their everyday knowledge, to prior experience on both sides of the border, between different texts they read, and also between how and what they learned in one content area related to another. The strategy of "making connections" was a way of recontextualizing knowledge, discourses, and text. Recontextualizing these meant crossing national, home-school, and disciplinary borders. The theme of "making connections" was salient throughout Ms. O's interviews, as it was during our observations of her teaching, as an essential tool to navigate the English-dominant and culturally different school context.

Reflecting on her own transfronterizx experience and on the fact that some of her students spontaneously transferred native language knowledge to their learning of English, she tried to be "a model" so students could also make their connections. Ms. Ornelas was aware that students used Spanish syntax when they spoke or wrote in English. She took that as an opportunity to explain the similarities and differences between the two linguistic systems' syntax. She also capitalized on the children's spontaneous strategies of crossing disciplinary boundaries, as can be heard from her words below:

> Sometimes I have to be very intentional and do it in front of the class, but sometimes I see the students doing it on their own. For example, when I check their writing, I see how they make changes, how they use the readings, books

they have read as examples to follow in their own writing. We see for example when we have visuals on the wall if they don't know how to say something they go and check on the posters. And they look at the words, or they check something they have already written before.

Ms. Ornelas's perception of Spanish as a resource was evident in the students' writing in English. She allowed students to code-switch in their writing, using Spanish words if they needed to and vice versa. She regularly taught the use of cognates in different academic areas, in particular for concepts of science and math. She also let class discussions occur in both English and Spanish, notably if translanguaging was the strategy that specific students needed to participate in the instructional conversation meaningfully.

In this classroom, "making connections" was part of the process of her students' learning, and, ultimately, it was her aim in teaching, as she said, "As a teacher, that is what you want for your kids. They think that [the academic knowledge] will be used only in school, but you want them to use it outside of class." From the teacher's perspective, "making connections" to the students' language and everyday lived experiences was "natural" for her as a transfronterizx. Furthermore, she promoted her students' recontextualizing of Mexican school knowledge and discourses. She allowed this process in her class not only because she saw the students' eagerness to share their knowledge but also because she saw this transfronterizx knowledge as a valid resource that students could use as tools to learn academic content. Making connections between school knowledge learned in Juárez and the content learned in the DL classroom is a practice that shows the bifocality (Smith 1994) and simultaneity (Levitt and Glick Schiller 2004) of transfronterizxs' lives:

> Another type of knowledge that they use in class is the academic knowledge that they bring from Juárez. They want to use that here. (Do you have examples?) Yes, I see that they want us to know that they did learn over there, and they show us . . . I have students who want to share almost by force: "Ms. Ornelas, in Ciudad Juárez we would do it like this." And of course, I let them go to the front of the class to show us and share so that they know that what they learned over there was not a waste of time, that it helps them and can still use it. I always tell them: "Kids, if you know it, use it. You don't always have to

do it my way. If you learned it differently, that is okay." . . . I feel that for them it is important that one recognizes that what they learned over there is valid and that they can still use it and so they don't think that we are going to forget that and from now on it is only about what we learn here.

In our observations, we could corroborate that Ms. Ornelas did facilitate students using their school knowledge from their experience in Juárez and that she continuously communicated the message that students could solve problems and do things in diverse ways. When writing, students had the freedom to select their topics and to choose their ideas of "enganchar al lector" (hook the reader). When solving math word problems, Ms. Ornelas encouraged students to share with the whole class their particular diverse ways of coming up with the result. When sharing their responses, Ms. Ornelas helped the students to write and draw their different solutions to their math problems on the projector for everyone to see. She did something similar with students' stories. In this way, Ms. Ornelas promoted children's recontextualizing their literacy and numeracy practices learned in Juárez in her classroom.

Recontextualizing Transfronterizx Literacies and Content

Using Transfronterizx Content When Writing Academic Texts

Students recontextualized their stories (their content) when learning how to write the narrative school genre. In addition to drawing on the features of the narrative genre and the writing process provided by the teacher, Ms. Ornelas's fourth grade students drew freely on their transfronterizx experiences and their stories in their native language in order to write their narratives. They learned language arts concepts and writing strategies in Spanish, such as:

1. Seleccionando el tema [i.e. "¿De qué pueden escribir los autores?" "¿Cómo generan los autores ideas para escribir?" "Coleccionar ideas," "Seleccionar

una idea"]; 2. El propósito de la escritura [i.e. ficción, ficción realista, ficción histórica, texto expositivo]; 3. El uso de organizadores gráficos en diferentes fases de la escritura y para diferentes géneros; 4. Recursos literarios [uso de diálogo, descripciones, metáforas, símil y animación para "enganchar al lector"]; and 5. Aspectos formales de la escritura [oraciones completas, "palabras elegantes," signos de interrogación y exclamación].

(1. Choosing the topic [i.e., what can the authors write about? How do authors generate ideas to write? Collecting ideas, Selecting ideas]; 2. The purpose of particular written genres [fiction, realistic fiction, historical fiction, expository text]; 3. The use of graphic organizers in different phases of the writing process and for different written genres; 4. Literary resources [the use of dialogues, descriptions, metaphors, similes, and animation in order to "hook the reader" or get the reader's attention]; and 5. Writing mechanics [complete sentences, elegant words, interrogation and exclamation signs]).

Students often learned these language arts concepts through the use of their transfronterizx experience and content.

On various occasions, students chose writing topics related to their lives in Ciudad Juárez. Sometimes the writing took the shape of a memory, remembering events that happened before the student moved to the United States. Other times, students wrote about events that they lived through during their regular visits to Mexico, either on weekends, summer vacations, or any day of the week. Visiting relatives in Ciudad Juárez was a frequent theme. Transfronterizx students lived on both sides of the border. Many lived with relatives, while their parents were still in Ciudad Juárez. In other cases, even if they moved with their parents to the United States, an essential part of their family was still living in Juárez. Thus "visiting relatives" took a particular connotation of everydayness, or *cotidianeidad*. Students also wrote about various fiestas in Juárez and other northern Mexican cities and about preparing and sharing their favorite Mexican food with their family and friends. Writing about celebrations and sharing food with relatives in Mexico is not just an everyday activity; it is intimately related to the identities of transfronterizx children.

For example, Valeria wrote about her father's birthday in Juárez and described her activities to get the ingredients for the birthday cake. In her writing, she uses her Spanish everyday discourse in the description of the local context of this event. We have not corrected her spelling or punctuation; however, we include an edited version of her writing in the footnote.[†]

La mañana habia amanecido muy magnifica: el sol brillante, fresco nada podia arruinarlo. Era el cumpleaños de mi papá el se había ido a su labor. Mi hermana y yo le quisimos hacer un pastel pero no teniamos los ingredientes. Asi que nos fuimos inmediatamente a alistarnos para ir a la tienda. Diez minutos después, nos fuimos a la abacería para comprar los ingredientes . . . La botica estaba llena, los pasillos llenos de gente ni podías pasar. Al fin pudimos pasar al pasillo de los pasteles. Escogimos los colores los ingredientes y la harina. Nos dirigimos hacia la cajera en la hilera había mucha gente. Rato despues pudimos salir de la tienda. Corriamos hacia la casa, atravesamos calles y banquetas hasta que llegamos.

(The morning had come magnificently, the sun was bright, fresh and nothing could ruin it. It was my dad's birthday, and he had gone to work. My sister and I wanted to bake him a cake but did not have the ingredients. So we immediately got ready to go to the store. Ten minutes later we left to the store to buy the ingredients . . . The store was full, the aisles were full of people and we could barely walk. Finally we made it through to the cake aisle. We chose the colors, the ingredients, and flour. We went to the cashier and there were a lot of people in line. Sometime after we were able to leave the store, we ran to the house, and crossed the street and sidewalks until we got there.)

[†]La mañana había amanecido muy magnifica: el sol brillante, fresco; nada podía arruinarlo. Era el cumpleaños de mi papá. Él se había ido a su labor. Mi hermana y yo le quisimos hacer un pastel, pero no teníamos los ingredientes, así que nos fuimos inmediatamente a alistarnos para ir a la tienda. Diez minutos después, nos fuimos a la abacería para comprar los ingredientes. (. . .) La botica estaba llena, los pasillos llenos de gente, ni podías pasar. Al fin pudimos pasar al pasillo de los pasteles. Escogimos los colores, los ingredientes y la harina. Nos dirigimos hacia la cajera; en la hilera había mucha gente. Rato después pudimos salir de la tienda. Corríamos hacia la casa; atravesamos calles y banquetas hasta que llegamos.

Valeria's account of a particular day in her life in Juárez shows her walking comfortably in the streets of this city with her sister and describing detailed scenes that are familiar to her and other transfronterizx. In this way, the teacher creates a space where Valeria feels free to recontextualize her everyday practices in her academic work. Through their writing, children were sharing what was important to them as transfronterizx, members of border families that maintain or renew familial links through these family events and rituals.

Using Transfronterizx Texts When Writing Academic Texts

Children also wrote about their favorite bands and singers. For example, for a "compare and contrast" writing assignment Tiffany selected two singers of Mexican northern music, Gerardo Ortíz, who sings *corridos*, and Jenny Rivera, who sings *rancheras*. Some singers, like Gerardo Ortíz, also sing *narcocorridos*, which very explicitly tell stories of drug traffickers. Tiffany's writing speaks to the knowledge and interest that other students also have about the *corrido*, *ranchera*, and *narcocorrido* genres. Some children chant these songs while they are doing their academic work. Frequently, we observed that when one child, usually a boy, started to sing a *narcocorrido*, then a group of students nearby, both boys and girls, would follow. If we did not pay attention to the lyrics of the song, this behavior would parallel the preadolescent conduct of any other group of children sharing music from the radio or YouTube. However, the words are an essential feature of these songs. They name traffickers, their territories, their rival groups, the weapons they use, their killing and torture strategies, and so on. Students do not just repeat these songs; they understand the characters, practices, and places portrayed in them.

Transfronterizx children learn these texts through the mass media and Internet, in particular through their access to YouTube, as was explained in the previous chapter. They discovered the lyrics by listening to the songs, by reading them on the Internet, by listening to relatives and friends, and when they went to Juárez. Reading, writing, and listening to this genre are parts of the vernacular literacies students engaged in outside the school and were a result of their life experience. It is alarming that transfronterizx children have firsthand knowledge of the violence lived "locally" in Juárez but also globally throughout the Americas. Disturbingly, these are part of the knowledge children bring with them to the classroom, as transfronterizx of this region, and we feel the need to document them and to think about what can be done to help students who are frighteningly learning how to deal with that reality.

In her writing, Tiffany recontextualized these transfronterizx texts in order to write a compare and contrast essay. She wrote about her admiration for Gerardo Ortíz, noting that she is his fan and would like to meet and sing with him. In her composition, the girl included titles of *narcocorridos*, such as "El cuerno de chivo" (AK-47 machine gun), but she did not write the lyrics. When we asked her about her essay, Tiffany simply clarified that it was not the *narcocorridos* she liked but the love songs he wrote. Children know that in their teachers' eyes, this music genre is not seen in a positive light. According to Ms. Ornelas, students felt ashamed of the transfronterizx reality of narco-violence, but they also enjoyed singing these songs and sharing them with their friends. This ambiguity reflects issues of identity formation of adolescents in our border region.

Because of its prevalence in the children's repertoire, even if *narcocorridos* include violent language, it should be a theme carefully discussed at school with the children. Ms. Ornelas addressed the subject of narco-violence when reading a book about gangs with her fifth grade class. Students "made connections to family members that are involved with gangs." Students were eager to share their stories. In the context of a language arts activity the teacher created a safe space for students to share their experiences, fears, and concerns resulting from the global aspects of drug trafficking–related violence felt throughout South, Central, and North America. The recontextualization of literacies and content into classrooms is important, as we have been demonstrating throughout the chapter. We propose that in the case of content and literacy practices embedded in situations of violence it is urgent that teachers help students to recontextualize these texts and practices. There is the need to create a safe space for dialogue and revision of the (global) social problem of violence manifested locally in this region, and these transfronterizx texts could become valuable tools for analysis.

However, this should be carefully planned and implemented by caring professionals who are well-informed of the reality.

Pedro's Story: Recontextualizing in Action

Next is a detailed example of how students learned language arts concepts through the use of their transfronterizx experience. It is similar to the others described earlier; however, we develop this one in more detail, presenting the interactional aspects of the writing lesson in order to discuss recontextualizing.

Ms. Ornelas's fourth grade class wrote about a hero in the students' families. Before the lesson described here, students had used graphic organizers to plan and organize their ideas. Depending on the selected written genre, students used a circle map, a climax organizer, a Venn diagram, or a cause-and-effect diagram. Most students chose to work on a narrative and started with the circle map and the climax organizer.

When students had written their first draft, Ms. Ornelas used the overhead projector to show the students how to develop the climax of a narrative fully. As she projected students' stories, she emphasized that students should slow down and add details to communicate the climax: "Muchos no me están dando el clímax, no le están sacando el jugo a ese limón." ("Many of you are not giving me the climax, you are not getting all the juice from that lemon.") She modeled having students asking questions of themselves, such as "Did I tell it too quickly?" or "Does it make sense?" and advised them to take their time to develop the climax of their story. She went over the first narrative, making sure the students understood what a climax was and how to develop it. Ms. Ornelas shared the second story from Pedro. He wrote about his father, who saved him from getting shot by a group of "narcos." Ms. Ornelas read the story aloud from the overhead. She reminded students again: "Entramos al clímax y nos tenemos que ir despacio y lo platicamos muy despacio." ("When we enter the climax, we slow down and tell it very slowly.") The students engaged in the discussion about the narrative feature. Pedro remarked that he was not sure if his story had a climax. Another student stated that this was probably correct because he did not plan his writing appropriately and added, "Solo las narrativas tienen clímax." ("Only narratives include a climax.")

Students also discussed the meaning and purpose of the story. Andrés asked, "Tengo una pregunta para Pedro: ¿Cómo está tu papá?" ("I have a question for Pedro: How's your dad doing?") Pedro responded that this event happened in 2006, that his father has a hole in his foot as a consequence of the shooting, but that he is doing fine. Andrés, engaging in a conversation and explaining his question, answered, "No sabía si quizá estaba en silla de ruedas." ("I did not know if maybe he was in a wheelchair.") At this point Pedro clarifies: "Mi historia no es completamente verdadera, es ficción realística. Lo que sí fue verdad fueron los balazos, pero que mi papá me salvó no era cierto." ("My story is not completely true; it is realistic fiction. What did happen was the shooting but my dad saving my life was not true.") He then continues to make the relation to the language arts concepts worked during that class as he adds, "Sí me doy cuenta que conté el clímax muy rápido, necesito contarlo más." ("Yes, I see now that I did tell the climax too quickly, I need to add more details.")

The following is an excerpt from the last draft of Pedro's story, which he wrote after working on his story's climax and before publishing it. We have not corrected Pedro's spelling or punctuation; however, we include an edited version of his writing in the footnote.[‡]

> Aviamos acabado de comer y mi papa nos dijo quien quiere ir al parque y todos asentimos la cabeza. Cuando aviamos llegado estábamos caminando pero de repente todos estaban temblando de terror otros corrían y también se tiraban al piso mientras los narcos venían hacia mi. Yo no sabia que pasaba

---

[‡] . . . habíamos acabado de comer y mi papá nos dijo: "¿Quién quiere ir al parque?" y todos asentimos con la cabeza. Cuando habíamos llegado estábamos caminando, pero de repente todos estaban temblando de terror. Otros corrían y también se tiraban al piso mientras los narcos venían hacia mí. Yo no sabía qué pasaba, así que yo solamente estaba jugando soccer hasta que se oyó: ¡Pam, Pam! Eran balazos. Yo salí corriendo, pero me tropecé. Cuando me levanté, un narco tiró el gatillo apuntándome, así que mi papá saltó hacia mí enviando la bala en contra de su pierna. No podía creerlo. ¡Mi papá me había salvado la vida! En un "flash" vino la ambulancia a atender su pierna y le pusieron yeso en el pie ¿Ya sabes quién es el héroe de tu familia?

así que yo solamente estaba jugando soccer hasta que se oyo -Pam Pam eran balazos. Yo salí corriendo pero me atrópese. Cuando me levante un narco tiro el gatillo apuntándome. Así que mi papa salto hacia mi impidiendo la bala en contra de su pierna. No podía creerlo Mi papa me había salvado la vida! En un "flash" vino la ambulancia a atender su pierna y le pusieron yeso en el pie ¿Ya sabes quien es el héroe de tu familia?

(He had finished eating, and my dad asked us, "Who wants to go to the park?" and we all bowed yes with our heads. When we got there we were walking, but all of a sudden everyone was trembling with terror; others ran and threw themselves to the floor while the narcos came after me. I did not know what was going on, so I kept playing soccer until I heard, "Pum, pum." It was the blast of a gun. I started running and I fell. When I got up a narco was pointing his gun at me. My dad jumped toward me as the bullet went into his leg. I could not believe it. My dad had saved my life! The ambulance came in a flash to take care of his leg, and they put a cast on his foot. Now do you know who is your hero?)

Some days later, Pedro told us that some elements of the story were real and others were fiction. He was with his father at the park playing soccer and ran to look for cover when they heard gunshots; however, his father was not truly shot. In the following days, other classmates also commented on this "realistic fiction" piece, which caused an impression and motivated conversations.

As seen from this example, the students are making meaning of the story, learning the structure of a narrative, and making connections to their transfronterizx texts, not only to write the story but also to ask each other questions. It shows how Pedro recontextualized a situation that happened in Juárez in an out-of-school context into a classroom practice.

Discussion

Seen through the lens of the continua of biliteracy model, the teacher created an instructional context where students developed biliteracy "along reciprocally intersecting first language-second language, receptive-productive, and oral-written language skills continua" (Hornberger and Link 2012, 265). This particular biliteracy context was characterized by a combination of monolingual and bilingual, as well as oral and literate language practices, according to the grade and the subject area covered. The students used translanguaging (García 2009)—as will be shown in detail in the following chapters—in order to learn the different content knowledge (medium). They also called on their understanding of the Spanish written system whenever they tried to make sense of the English linguistic structures and the similarities and differences between both languages' scripts. The use of cognates and the explicit instruction of the similarities were especially evident.

Although Ms. Ornelas's classroom was a local (micro) context, macro-levels in the form of the state policies and curricula made their way to the everydayness of the classrooms. This process explains the vertical recontextualization introduced by Kell (2011). The micro-levels were also present in the local context because of recontextualization, as children brought transfronterizx literacies. Recontextualizing literacies shows the DL classrooms observed as globalized worlds characterized by mobile linguistic resources.

The analysis of the students' notebooks and observations during class suggests that in Ms. Ornela's classroom, students learned the language arts concepts and skills required by the state-mandated curriculum and assessed by the then new test, the State of Texas Assessments of Academic Readiness (STAAR). In this particular year, the pressures to prepare students for the exams were evident at the district level because this was the first year of the STAAR's implementation. Besides, the district had adopted a new curriculum which, in the district's view, was a better match to the exam. Thus, teachers and students felt these new policies present in the local contexts of their classroom. The distant (global), disconnected, and powerful context of the Texas Education Agency with its policies written with no bilingual transfronterizx student in mind is, nevertheless, so profoundly present in the everyday local realities of the DL classrooms observed. The literacy practices and the "literacy technologies" (Brandt and Clinton 2002) promoted by these global institutional contexts in the form of standards, tests, and prescriptive curricula are very much there in the classrooms.

However, in her classroom, the teacher created a local context where transfronterizx content was also present. Students expressed content "encompassing majority to minority perspectives and experiences, literary to vernacular styles and genres, and decontextualized to contextualized language texts" (Hornberger and Link 2012, 265). In other words, students learned content that came through these literacy artifacts, such as how to write narrative texts, using various graphic organizers to support the writing process, and writing mechanics in Spanish through the use of content that portrayed their experiences as transfronterizx. As Pedro's example shows, this material was not only used for academic learning, but it was also shared and authentically discussed by teacher and classmates. Besides the formal aspects required by the language arts state curriculum, meaning-making of the content of interest to students was also a purpose for this activity.

In the examples of writing in the fourth grade classroom, students expressed content that encompassed "minority perspectives and experiences" (Hornberger and Link 2012, 265) as they learned literary and traditionally decontextualized forms of school writing:

> The continua model posits that what (content) biliterate learners and users read and write is as important as how (development), where and when (context), or by what means (media) they do so. Whereas schooling traditionally privileges majority, literary, and decontextualized contents, the continua lens reveals the importance of greater curricular attention to the minority, vernacular, and contextualized whole language texts. (Hornberger and Link 2012, 268)

We consider these texts written by transfronterizx children, in part, minority texts, because their authors are minoritized, they are written in the native minoritized language, and they are apparently written from their perspectives, accounting for meaningful experiences in their everyday lives. However, they are also texts constructed in the classroom context with the purpose of teaching the state curriculum.

In conclusion, through their written productions, students recontextualized their stories and lived experiences from Juárez into the context of this classroom in El Paso. We agree with other researchers (Kell 2000) that this process is complicated because of the differential status between the dominant language arts state curricula and the transfronterizx stories and contents children recontextualized. However, we also believe that in this particular classroom the space created by moving specific transfronterizx discourses was filled by an ideology that favors bilingualism and children's funds of knowledge (González, Moll, and Amanti 2005), including transfronterizx funds of knowledge and experiences. See chapter 4 for a description of ideologies of empathy and care, as well as chapter 9 for other examples of funds of knowledge utilized in the classroom.

Through her "making connections," "crossing borders," or recontextualizing strategies, Ms. Ornelas valorized many points along the continua of contexts, media, content, and development. The "making connections" practice in this local classroom was a hybrid practice (Gutiérrez, Baquedano-López, and Tejeda 1999), one that occurred in multilingual classroom ecologies (Creese and Martin 2003) that "offer possibilities for teachers and learners to access academic content through the linguistic resources and communicative repertoires they bring to the classroom while simultaneously acquiring new ones" (Hornberger and Link 2012, 268).

7

Translanguaging

Access to Science Discourse

IN THIS CHAPTER, we analyze meaning-making practices in a fourth grade two-way dual language (TWDL) classroom. We show that emergent bilingual learners and their teacher participate in activities that mediate the understanding of science content. The teacher creates a borderland space in which the full repertoire of students' languages, including translanguaging, is recognized and validated. We illustrate how the teacher guides students to use strategies and meaning-making tools in both languages to construct meanings of the science content. We also demonstrate how she scaffolds students' language development, develops students' higher-order thinking, and involves all students in constructing understanding. We end with a discussion and suggestions for DL teaching.*

Emergent bilingual students face the challenge of developing disciplinary knowledge in content areas such as science. While dominant ideologies that favor English-only approaches consider these students merely as English Language Learners (ELLs) (defined by their relationship to English), other approaches consider the wealth of meaning-making resources emergent

---

*This chapter is derived in part from an article by Esquinca, Araujo, and de la Piedra (2014) published in *Bilingual Research Journal* on August 8, 2014, available online: http://www.tandfonline.com/doi/abs/10.1080/15235882.2014.934970.

bilingual students already possess. In this chapter, we illustrate how emergent bilingual participants of this study, with the guidance of their teacher, learn to use the full range of meaning-making tools—including translanguaging—to mediate understanding in science. The questions that guided the analyses include the following: How do children in TWDL classrooms construct school science knowledge in a program in which science is taught in English? How does a language-separation approach impact TWDL students' construction of science content understanding? Focusing on the classroom interaction in one TWDL classroom, we show how the teacher, Ms. Ornelas (Ms. O), creates a borderland space in which the full repertoire of students' semiotic resources is recognized and validated. We illustrate how Ms. O guided students to use translanguaging and other mediating tools such as multiple modalities to learn science content. In what follows, we briefly review the literature on science education and then present the findings.

Sociocultural Perspective on Science Education

A sociocultural perspective of science education, according to Lemke (2001), views human social activity as central to science and science education and contextualizes those activities sociohistorically. Human interaction in institutional contexts, such as schools, takes on a weighty role because it is within the context of those human interactions where learning occurs. Similarly, Lave and Wenger (1991) showed how social interaction, occurring in communities of practice, promotes meaningful learning. Indeed, as Lemke (1997) has written, thinking is tied to human participation in activities with persons, tools, symbols, or processes.

Thinking and learning, in a sociocultural view, has a social origin, as neo-Vygotskian scholars have shown (Moll 2014; Smagorinsky 2011; Wertsch 1991). The notion of scaffolding relies on the Zone of Proximal Development (ZPD), an idea based on the observation that there are

two levels of development in a learner: the actual developmental level, which is determined by what the learner can do alone, and the potential level of development, which can be established by observing what the learner can do when assisted by an adult or a more capable peer. (de Guerrero and Villamil 2000, 51)

Scaffolding refers to the activity that takes place at the ZPD as a more capable peer or adult, in social interaction, assists the learner in an activity that the individual will eventually be able to do alone. Wood, Bruner, and Ross (1976, 98) cite six essential elements of scaffolding: (1) recruiting interest in the task; (2) simplifying the task; (3) keeping to the goal; (4) marking critical features of discrepancies between the produced and the ideal solution; (5) controlling frustration and risk during problem solving; and (6) demonstrating an idealized version of what is produced. In order for the scaffolding process to work, the learners' emergent autonomy should be supported and encouraged by the teacher until mastery of a certain task occurs.

To become independent problem-solvers, students need assistance from an adult or peer collaboration through the use of scaffolding. Given the Vygotskian notion that the individual internalizes functions that first appear in social interaction, guiding learners toward appropriation involves the creation of activities that will promote it. These activities can be carefully planned and structured, or they can be loosely organized and unpredictable. As learners become autonomous, they regulate their own activity. Self-regulation takes place when children begin to use for themselves the signs that adults used to regulate their activity (Díaz, Neal, and Amaya-Williams 2001; Tudge 2001). Díaz, Neal, and Amaya-Williams (2001) define self-regulation as "[a]dult teaching characteristics that promote self-regulatory development—verbalization of plans, rationales, and goals, and the adults' gradual and sensitive withdrawal from the regulatory role" (140).

Meaning-Making by Bilingual Children: A Sociocultural Perspective

Learners have been shown to draw on a full range of meaning-making abilities in a learning activity. In studies of bilingual children in literature discussions, children are shown to use Spanish to interpret materials in English (Reyes and Azuara 2008), to use both languages to retell narratives written in one of the languages (Martínez-Roldán and Sayer 2006), and to use Spanish to make sense of English narratives (Moll 2014). As Moll (2014) notes, such studies demonstrate a Vygotskian principle "that what is possible to achieve in the end is already available in some form in the beginning, in the immediate environment" (79).

In addition, bilingual children provide scaffolds for each other in order to help each other understand, including the use of translation or paraphrasing. Language mediation among bilingual children includes processes and strategies such as what Olmedo (2003) terms "the bilingual echo," which is when "a child spontaneously tries to mediate the language comprehension or concept learning of a peer through a variety of linguistic and paralinguistic strategies" (150). In Olmedo's study, students used diverse strategies such as translation, scaffolding, and modeling behaviors. According to Olmedo, "the strategies addressed either an actual instance of miscommunication or situations in which a child perceived that a peer needed assistance, either because of lack of comprehension, lack of knowledge, or failure to respond appropriately" (151). The "literate talk" (Gibbons 2009) or "science conversations" (Kurth et al. 2002) that we observed in this particular classroom are examples of strategies that help children move from apprenticeship to appropriation. As described by Gibbons (2009), through these strategies teachers model the language and thought processes of the discipline. In the TWDL classroom we observed, such strategies took place through translanguaging.

From a sociocultural perspective, learning comprises a change in the relationship between the learner and the world (Hedergaard 2001). This change happens "through the subject's appropriation of tool use and artefactual knowledge" (15). In the study presented here, students work toward accomplishing knowledge construction. The sociocultural perspective on learning has helped us see how the teacher and the students use their diverse resources "to create environments in which old and new knowledge can be marshaled to achieve optimal achievement" (Vásquez 2006, 52).

Translanguaging as Mediation

As discussed, language mediates learning. The flexible and dynamic use of bilingual discourse practices, hereafter referred to as translanguaging, mediates learning for bilingual learners. The idealized notion of a balanced bilingual, one who keeps two languages separate and never mixes the two, has traditionally been lionized as the hallmark of a "true" bilingual (Valdés 2003). Translanguaging, however, challenges monolingual bias (García 2009, 2012); monolingual bias censures it and frames it from a deficit perspective. Defying deficit perspectives, we instead use the term emergent bilingual (García 2009), which is an asset-oriented perspective.

A translanguaging framework proposes that bilingualism is a resource that can be developed and conserved by educators (García 2012). According to García and Kleifgen (2010), translanguaging includes practices such as: (1) shifting between text in one language and discussion in another; (2) moving across texts that feature different languages; (3) discussing in one language but checking comprehension in another; (4) reading in one language and writing in another, discussing in one language and writing in another (see also Esquinca 2011); (5) integrating students' language resources; and (6) using both languages flexibly in microalternation, or code-switching. "A translanguaging approach to bilingualism extends the repertoire of semiotic practices of individuals and transforms them into dynamic mobile resources that can adapt to global and local sociolinguistic situations" (García and Wei 2014, 18).

Researchers who propose the concept of translanguaging or similar terms such as polylanguaging, heteroglossia, codemeshing, and translingual practice (see Lewis, Jones, and Baker 2012, 649) argue that it "better captures the sociolinguistic realities of everyday life" (García and Wei 2014, 29). Studies have found translanguaging practices outside schools in different contexts and for diverse functions, such as communication in the family (Orellana 2009) and multimodal writing through instant messaging (Lam 2009). Other researchers have focused on translanguaging in school environments (Canagarajah 2011; Creese and Blackledge 2010; García and Sylvan 2011; Martínez 2010). These authors concur that translanguaging is generally used by bilingual and multilingual speakers, even in situations where curriculum planned the separation of languages. These studies document the fluidity and flexibility of language use in classrooms when bilingual teachers and students use different communicative resources at their disposal in order to create understanding, connect with one another, and make sense of their bilingual worlds.

In particular, a few studies focus on Content and Language Integrated Learning (Coyle, Hood, and Marsh 2010), where students use their languages and semiotic resources for different academic activities and purposes, and where language scaffolding (Gibbons 2009) occurs in a safe and supportive environment. According to Baker (2006), one of the advantages of translanguaging is the promotion of a deeper understanding of subject matter through the use of ZPD and cross-linguistic transfer. If students do not understand the language they are being taught in, it is next to impossible to construct meaning and learn meaningfully. Using the full range of bilingual meaning-making resources, including translanguaging, expands thinking and understanding. It gives teachers and students opportunities to build on their strengths and to acknowledge and use a full range of linguistic practices to improve teaching and learning. This study adds to the literature that describes and analyzes translanguaging practices and their potential for content learning and academic achievement.

Using Translanguaging as a Pedagogical Practice

As noted earlier, science was taught in English in the TWDL setting we researched; the language of instruction and course materials were all in English. Ms. O presented, explained, and gave instructions to students using English. As for the students, some would also participate in English, but many would use Spanish in classroom communication with peers and with the teacher. Rather than ignoring Spanish contributions or consistently asking students to repeat the message in English, Ms. O acknowledged and responded to students. Ms. O took students' ways of knowing and talking seriously and engaged with them mediated by translanguaging and multiple modalities.

For instance, in a science unit on forms of energy, Ms. O led a discussion aided by a multimedia lecture on the same topic. Streamed from the Internet, the lecture was available directly through a district subscription service. It relied on animation and hypothetical scenarios to guide students to become aware of the different forms of energy in the world around them. Using the scenario of a rock concert, the lecture identified different forms of energy.

Ms. O chose excerpts of the video for discussion. Perhaps due to the length of the video and the complexity of the concepts being presented on this occasion, we observed Ms. O stopping the video seven times. Each time she stopped it, she went over the concept, extended the dialogue, and encouraged students to make connections to their everyday life or to other concepts, with discussion taking place in both languages. Social interactions in both Spanish and English about the content of the video allowed students to construct understandings about concepts discussed in the video. Spoken interaction among the participants, visual representations from the video, sounds, images, and recollections all became meaning-making tools for students. Thus, translanguaging and multimodality (Kalantzis and Cope 2012; Kress 2010; New London Group 1996) were used throughout the episode.

The following excerpts show how in the discussion between Ms. O and her class, students' participation was recognized and used to further the group discussion. To define insulation and conduction, the video referred to several examples of insulation of different forms of energy: plastic-insulated copper wires that powered the musicians' instruments and a thermos onstage. Namely, copper conducts energy, and plastic insulates the energy.

After she stopped the video again, Ms. O refocused the class's attention on the broader topic, different types of energy. She asked the class, "What about sound? Between a foam or a wooden door, which insulates or conducts sound energy?" Through this refocusing, she connected the topic of light energy to different forms of energy, including sound energy. Students were initially quiet since the excerpt they had just seen was on the topic of insulating light energy. Ms. O told them after a while, "Wood is a good conductor of sound." Once Ms. O said that, students became animated and interested in the topic of sound conduction. One girl went to the wooden door of the room and knocked on it. At this action, a second girl asked, "¿Entonces por eso se oye?" ("Is that why it makes a sound?"), to which Ms. O answered, "Molecules are packed together [in wood]."

The realization that materials conduct sound energy caused students to ask a number of questions about the topic. While the teacher spoke English and the video was in English, the students almost all participated in Spanish. One student, for instance, asked what the best conductor is, a paperback book or a plastic pencil box. To help the student answer the question, Ms. O then knocked on a book and on a box and asked, "Which is the best conductor? Why?" A girl answered, "Porque aquel agarra aire [entre las moléculas]. Es un tipo de material diferente." ("That one has air [between molecules]. It's a different type of material.") Probably wanting the student to refer to molecular structure, Ms. O asked, while pointing to the plastic pencil box, "How are the particles here?" Together, several students answered. The episode exemplifies how bilingual conversations about molecular structure maintain a conversational coherence. Instead of interrupting the flow of the conversation, Ms. O continued the discussion using translanguaging as a tool. Namely, she did not interrupt students if they did not use English. Thus, she engaged with students in English; some students participated in Spanish and others in English. Translanguaging was a tool she was able to use to get students to understand the concept of molecular structure.

Furthermore, we also observed Ms. O simultaneously modeling the process of observing the natural world, making hypotheses, and explaining why observed phenomena occur. After the previous episode, Ms. O pointed to the two objects again, the book and the plastic box. "Both of these are solids. This one [pointing to the paperback book] is flexible. This one [plastic pencil box], I can't bend it. [The box] is a more rigid solid. Which one is louder? Why again? This one [hardback book] is rigid. This one [paperback book] is soft. This one is cardboard, como cartón." This was one of the few times we witnessed Ms. O translating a term, cardboard, into Spanish. The episode also shows that translanguaging was used to clarify the meaning of a term.

The episode suggests that participants interact around meaningful ideas in a way that allows them to understand the concept at hand. One of the most effective tools here is translanguaging. It allowed students to construct meanings drawing on their background experiences while the teacher guided students to develop higher-order thinking, particularly explaining observed phenomena in the natural world using scientific concepts (Sandoval and Millwood 2005; Schleppegrell 2004), including molecular structure. The fact that the class was able to make meaning in two languages suggests that translanguaging promoted meaningful understanding of the conductors of sound energy. Through the use of key questions and translanguaging, Ms. O was able to facilitate movement across the ZPD for her students. As Warren et al. (2001) state, it is vital to take seriously students' ways of knowing and speaking. All too often, they argue, scientific ways of knowing are seen as entirely distinct from everyday practices, especially when they come from minoritized communities.

A Social Interactive Approach to Develop Students' Science Thinking

Meaningful activities to support learning, and in which a more capable other can scaffold learners' thinking, are vital. To that end, Ms. O designed collaborative science activities in which she could guide individual students to construct understanding using their two languages. In her discussions, she often exhorted students to use their prior knowledge and to use science principles to explain why observable facts take place, as the next example suggests. Moreover, she guided students to become aware of their own thinking processes and raised their awareness of the value of making connections.

We identified many different instances in which Ms. O organized instruction for children to dialogue meaningfully. Not only did students respond to teacher-posed questions, but they also posed real and thoughtful questions to the teacher and to the class as a group. For instance, during a science class on physical properties of soil, we found that Ms. O deliberately presented "high support along with high challenge" (Walqui and van Lier 2010, 7). After conducting an experiment and recording students' observations about physical properties of soil, clay, sand, and gravel, Ms. O asked them to orally answer the question "How do humans use soil? Think in real life." Children started to call out brief answers such as "for plants" and "construction." Alejandra offered "for compost." Her intervention started a conversation about compost, which was a topic most of the children did not know much about. Ms. O asked her to define what compost was, and she offered: "It's some dirt to use for the worms." Next, Ms. O and Alejandra had the following exchange.

MS. O: You mix soil with . . .
ALEJANDRA: With trash.
MS. O: What kinds of trash?
ALEJANDRA: Peeling bananas.

Ms. O followed the exchange with a more detailed definition of compost, adding that compost is soil that is good for plants. She then asked children a kind of question that required thinking: "Why do you think that soil is better to grow plants?" When Ms. O noticed the students still did not quite understand the meaning of compost, she drew compost on the board (soil, vegetables, and fruits), and added that compost is soil to which "food left-overs" are added, specifically "vegetables and fruits." She then repeated the question: "Why do you think that soil is better to grow plants?"

At this point, students started thinking and risking their answers even though they were not entirely sure if they were correct. Vanessa stated the following: "I think, no estoy segura, pero yo pienso . . . because no dirty, no está sucia, porque es como tierra blanda, abajo puedes enterrar semillas." ("I think, I'm not sure, but I think that . . . because it's not dirty, but it's like soft soil and you can plant seeds.") Ms. O restated her question: "Pay attention to my question; when you mix soil with food leftovers, banana, tomato peel, if you plant a seed a plant will grow. Why?" After some time, a boy responded, "Because it's good soil; [it] has leftovers." Through her line of questioning, the teacher scaffolded students' thinking to make connections between students' prior knowledge of science and the topic at hand:

MS. O: What do leftovers give soil?

BOY: Energy, vitamins.

MS. O: Vitamins, minerals, nutrients! (Writes these words down next to the drawing of compost she made on the board.) Those vegetables and fruits, that food has energy in them. Those vitamins, minerals, and nutrients will mix with the soil, and the plants are going to absorb them.

This event shows the way the teacher scaffolded the students' under-standing of the concept of soil nutrition. With regard to this finding, the teacher also reinforced connections that students made between Spanish and English vocabulary, when Vanessa asked, "¿Qué significa vitamins?" ("What does 'vitamins' mean?") and other students answered, "¡Vitaminas!" The teacher explicitly points out the cognate: "Vitamin, it looks like a word in Spanish," scaffolding translanguaging. Thus, Ms. O made connections across languages and across scientific concepts. Moreover, it shows how creating spaces for students to think aloud under the guidance of the teacher allows students to refine their thinking and clarify their insights (Keys 2000).

Three weeks later, during a unit about constructive and destructive forces that change the surface of the earth, Ms. O continued to guide students to make more connections. The following episode illustrates ways in which students appropriated the practice of making connections. On a lesson about volcanoes, students were able to connect to the previous lesson about soil. During the observation, the students were very interested in the topic and asked each other and the teacher if there was a volcano in El Paso. At one point, Juliana made a spontaneous and autonomous connection, which the teacher followed by a third connection:

JULIANA: Un día leí un libro de volcanos y saqué mucha información. La lava es buena para los animales y para las plantas. ¿Por qué aquí no? (One day I read a book about volcanoes, and I got a lot of information. Lava is good for animals and for plants. Why not here?)

MS. O: I'm happy you say that. Let's make a connection with the unit of soil. Remember which is the best kind of soil?

As Juliana's questioning suggests ("Why not here?"), she was curious as to how her research contradicts how volcanoes are being characterized in the discussion, where volcanoes are described as destructive and therefore not good. Juliana was exercising agency by challenging the information being presented. Other students chimed in and connected that day's discussion to the discussion that took place three weeks prior. Other students recalled that the best soil is the one that has dead animals and plants. The teacher confirmed and explained that these transform into lots of minerals: "Plants and animals eventually mix with soil," and she added, supporting Juliana's idea, that although at the beginning a volcano generates destruction, it also enriches the earth afterward. A student concluded, "It's like a cycle."

Students' incipient scientific reasoning is intimately tied to social, cultural, and historical contexts (Lemke 2001). In the previous excerpt, students made connections to real-life places and events. In addition, the group discussion, one of many we observed in Ms. O's classroom, allowed students to ask questions, hypothesize, formulate ideas jointly, and explain (Rivard and Straw 2000), all hallmarks of scientific reasoning. Moreover, such inter-actional activities allowed students to display their competence as science learners (Crawford 2005) using language and references that are meaningful in their local context.

Involving All Students in Constructing Understanding

As we have shown, Ms. O involved all students in class discussion and guided them to observe, question, hypothesize, and explain using translanguaging as pedagogy. As students began to appropriate science concepts and learning strategies, Ms. O involved them all so that they could help each other using whatever meaning-making strategies were useful. In other words, she cre-ated a community of practice (Lave and Wenger 1991) in which learners at different stages of development could provide aid for one another.

On one occasion, during a lesson on the phases of the moon and the position of the moon in relation to the earth and sun, we documented an example of peer scaffolding mediated by multiple meaning-making tools, including translanguaging and multimodal representations (Kalantzis and Cope 2012; Kress 2010; New London Group 1996). On the day of the obser-vation, we noted that the class had spent some time previously talking about the pattern in the phases of the moon, and that day students were defining each moon phase. Guided by Ms. O's drawings, students went up to the board to define each phase, while the other students worked independently at their desks.

Ms. O also handed out a piece of paper with written definitions of each phase. Students had to read and demonstrate understanding by drawing what was on the paper. Next, Ms. O demonstrated the task as follows. Using one of the definitions, Ms. O underlined the phrase "not reflecting light" and then asked one student, Maricruz, to draw a moon that matched what she had read.

MS. O: What does "not reflecting light" mean to you?
SEVERAL STUDENTS: No light.

MS. O: In your notebook draw the moon, and we are going to show it not reflecting any light. Cut the description [from the handout] and glue it here [on the science journal]. Let's do a second one, and let's see who can help me. [Reading the next definition] "One quarter of the side of the moon that is facing earth appears to be reflecting light from the sun. The light is increasing." You want to come and help me, Regina?

REGINA: Yes. [Student goes up to the board to draw.]

MS. O: [Reading] "Only one half of the side of the moon facing earth appears to be reflecting light from the sun. The light is increasing."

Next, Regina drew on the board to match the definition. At the same time, kids drew the moon independently at their desks. She then asked a couple more students to draw on the board just as Regina had. Matching across meaning-making systems, linguistic and visual, allowed learners to attend to the meaning of the scientific concepts (Kalantzis and Cope 2012; Kress 2010). Multiple modalities mediated understanding of the concept of the phases of the moon.

As students worked in their science journals, Ms. O circulated around the room. Next, she noticed that one student seemed stuck because she was not drawing, reading, or saying much. She reminded students about the reading strategies she had shown them before. "Look for keywords that can help you." Next, she addressed the student who seemed stuck directly. "Are you struggling, Tiffany?" Ms. O then approached Tiffany to help her. When another student, Vanessa, also noticed that Tiffany was struggling, she approached Tiffany and spoke up: "Así como usted nos dijo que tacháramos las palabras que no sabemos. (Just how you told us to do: to cross off the words we don't know.) Focus on the words you know. Underline the words you know." It is important to emphasize that these were words that the teacher had used previously to guide students' reading comprehension. Vanessa's languaging suggests that she inserts into her own speech the words of the teacher and is appropriating the meaning of the reading comprehension strategy; her utterance is heteroglossic (Bakhtin 1981) and strategic. Second, this instance shows how bilingualism is a resource for learning in Ms. O's class. Vanessa translanguages with ease, using Spanish and English to quote Ms. O's reading strategy in the source language. As the literature has shown consistently, quoting is a frequent motivation to code-switch (Martínez 2010). It suggests as well that Vanessa has appropriated the reading strategy to such an extent that she is capable of quoting it when necessary.

Vanessa's aid to Tiffany demonstrates two aspects of this learning situation, akin to Olmedo's (2003) concept of the bilingual echo. It shows how peers can scaffold each other's reading comprehension. Vanessa took the cue from Ms. O regarding keywords and, confident that Ms. O would value her contribution, helped her peer. The example shows the result of the practice of scaffolding translanguaging: student self-regulation.

Discussion

Meaning-making in science in this TWDL classroom involves a dynamic use of language and other semiotic resources. Translanguaging is a recurring discourse practice as well as a pedagogical tool that the teacher uses. Namely, Ms. O guides students to explain using scientific principles, all mediated by oral language, narratives, visual representations, and sounds. Also, students participate in learning communities in which they share learning with each other and help each other to learn as well.

Meaning-making by translanguaging is a vital discourse practice in TWDL classrooms. Languages do not remain separate in classroom talk even though the language-separation approach is often considered an essential component of TWDL programs, owing to the theoretical assumptions about second-language learning (Krashen and Terrell 1983), as well as the need to safeguard spaces for nondominant languages. The vitality of multiple languages and voices can become a pedagogical practice for teachers like Ms. O to help students learn content. As we have shown here, there were numerous and varied examples of students' use of the full range of language and other meaning-making practices, which included the use of cognates, breaking down procedures into steps, and appropriating learning strategies. These practices helped students to learn science content, and they went on regardless of the fact that the teacher delivered instruction in one of the languages. Students used translanguaging practices in science, including translating, multimodality, paraphrasing, and code-switching, in every class meeting. This finding is consistent with recent research that draws on interactionist theoretical perspectives and shows that bilingual pedagogies (Gort and Pontier 2013; Reyes and Azuara 2008) mediate understanding and mastery of academic content in TWDL programs.

Language mediates students' understanding when they are guided to analyze, interpret, and communicate scientific ideas (Glynn and Muth 1994) or when students are guided to use language "to explain, predict and integrate new information into existing schemas" (Fellows 1994, 999). These higher-order thinking practices promote a "minds-on" role in learning science. We show that bilingual practices are tools for mediating understanding. Students used these tools to develop academic discourse, but also as a tool for understanding science content. The two cannot be separated. As emergent bilinguals, they learned about physical properties of clay, sand, and gravel. Ms. O's verbal questioning guided them to explain processes ("you mix soil with trash") and to posit hypotheses. For instance, students' explanation of what constitutes "good soil" required them to think beyond how compost is made and to move toward why compost provides nutrition for plants. Thus, rather than simply focusing on providing students English input, Ms. O used verbal and written language as a mediating tool for understanding science (Klein 2004; Sandoval and Millwood 2005). Ms. O avoided conveying to students the idea that there is only one right answer or one way to speak in science class, since that might communicate to students that language is fixed, rather than dynamic, socioculturally constructed, and multivoiced (Moje 1995). Moreover, she provided opportunities for students to write their understanding in their science journals, a practice that can also enhance students' science understanding (Hand, Hohenshell, and Prain 2004; Holliday, Yore, and Alvermann 1994; Keys 1999; Rivard 1994; Shepardson and Britsch 2001).

Findings presented in this chapter show how Ms. O and the students built a network of learners in which different levels of expertise were recognized. Sociocultural studies of learning have for a time now proposed that learning is situated in communities in which learners may participate in any number of ways (Lave and Wenger 1991). Knowledge is (re)produced through participation in meaningful activities. Therefore, the example of Vanessa coming to the aid of another student exemplifies the ways in which a student uses language mediation bilingually: "Así como usted nos dijo que tacháramos las palabras que no sabemos, focus on the words you know." Thus, rather than understanding learning among emergent bilinguals as a change in mental structures, we show how the classroom is organized so that students can learn from, as well as teach, each other.

In conclusion, language mediates understanding, according to sociocultural perspectives on learning. Student participants of this study used both languages to learn. The classroom was an environment in which student participation in either Spanish or English was recognized, modeled, and scaffolded. However, we observed more than that. We also documented that the teacher and students created a social environment that promoted higher-order thinking and in which all students engaged in constructing their own and their peers' understandings. This social environment aided students to move from the position of an apprentice to an autonomous learner. Thus, language mediation served not only the purpose of comprehension of the content but awareness of the communicative needs of their peers. Bilingual children can monitor other children's comprehension and can provide scaffolds for others by modeling strategies (Olmedo 2003). We witnessed the process in which students started to appropriate the practice of accounting for observations using scientific reasoning. In a TWDL classroom, in which both languages are valued, it becomes easier to use both languages to construct the understanding of science concepts. In comparison, monolingual English-only classrooms do not permit this possibility for emergent bilinguals (García and Kleifgen 2010).

8

Multimodality as a Resource for the Social Organization of Learning

AMONG THE TOOLS TRANSFRONTERIZX STUDENTS used to navigate U.S. schools, we found multimodal literacies and translanguaging. Drawing on literature on multimodality (Dicks et al. 2011; Gutiérrez et al. 2011) and recent research on translanguaging practices (García 2009), in this chapter we analyze one multimodal literacy event which is representative of many we observed in this DL program. Although this chapter centers on multimodality, translanguaging was also analyzed here as part of the multiple semiotic resources used in communication (Kress 2010; New London Group 1996). Language does not operate in isolation from other modalities but is one of a host of semiotic resources. A translanguaging framework recognizes that an assemblage of modalities constitutes bilinguals' repertoires: "Multimodal social semiotics views all linguistic signs as part of a wider repertoire of modal resources that sign makers have at their disposal, and that carry particular sociohistorical and political associations" (García and Wei 2014, 29). In this context, one transnational teacher's ideas about how best to teach literacy to emergent bilinguals and transfronterizx students supported her organization of authentic learning environments where students could use their repertoires of semiotic resources. We contend that Ms. Ornelas cre- ated—in her own words—"safe spaces for learning" in her DL classroom. These findings contribute to the conversation on how multimodal literacies challenge traditional views of literacy as isolated skills and construct safe spaces for learning, especially for emergent bilinguals.

When we talk about text in this chapter, we refer to textual practices (Arnold and Yapita 2000), broadly defined, which include multiple semiotic forms such as pictures, poetry, song, body movement, photographs, graphics, models, videos, video games, computers, and so on.* People transform what is "presented to them via a range of modes—in image, in speech, in experiment/demonstration, with models—into a new sense, their sense, representing their interests in their world" (Kress 2000, 339). This view of children's roles when engaging with multimodality accounts for their agency in these practices. For example, Tackvic (2012, 427–28) reported the use of multimodal literacy practices by elementary students in order to create their own stories for storytelling in class. They used digital images, sounds, and their voice, which helped them to imagine, produce, and publish original stories.

Gumble (2012) also presents the use of multiple modalities to gather information and synthesize ideas in order to write a video script about war. Junior high school students were asked to create their own videos about their interpretation of war. For this particular project, students used letters, journal entries, songs, political cartoons, and photographs. Within this project, students engaged in following the copyright laws of the files, as well as critical thinking when asking questions and looking for evidence to support their ideas. Thus, students not only developed literacy skills by using the different kinds of digital media for the production of these projects, but they also used their ideas and critical stances in the production of these multimodal texts. In chapter 5, we analyzed one multimodal event that shows children appropriating semiotic resources from the diverse settings that they traversed, crossing national, genre, and school-home boundaries. Understanding the agency and roles of students in these literacy events is particularly important for emergent bilinguals, who must use every resource available to them within their communicative repertoires in order to make sense of texts (broadly defined) at schools and out of schools, in any of their languages. Furthermore, these events show the emergence of hybrid forms of communication in the moment of interaction (Pennycook 2010).

---

* See chapter 2 for more information about this definition.

Multimodal literacies may aid meaningful learning with emergent bilinguals. Ajayi (2009) recognized that multimodal literacy pedagogy could be used to facilitate the learning process of literacy, precisely because multimodality allows using different types of texts that promote students' learning using various methods. Multimodal literacies can be used by teachers to communicate their ideas using different types of resources, but more importantly, critical thinking is evident in the use of multiple modes of communication (Lotherington and Jenson 2011). de la Piedra shares examples of a teacher who works with borderland adolescents. The teacher "built upon the students' interests in Mexican popular culture and peer-group literacy practices (e.g., reading about favorite Mexican bands on the Internet) to engage them in academic tasks such as reading, writing, and conducting research" (de la Piedra 2010, 581). These examples illustrate how recent immigrants were able to translanguage and produce PowerPoint texts which included content researched on the web, pictures, and written text in both Spanish and English languages. Spence (2009) reports on a project in which four students created a web page titled "Mexican Heritage" for a contest. In order to develop the web page, students used English and Spanish, as well as multiple literacies. Honeyford (2014) presented a study in which a group of emergent bilinguals used various modes to create a mural in which they represented their language, culture, and identities. Students in this project produced digital poems, letters, and essays. Using multimodal practices, these students used literacies to think in different ways about their position in society. These studies demonstrate that emergent bilinguals "are often more likely to experiment with English and academic genres, while also taking on powerful identities as learners and language users, when formal and informal modes of communication are leveraged, multimodality and language-crossing encouraged and the use of both home and academic vernaculars promoted within a context that values social relationships and the playful imagination" (Gutiérrez et al. 2011, 232).

The thematic analysis of our data provided a large number of categories that were selected to explore in depth. From the analysis of literacy events, we identified categories such as "multimodality" and "translanguaging." After performing focused coding, we realized that there were many instances in which both multimodal and translanguaging practices were used as resources for teaching and learning. As seen before, translanguaging does involve multiple semiotic resources; thus, it includes multimodal literacies. This chapter describes several examples of activities in the classroom that included and encouraged multimodal practices.

Creating an Authentic Learning Environment: Orchestrating Learning Through Multimodality

Ms. Ornelas's classroom and her teaching practices involved many modalities. The lessons included, among other activities, the use of oral language when engaging in explanations, class discussions, modeling, and questioning. We observed a variety of printed and written materials; for example, graphic organizers in all subjects such as charts, bubble maps, treemaps, Venn diagrams, and poster boards written by the teacher and the students, sometimes including pictures.[†] The teacher also projected written text on a screen for students to use. Teacher and students also utilized digital media such as video, computer software, and Internet web pages frequently.

The teacher had a dynamic word wall which she updated continuously with new words learned during her lessons. She made a point of having both everyday and academic concepts in English for students to use as resources. During our interviews, Ms. Ornelas reported that emergent bilinguals needed not only the vocabulary of the discipline, but also the everyday vocabulary they found in content area texts, and that hindered their ability to understand the particular text. Thus, she had built a word wall that included everyday words, such as "playground," "chips," and "temperature," for students to use during lessons, in addition to the scientific words related to the content areas. During our observations it was common to find students using the word wall as part of the semiotic resources available to them; for example, it was common to see them pointing at the words, copying the

---

[†]In most of the observations conducted in language arts and social studies, Ms. O used Spanish to name these graphic organizers because these subjects were taught in Spanish in fourth and fifth grades: *organizadores gráficos, mapa de círculo, mapa de árbol, mapa de doble burbuja, mapa de causa y efecto.*

spelling, or searching their memory for a concept and then matching it to the word on the word wall. In our observations, we noted that students had acquired many of these complex disciplinary concepts in Spanish and used cognates as resources for these types of words.

We observed the teacher *orchestrating* multimodal lectures. We use the word "orchestrating" because it portrays the teacher as an orchestra director, mediating students' learning, while students were engaged in playing their individual roles in the learning process. The lessons were individually performed, but at the same time guided by the teacher. As a result, we often observed collective products that were not necessarily possible by individuals performing their part in isolation. It had to come from the co-construction of knowledge during the interactions, with skillful guidance by the teacher.

As we showed in previous chapters, the orchestration of lessons often included translanguaging practices using diverse modes of communication. Ms. O. used every multimodal resource available in her classroom, her own as well as her students' repertoires to orchestrate instructional conversations (Tharp and Gallimore 1991). That is, "talk in which ideas are explored rather than answers to teachers' test questions provided and evaluated" (Cazden 1988, 54). Instructional conversations in this classroom included, for instance, oral explanations, written text on the walls, a word wall, and a video projected on a screen or the teacher's computer. Most importantly, during her lessons, the teacher modeled the use of environmental print in her walls, frequently pointing at pictures hanging on the walls, drawings on the whiteboard, or relevant text produced by teacher or students. Lessons also included a great variety of models, as well as electronic equipment that allowed the teacher to use digital images and texts, such as smartboards and projectors.[‡]

During these carefully orchestrated instructional conversations, teacher and students jointly produced collective multimodal texts which they could later use during present or future lessons. Jointly produced texts became part of the array of textual practices available for learning and were used by teacher and students alike during literacy events. The teacher modeled how

---

[‡]For example, in order to teach the phases of the moon, she used a model of the earth and the moon, and a flashlight.

to use these multimodal resources for learning. Students also used these resources spontaneously, when they needed a particular word or concept from any of these multimodal literacies around them. Thus, we observed multimodality in "joint activity" (Tharp and Gallimore 1988) as has been defined by sociocultural theories of learning, as well as "guided participation" as defined by Rogoff (1990). As Rogoff (1990) states, "Children's cognitive development is an apprenticeship—it occurs through guided participation in social activity with companions who support and stretch children's understanding of and skill in using the tools of the culture" (vii). Also, we observed instructional conversations as significant parts of the joint activity in these classrooms.

Not only did Ms. Ornelas use a wide variety of multimodal practices in her lectures, but she also, and most importantly, organized learning activities where students were expected to use multimodality. For example, students prepared posters (writing, drawing), engaged in role-playing, used music, and produced videos. Also, Ms. Ornelas explicitly taught the students the importance of multimodality and modeled for them. For example, during a particular observation, she gave the following instructions: "I want you to include writing and pictures. Remember, pictures are important because they help us understand better. At the end of the project, you will present and teach the others. You will be the teachers for that time. Does anybody have a question?" These words precisely capture the message of a teacher communicating to her students the importance of including multimodal repertoires for learning. We observed Ms. O giving similar instructions on several occasions. The teacher regularly reminded students to take advantage of valuable artifacts in the classroom that are there to help them make connections in two languages, as well as to make a connection to the real world. Similarly, in a study conducted in a two-way-immersion German-Italian classroom, Budach (2013) argues that not only language choice but also multimodality and artifacts are mediators for learning; in this case the inclusion of a "rocket" (rock candy), flashcards, and a school bag played important roles in the literacy event analyzed. In the following pages, we will present rich examples of this "orchestration."

As García and Wei (2014) point out, translanguaging includes "all meaning-making modes" (29). As addressed previously, this DL classroom was a place where translanguaging occurred freely and spontaneously. Multimodal literacy practices were meaningfully included in the different literacy events we observed.

Analysis of a Multimodal Project Presented During "Science Extravaganza"

Every year the district celebrated "Science Extravaganza," a science activity where teachers and students created collective projects to share with other grades. The Science Extravaganza activity lasted all day and teachers and students prepared their projects weeks in advance. In this school district's DL program, science is taught in English only; thus the presentations and showcases were to be conducted in this language. During the course of the research, we were able to observe three Science Extravaganza activities—one in each year of the study. In this section, we present the analysis of one activity in particular which occurred in June 2010. This is one of many examples of literacy events we observed where multimodality was intrinsic to the construction and organization of learning.

Ms. Ornelas and her one-way DL fifth grade class prepared a presentation for the whole school, just like every other class did.[§] Students in this one-way fifth grade class were notoriously (and understandably) nervous about presenting in English. One-way DL sections in this school received recent immigrants, as well as students who had been in the United States for short periods of time; thus students felt that Spanish was their stronger language. Knowing that students felt nervous about presenting in English, Ms. O intentionally planned this activity allowing ample opportunities to prepare. Ms. Ornelas thought a video was an excellent presentation tool, one which students could develop in advance and video-record their presentation instead of solely relying on their oral expression skills during the Science Extravaganza presentation. The video would present the main ideas and scientific concepts related to the topic at hand: inherited and learned

---

[§]As introduced in chapter 3, most students in one-way DL classrooms in this school were newcomers or had been in the United States for just a few years.

characteristics of living beings. In addition to the video, students would prepare a game for the audience to play, which would be linked to these concepts.

Many of the other classes relied on videos from a prepackaged virtual interactive resource available to them from the school district (EduSmart module).[*] Ms. O communicated that instead of using those videos, she wanted students to use iMovie to create and edit a video clip featuring students providing explanations of the concepts.[**] After projecting the video clip they produced, they would be able to use the game that came with EduSmart. Ms. Ornelas explained her rationale to the students:

> What I want to do is for us to create a video (using iMovie). I don't want to show the whole video (from EduSmart) because it's very long and we don't want the kids to get bored. We are going to create a video clip with you explaining the concepts; we are going to show them (other students) that video clip, and then we are going to use the game (provided by EduSmart Science), and you can use the questions, the quiz, and that's it.

Note that the teacher spoke in English most of the time because science was taught in English. In addition, the presentations at Science Extravaganza were expected to be in English. However, the preparation of the activity involved translanguaging practices. Multimodality and translanguaging allowed students who were in the initial stages of English development to participate.

This multimodal project occurred in a series of literacy events throughout two days. We have identified and analyzed these individual literacy events in order to make the whole experience of preparation and presentation of Science Extravaganza more comprehensible to the reader. As will be seen in

---

[*]EduSmart Science is a multimedia science resource that this particular school district bought for teachers and students to use for science instruction. According to the teachers, the product was aligned with the Texas State standards or TEKS (Texas Essential Knowledge and Skills). For more information, visit the web page, http://www.edusmart.com/tx?t=x.

[**]iMovie is video-editing software by Apple Inc.

the following pages, each one of these literacy events constituted part of the same larger project: Science Extravaganza. However, each literacy event also had its own characteristics, and it made analytical sense to conceive it as a whole. The following are the six literacy events:

1. Preparation and Modeling of the Technology
2. Scaffolding and Translanguaging During Video Viewing in EduSmart
3. Practicing the Interactive Game
4. Script Production in Teams
5. Whole-Class Production of the Script
6. Rehearsal of Each Student's Line in the Video Clip

Literacy Event 1: Preparation and Modeling of the Technology

The first thing students needed to learn was how to use the equipment during the presentation, and a literacy event with this purpose occurred, where the use of Spanish dominated. It was the first time for students to use the smartboard and operate the EduSmart software by themselves, without assistance from the teacher. Thus, Ms. Ornelas designed a brief lesson to prepare students to use the equipment. During this event, Ms. Ornelas taught students how to connect the electronic board and how to use the electronic pen to make the EduSmart game work. This event was multimodal; it involved oral language, such as explanations about how to hook up cables and turn on the machine, and demonstrations on how to perform these activities; not to mention the fact that it was done in two languages—although, during this time of the multimodal literacy event, Ms. Ornelas used Spanish almost exclusively. We interpret that the teacher did not conceptualize this event as academic per se. This is the reason she chose Spanish, even though science is officially taught in English, as will be apparent in the rest of the literacy events where she used English most of the time. Children actively participated in this literacy event, genuinely engaged in learning how to operate the smartboard as well as the EduSmart science module. For example, we heard students making comments about the equipment, trying to understand how it worked, and comparing the smartboard to their Nintendo DS game console.

Literacy Event 2: Scaffolding and Translanguaging During Video Viewing in EduSmart

Ms. O organized the next literacy event to include video viewing and scaffolding through translanguaging practices. The fifth graders watched the module in EduSmart. The module consisted of a video about the science concepts of "Inherited Traits vs. Learned Behaviors" and games about the content of the video. The video was delivered entirely in English. The teacher supported the comprehension of the video contents by asking questions of the students, also using oral English. During the observations in her classroom, we noticed Ms. Ornelas used these kinds of listening comprehension and reading comprehension questions as a form of scaffolding. She designed interactions in order to monitor and support emergent bilinguals' participation in academic activities. During these interactions, students usually answered using both languages.

The next excerpt is one example of many multimodal interactions that occurred during the video viewing when the teacher stopped the projection after a few minutes of video viewing to monitor and scaffold comprehension:

1   MS. O: What is another learned characteristic?

2   GIRL 1: Swim?

3   MS. O: Swimming, but other than those pictures [shown in the video]? Tell me something that you learned.

4   BOY 1: Caminamos (we walk)

5   GIRL 2: Andar en la bicicleta (riding the bike)

6   MS. O: Walking

7   GIRL 3: Andar en patineta (skateboarding)

8   MS. O: Yes, very good.

9   MS. O: What about the fur of the bear. Is that inherited or learned?

10   CHILDREN: Inherited

11   MS. O: Remember, I told you in class that animals and plants have special characteristics. Why is that?

12   BOY 2: To survive

13   [Teacher starts the video. The video continues on animals and plants' unique traits. After a few minutes, the teacher stops the projection of the video and turns to the students.]

14   MS. O: What about plants? Do they have inherited traits, or do they also learn behaviors? [silence] Let's vote. How many of you think that a plant can learn a behavior? How many of you think they inherit traits?

15   [Children raised their hands to cast their votes. On the screen, there is a picture of a cactus. Ms. O explains that plants inherit but do not learn traits.]

16   MS. O: They have special characteristics, like this cactus right here. Who can mention to me the special characteristics of this cactus?

17   BOY 1: To steal the food, digo (I say) the water

18   MS. O: To conserve water

19   BOY 1: Conserve

20   MS. O: What do they have to conserve water? Where do they keep the water?

21   GIRL 1: In the roots

22   BOY 2: In the leaves?

23   MS. O: [Pointing to the picture.] Right here, right? In the inside. They keep water inside so they can survive. What about the spines, why do they have those?

24   BOY 1: So the animal do not eat it?

25   MS. O: Exactly, for protection.

This excerpt shows the kind of scaffolding that Ms. Ornelas engaged in almost daily, in the various subjects she taught, which involved translanguaging, including multiple modes of communication (García and Wei 2014). The multimodal and translanguaging interactions were particularly important when the official language of the lesson was English, as in the case presented here. The interaction included the use of translanguaging and multimodality; we identified the use of oral language (English and Spanish), images and oral language through the video (in English), and written text on the screen (in English). In addition, body movements were part of this event; for instance, children casting their votes by raising their hands. In this case, although students did not use their words in order to respond to Ms. O's question ("What about plants? Do they have inherited traits, or do they also learn behaviors?") they used the gesture of raising their hands to communicate their thoughts. Ms. O used this strategy frequently when she saw insecurity or doubt in her students' faces. This move served to provide some time for thinking and responding with body movement. In line 3, Ms. O acknowledged the girl's response "swim," and modeled the complete form in English, "swimming." Additionally, she pushed students not to rely solely on what the video told them, but to look for their own experiences and knowledge by saying, "Tell me something that you learned." This encouragement appeared to work since students did provide personal examples of learned traits.

Note that when referring to their own experiences and knowledge the students' participation in lines 4, 5, and 7 were in Spanish. The teacher modeled the English form for one of these in line 6: "walking." In line 11, the teacher connected the video content to what they had already covered in class; as a result, students remembered the content they had learned: that animals and plants do have special characteristics in order "to survive." Students used English in lines 10 and 12. Ms. O and her transfronterizx emergent bilinguals engaged in a wide variety of semiotic resources from their repertoires in order to undertake academic work to be delivered in English. Ms. O orchestrated a multimodal instructional conversation where students brought their knowledge of the topic and used it in their translanguaging practices. Ms. O's questions, the presentation of the subject through diverse modalities (pictures, video, oral language, written language), the use of students' dynamic bilingualism, their knowledge of the desert plants (cactus), and their school knowledge of science all together allowed for this literacy event: the joint construction of understanding of the concept of learned and inherited traits.

Literacy Event 3: Practicing the Interactive Game

Once students had reviewed the main ideas and scientific concepts to be presented during the Science Extravaganza through watching the EduSmart video and frequent scaffolding by the teacher and their peers during interactions that resembled the excerpt analyzed above, the teacher and students practiced the interactive game. The purpose of the game was to match the concept "inherited" or "learned" trait with a picture, by using a large smartboard and electronic pen. In this literacy event, most of the interactions were in English. Ms. O modeled and taught how to use the pen on the electronic board. By using the pen, the members of the audience had to drag the picture to the corresponding area, identified by the labels "Learned Behavior" or "Inherited Traits." The teacher modeled this action and showed the sounds that the game made when the responses were identified as "correct" or "incorrect." When he heard these sounds, a boy yelled excitedly, "Como en el Pac-Man!" ("Like in Pac-Man!"), drawing from his previous experience with video games. Students enjoyed this part of the project because they got to use these new technologies, which they related to their digital literacies.

Literacy Event 4: Script Production in Teams

At this point, students had learned how to operate the equipment (Literacy Event 1), watched the EduSmart video, and discussed the concepts (Literacy Event 2). They had also practiced the EduSmart game that they were to have other students play (Literacy Event 3). At this moment, the teacher organized the student-produced video in which fifth graders would present the scientific concepts. For this, and, before recording the video, students had to write the script. With this in mind, Ms. O organized a script-writing activity by teams. The following two excerpts show the translanguaging practices that occurred while doing group work without the support of the teacher. In both passages, the teams worked to produce a written text to be rendered in oral language during the video recording. The uses of translanguaging, as well as oral and written modes of communication, are evident in both excerpts. These excerpts are themselves multimodal and are part of the multimodal larger project analyzed here: Science Extravaganza. Although we are sharing data from fifth grade in this chapter, we observed similar events in fourth, fifth, and sixth grades, both in one-way and two-way DL classrooms.

1   BOY 1: ¿Qué vamos a decir? (What are we going to say?)
2   GIRL 1: My name is Patricia and I am here for explain you the difference of inherited and learned traits.
3   GIRL 2: Cada uno debe de decir (each one should say) inherited, otro (another) learned.
4   BOY 1: Yo digo (I say) inherited
5   GIRL 1: Yo (I) learned.

6   GIRL 2: [Pointing at two members of the group] Ella va a hacer las carac-
terísticas de los animales y el de plantas, ¿no? (She is going to do the
animal and plant characteristics, no?)

7   GIRL 1: Okay, yo voy a comenzar. (I will start.) Today I am going to talk
about y luego yo digo todo lo que salga ahí (I will say everything that
comes up in the paper) [pointing to the paper where Girl 2 is writing].

8   GIRL 2: Espérate, pero tiene que ser simple porque va a ser para pequeñi-
tos. (Wait, it has to be simple because it is for the little ones.)

9   GIRL 1: My name is Ms. Fernandez. Today we are going to talk about the
learned behaviors.

[Girl 2 writes each member's introduction.]

We have included this excerpt because it shows how students start using translanguaging and multimodal modes of communication even for planning their introductions. Introductions might be a part of an oral presentation that we may not find if we observe classrooms with no emergent bilinguals. However, for emergent bilinguals in this group, it was important to plan every step of their oral presentations.

Different groups were working on their scripts; some of them spent time on their introductions, like the group shown in the excerpt above; other teams went directly to write their presentations of the scientific concepts to be covered during the presentation. The following passage demonstrates how students wrote their scripts collectively. It illustrates a pattern we identified, where usually one of the students was the scribe of the group. In this particular example, Ms. O left it to the group to decide who the scribe would be. The rest of the team members dictated sentences for the written work or offered ideas for the scribe to compose sentences and write them down. As shown below, translanguaging practices were frequent in these interactions, where most text had to be written in English—in this case, the presentation had to be rendered in this language—while students used a variety of multimodal resources at their disposal in order to co-construct the text. As you may see below, the interactions before, during, and after writing the English academic text involved Spanish oral language:

1   GIRL 3: [Dictating to Girl 4] Learned, vamos a decir que lo aprendió de
su (let's say that he learned it from) environment.

2   [Girl 4 writes in her notebook, "They learned in his [*sic*] environment."]

3   GIRL 3: Necesitan el sol. (They need the sun.) [Dictating to Girl 4] They need the sunlight.

4   BOY 1: Otra tiene que ser (another has to be) they need protection.

5   GIRL 3: Protection [dictating the word to be written in the script but using Spanish phonology].

6   GIRL 4: [While writing] They need food. Listo! (Ready!)

7   GIRL 3: Otro . . . mhhm. The animals are equal to their parents.

8   GIRL 4: ¿Iguales? (Same?)

9   GIRL 3: No, [dictating to Girl 4] same.

This excerpt shows how students co-constructed the ideas to write the video script. Translanguaging practices had different functions in this interaction. It is evident that in general, students used English to dictate a sentence or suggest an idea that could be written in the script, while using Spanish to give context to the future English text, always making sure other students understood what was said, or to clarify vocabulary choices. For example, in line 4 Boy 1 indicates in Spanish, "Otra tiene que ser" ("Another characteristic should be"), followed by what he suggested to include in the written script in English: "they need protection." In line 1, Girl 3 thinks aloud in Spanish in order to come up with the English sentence she dictated to the scribe. Girl 3 starts using English when she said "learned" to dictate a line to Girl 4, and quickly changes to Spanish: "vamos a decir que lo aprendió en su," and then goes back to English: "environment." Girl 4 understands what Girl 3 thought and communicated, which is evidenced when she wrote the complete idea: "They learned in his [*sic*] environment." Similarly, we observed the translation of a complete idea in line 3. Girl 3 starts her intervention in Spanish, maybe thinking aloud her idea, but then uses English in order to say the sentence to the scribe out loud. In line 5, we observe that Girl 3 feels the need to support the scribe. Boy 1 had contributed the last sentence "they need protection" in line 4. Girl 3 repeats the last word that boy 1 said but uses the Spanish phonology in order to dictate a cognate (*protección* and protection). By doing this, she differentiates between the words in Spanish and English and makes sure Girl 4 spells the word using English spelling as opposed to Spanish spelling. In line 6, translanguaging was used to signal that the scribe (Girl 4) was finished with writing the last sentence and she was ready for another one. Finally, lines 7, 8, and 9 show translanguaging when negotiating the choice of words for the script. The movement across the continua of languages (English and Spanish), registers (what has been constructed as "standard" and "vernacular" languages), multiple modes, thought and language, and the present and the future times is evident in this episode. At the same time, students are not just using language in a vacuum, but they are "doing" with their language practices (Pennycook 2010) as they become students in this DL program. They were clearly "doing being bilingual" (Gort 2015).

As García and Wei (2014), drawing on Swain (2000), Cook (2012), and Maturana and Varela (1998) stated, "all languaging is knowing and doing, and all knowing and doing is languaging" (11). This explains the intertwined nature of language and cognition, which we repeatedly saw in examples like the one analyzed above. Translanguaging practices were part of the thinking, talking, writing, and doing the English academic text. The text was collectively written on a piece of notebook paper, using all diverse repertoires in the linguistic borderlands (Martínez-Roldán and Sayer 2006) children have at their disposal, to be then rehearsed and enacted in a video that was also going to be delivered in English.

Literacy Event 5: Whole-Class Production of the Script

After observing the interactions and the texts of the small group work, the teacher decided to change the activity from a small-group script-writing project to a whole-class script-writing undertaking, where she could scaffold the writing some more. In this literacy event (Whole-Class Production of the Script), we also observed translanguaging and multimodality. The next example shows a few minutes of interaction that serves as an example of how the teacher and students co-constructed the collectively written text to become the video script for the Science Extravaganza project.

1   MS. O: I see you are a little bit lost. Why not the whole class write the
        script together? We are going to do it a little bit more guided.

2   [Teacher asks questions. With students' responses, students and teacher
        compose the script. Students take turns writing the sentences on the
        board. The teacher dictates.]

3   GIRL 5: The difference is that in inherited they are born with that and learned is in his environment?

4   MS. O: Okay, I like that. Let's put it together. Let's explain what an inherited trait is first. [Dictating] *An inherited trait is. . .*, and Valeria says that an inherited trait is something that you are born with. Is that true?

5   CHILDREN: Yes!

6   MS. O: Let's write it. *An inherited trait is a trait*, or let's say it's a characteristic, so we don't say the same word twice. And who is born with the inherited trait?

7   BOY 2: Offspring

8   MS. O: But who is an offspring?

9   CHILDREN: El hijo (the son), children

10   MISS O: What are animals, plant, humans called together? What is the science word for these?

11   BOY 2: Organism!

12   MISS O: Thank you! [Dictating] *An inherited trait is a characteristic that an organism is born with.*

This is a short excerpt from a productive interaction, which represents a much more prolonged interaction that teacher and students engaged in before producing the written text in English—the language of the final product. It is crucial to emphasize the role of the teacher in the organization of this translanguaging literacy event. The teacher actively monitored the comprehension of emergent bilinguals' and their performance in the activities she had organized; when she observed things were not working out as planned, she immediately changed the activity to one that entailed more scaffolding on her part. Thus, the teacher leveraged "emergent bilingual students' complex discursive practices to develop new understandings, expand students' linguistic repertoires and metalinguistic awareness, and incorporate and build on student knowledge and expertise" (Gort 2015, 3).

In the excerpt above, the teacher asked questions in order to get students to think and compose their ideas for the script; all this was done using oral and written language. Also, students were encouraged to apply their diverse linguistic repertoires in both Spanish and English, including everyday and academic registers, to contribute to the multimodal collective product. Note in line 3, Valeria uses her English skills, although noticeably in emergence, and in line 9 students translanguaged when responding to the teacher's question about "who is an offspring." They offered "children" and "el hijo" (the son). The teacher guided the students' use of scientific concepts in lines 10 and 11. Finally, after some oral interaction and students' participation in the collective production of the video script, Ms. O stated the sentence aloud, and a student wrote it on the board. Translanguaging practices are mediating the co-construction of the video script. Although students only engaged in oral and written language modes, this interaction is part of the larger multimodal project analyzed here. Ms. O modified her lesson plans in order to support the emergent bilingual students' participation in this academic project, as they relied and built on their translanguaging and multimodal resources. The teacher was an important resource, helping students think and write the script for the final product: the video. Thus, here we observed multimodality in "joint activity" (Tharp and Gallimore 1988) and apprenticeship in Rogoff's terms (1990), where the more expert others "support and stretch children's understanding of and skill in using the tools of the culture" (vii). The tools used in this event were multimodal.

Literacy Event 6: Rehearsal of Each Student's Line in the Video Clip

Once the class finished the collective writing of the script, Ms. O continued scaffolding the multimodal larger project of the Science Extravaganza with the rehearsal of each student's line for the video clip. Ms. O. asked students to do a choral reading of the script they just wrote collectively in chunks. Choral reading alleviates the pressure that emergent bilinguals may feel when reading aloud in front of the whole classroom (Herrera, Perez, and Escamilla 2010). Furthermore, breaking down the texts in pieces facilitated the students' ability to read while comprehending the sentence they were reading. In addition, Ms. O prepared the students to rehearse their line in the video individually.

Once the script was finished and rehearsed collectively, Ms. O assigned one or two sentences to each student, ensuring the participation of all in the video. Each individual student rehearsed one sentence of the script for the video. This part of the literacy event was conducted mainly in English, as the students' lines were written in English; however, Spanish surrounded the English collectively written text, just as it has been shown in other literacy events of the project. After this rehearsal, the teacher and the students were ready to produce the final product. Ms. O. videotaped each student saying his or her line for the final video clip using her laptop computer. This part of the literacy event was done exclusively in English since the video script was expected to be all in English.

Discussion

This chapter shows how one teacher created a flexible, authentic, and safe learning environment for emergent bilinguals by orchestrating multimodal resources within translanguaging practices. These multimodal literacies, where translanguaging was not only allowed but encouraged, challenged traditional views of literacy as isolated skills used to decode print and bilingualism as solely the knowledge of two (separate) languages. The activities observed allowed for students' agency to use their repertoire of language and literacy practices. Students drew from multiple communicative resources (linguistic and cultural knowledge, multimodality) to engage, make meaning of, and produce texts (broadly defined). The production of texts in the literacy events analyzed was accomplished by the teacher mobilizing and "orchestrating" students' resources. Students were able to mobilize the resources available in their repertoires of language and knowledge because Ms. O not only allowed students to use them freely; she also explicitly instructed them to use all their resources and even modeled their use. As García and Wei (2014) described in their groundbreaking theoretical work on translanguaging, the students and Ms. O were "languagers" who used diverse and multimodal semiotic resources at their "disposal in strategic ways to communicate and act in the world, but which are recognized by the bilingual speaker, as well as by others, as belonging to two sets of socially constructed 'languages'" (10).

Multimodality played a crucial role within the translanguaging practices observed. The uses of oral language and written text, as well as the production of the students' video, all were diverse modes of communication that supported the success of this activity. After analyzing these interactions, we concluded that multimodality allowed for meaningful and engaged student participation among transfronterizxs. Similarly, for Wilber (2012) the new literacies produce changes in the lives of those who use technologies in literacy practices. The use of digital tools allows students to gain expertise that will be used for different types of practices. Although Wilber focuses on the use of many different digital tools like Glogster and Inspiration, as well as social media tools (like Twitter, Ning, and Facebook), and our example includes the use of video and video software, the results are similar in that students become engaged in academic activities through the use of multiple modes of communication.

The everyday construction of safe spaces for learning in DL classrooms through multimodal practices become possibilities for social change. García and Leiva (2014) note that such an agenda involves working with students as they build on their translanguaging resources to educate all students equitably, particularly transnational (and transfronterizx) students. Forzani and Leu (2012) emphasize the importance of using multimodal literacies in primary school. The authors emphasize that using new literacies in primary schools helps to assure equity and opportunity and to let students construct their knowledge while using technological tools that often include multiple experiences.

As we have argued throughout this book, transfronterizx students were able to use a variety of linguistic and cultural resources in order to make meaning of texts, broadly defined. Due to the context of the DL classroom, as well as the bilingual community that surrounded the school, students engaged in translanguaging practices every day. And these practices involved a wide variety of modes of communication.

9

Understanding, Valuing, and Modeling Transfronterizx Funds of Knowledge

Introduction

SOME OF THE ENDURING BARRIERS that students of color, in particular immigrant students and emergent bilinguals, experience are due to schools not valuing the knowledge that they acquire outside the academic sphere. In many U.S. classrooms, immigrant students and emergent bilinguals sit through teacher-centered lectures about material, subject areas, and topics that do not take into consideration their language, culture, or experience (Beyer and Apple 1998; García and Guerra 2003). For these students to be successful in schools, school systems must be restructured in a manner that includes all students, their families, their communities, and their lives (Anyon 1997; Chapman and Hobbel 2010; Darling-Hammond 1997; Moll et al. 1992; Sleeter 2005). In their groundbreaking book, González, Moll, and Amanti (2005) asked how practitioners "within the limits of their very real structural constraints, can realistically carry out emancipatory and libera-tory pedagogies when they themselves are victims of disempowerment" (2). In this chapter, we present an example of one teacher's pedagogical approach to using borderland students' funds of knowledge. We propose that peda-gogical approaches like the ones we highlight here may be the foundation to transform the current school structure into a more inclusive education, one that will allow all students to feel welcomed and cared for in schools, encouraging them to learn.

The benefits of including funds of knowledge in schools, in particular for students of color, have been addressed by numerous studies (González, Moll, and Amanti 2005). However, very few studies have focused on the simultaneity, fluidity, and mobility of this knowledge and these cultural practices (Lam and Warriner 2012). Here we emphasize the advantages of traveling and crossing borders through the case of a group of economically disadvantaged students who were fleeing violence in their home country. These students gained access to resources on both sides of the border through their border-crossings and a pedagogical approach that allowed them to capitalize on their funds of knowledge. As Vélez-Ibáñez and Greenberg (1992) note, transnational families can sometimes gain "access to personal or institutional resources on either side of the border" (317), providing access to a network of social and familial resources that can potentially leverage institutional, cultural, and linguistic advantages.

We document what we call the *transfronterizx funds of knowledge* and analyze the ways in which transfronterizxs use this knowledge for academic purposes in the DL program. We also document the importance of the teacher as a facilitator of this process.

Funds of Knowledge as a Theoretical Perspective

Many students use lessons taught at home by families and community members to navigate through different systems and institutions, including schools. Knowledge about such things as taking care of siblings or translating for family members, and values such as a strong work ethic are valuable funds that are learned by students through their lived realities. Vélez-Ibáñez and Greenberg (1992) coined the term "funds of knowledge," defining these as strategic and cultural resources that households contain. They state that "such funds are rooted in daily, useful skills and information of a very broad nature, and because they include mechanical, historical, creative, computational and design mastery, they are expressed in a broad range of contexts" (318). They also emphasize that the younger generation experiments with these in a variety of ways and that they change according to experiential reality.

An influential study in Tucson, Arizona, by Moll et al. (1992) further analyzed funds of knowledge by examining the social history of households and the labor history of the participating families. Their research revealed cultural and cognitive resources in each household that could be used for classroom instruction. Moll and colleagues (1992) define funds of knowledge as "the historically accumulated and culturally developed bodies of knowledge and skills essential for household or individual functioning and well-being" (133). Funds of knowledge are learned at home through students' interactions with other individuals. The authors describe two aspects of the funds of knowledge, which they emphasize contrast sharply with classroom practices. One is that funds of knowledge are "flexible, adaptive and active and may involve multiple persons from outside the homes" (133). In the authors' words, they are "thick and multi-stranded" (133). The second characteristic is reciprocity and establishment of relationships based on mutual trust, symbolizing human social interdependence. Thus, funds of knowledge provide contexts in which learning can occur. Furthermore, children are provided with many opportunities to participate in these with people they can trust; children are active participants in their learning process, which is mainly organized around children's interests and questions, rather than imposed by adults.

The guiding principle behind funds of knowledge is valuing the community as a resource of enormous importance, one that can create educational change and improvement (Moll et al. 1992). Moll et al.'s (1992) study reflected the experience of a teacher who shifted her deficit views and deconstructed previously held stereotypes about Latinx households. This teacher realized that her students' parents cared for and supported the education of their children; the teacher included the funds of knowledge she learned and observed at these Latinx homes in her class. She bridged the world of the students at home to the school environment. Through inquiry, she created a curriculum in which students became active learners. The lived experiences of the students were used in her classroom as topics and resources for teaching. González, Moll, et al. (2005) used these insights to train teachers as ethnographers to conduct visits to their students' homes and form curriculum units to tap into students' funds of knowledge.

There is a rich body of research focusing on students' funds of knowledge, with a wide breadth of contexts including college students (Marquez Kiyama 2010), science (Calabrese Barton and Tan 2009; Seiler 2001), early childhood (Gregg, Rugg, and Stoneman 2011), multiliteracies (Pirbhai-Illich 2010), family literacy (Dworin 2006; González, Andrade, et al. 2005; Longwell-Grice and McIntyre 2006), college preparation (González and Moll 2002), adult literacy learning (Kalman 2004, 2005), technology (Spence 2009), and dual language (Fitts 2009). These studies consistently show that when teachers incorporate funds of knowledge of students in the classrooms, the students are engaged and tend to excel in their studies.

There are few studies of funds of knowledge in transnational contexts (Andrews and Yee 2006; Hedges, Cullen, and Jordan 2011; Martin-Jones and Saxena 2003; Zipin 2009). For example, Andrews and Yee (2006) describe how UK teachers held deficit perspectives of their students. They studied the experiences of two transnational students (one Pakistani and the other Bangladeshi) and found that teachers had a limited picture of students compared to families' multifaceted and complex portrayal of the same students. While students were engaging and outgoing out of school, teachers described the two students as "shy," "doesn't put herself forward," and "lazy" (444). This example points to what Moll and colleagues (1992) describe as a typical teacher-student relationship, limited, or thin and single-stranded. Teachers know students only based on their performance in the classroom.

In contrast, other studies show specific student practices and pedagogical effort of teachers who incorporate funds of knowledge in their instruction. Cuero's (2010) research focused on Jennifer, a fifth grade student, who used her transnational funds of knowledge to craft her writing. Cuero identified metacognitive strategies and a strong written voice used by Jennifer through her writing. Writing about her transnational experiences in Mexico, Jennifer became a skilled writer. Her ability to draw on her transnational funds of knowledge, as well as on her linguistic skills, allowed her "to work wonders with words" (435). Browning-Aiken (2005) researches the border-crossing of the Aguilar family. Her findings reveal the knowledge the Aguilar children have about copper mining and the important effect this has had on the economic and political development of southern Arizona and Mexico. Because many of the men in the family worked in mines on both sides of the border, the children knew about the history of mining, the environment, the relationship between the industry and the state's economy, and the international exchange of technology and trade. Based on this information, the researcher developed a curriculum module relevant to students' lives and that built new knowledge and skills. This module was then used to teach about geology, mining, and ecology. In this case, Browning-Aiken saw the border as "a bridge for people trying to maintain their ties in two countries and to have the best of both worlds" (179). Finally, Zipin (2009) shows how middle school students in Australia are resources to write a health science curriculum that draws on their funds of knowledge. The author problematizes a single-stranded view of students and argues for approaches to funds of knowledge that incorporate even what might be considered "dark" funds of knowledge, those knowledges that result from difficult lived experiences such as poverty or violence.

Toward a Definition of Transfronterizx Funds of Knowledge

In this chapter, we build on previous research (Cuero 2010; Vélez-Ibáñez and Greenberg 1992) to propose that *transfronterizx funds of knowledge* is the ability to draw on geographic, linguistic, and cultural knowledge and to leverage transcultural and transnational gains in educational contexts. As the studies reviewed in chapter 1 show, transnational students bring unique assets to educational settings such as engagement of people in language and literacy practices that span national boundaries. In school, students draw on their textual resources "derived from their transnational fields of activity in approaching" literacy in school (Lam and Warriner 2012, 210). Transfronterizx funds of knowledge are a type of transnational funds of knowledge where transfronterizx experience is frequent and engaged in mobile experiences of border-crossing and travel activity. The concepts of *transfronterizx funds of knowledge* and *transnational funds of knowledge* differ in that the contacts between two countries and across borders are more intense and engaged in an embodied experience on the border. These contacts take place often, sometimes the same day or the same week, and entail back-and-forth movement from one country to another. We adopt Levitt and Glick Schiller's (2004) proposal that to understand the transnational experience it is important to capture "the experience of living simultaneously within and beyond the boundaries of a nation state" (1006). Tranfronterizx students crisscross international boundaries as part of their (sometimes daily) routines. For instance, they might use their observations and knowledge about Mexican grocery store shopping to learn mathematical content in their classrooms on the U.S. side, then go back to the grocery store *on the same day* and apply their mathematical knowledge to make calculations at the grocery store in Mexico.

Thus, transfronterizx funds of knowledge are "embedded in multilayered, multi-sited, transnational social fields" (Levitt and Glick Schiller 2004, 1003) so that activity straddles and traverses borders. In their work on simultaneity, Levitt and Glick Schiller (2004) define simultaneity as living life that incorporates daily activities, routines, and institutions located both in a destination country and transnationally. We draw on the concept of simultaneity to understand how transfronterizx practices are embedded in transnational social fields which function to mobilize knowledge and text across national boundaries. Another construct to understand transfronterizx funds of knowledge is recontextualizing. We will analyze examples where transfronterizx students engaged in recontextualizing their funds of knowledge from both sides of the border. Transfronterizx funds of knowledge are part of the community cultural wealth repertoires used by transfronterizx students in order to navigate U.S. schools. Encouraging students to use textual resources and knowledge that traverses boundaries is a pedagogical approach that facilitates transnational students' engagement in school.

Bridging Transfronterizx Knowledge and School Knowledge

As presented in chapter 3, Ms. O was transfronterizx and bilingual. Ms. O said that her bilingualism and her transfronterizx experiences helped her understand her students and the importance of constructing a safe learning environment by allowing them to "make connections" between school knowledge and what they already knew, and vice versa (see also chapter 6). During an interview with Ms. O, she explained how she continuously had her students "make connections" to their lives: "The concepts that I teach, I try to see, I try to teach them how they can use them in their daily lives, such as in their home, when they go to the store, when they go and buy something when they receive change. I try to have them make that connection."

Ms. O made the students think about how they could use what they were learning in school in their lives outside of school. She said that her students came back and shared with her the different connections they made between their academic work and their worlds outside of school. Ms. O then emphasized to her students that these types of monetary estimations are not only things they will use in school to get good grades in math, but a kind of knowledge they can use in their everyday lives. She supported teaching practices that use both community and school as resources (Moll and Greenberg 1990) and was able to see how her students used school concepts at home; she understood the importance of using home knowledge at school. Based on interviews and our classroom observations, it was clear that Ms. O highly encouraged the use of transfronterizx funds of knowledge in the classroom.

During our observations we noted numerous times that the class was frequently boisterous and talkative, revealing that much learning was going on as students connected their conversations to the lessons. Students talked freely in either English or Spanish without fear of reprisal. Most of the students were eager to share their daily lives, their families, and everyday activities, such as *telenovelas* (Spanish soap operas) or the latest popular songs and artists. The following are three instances of how the students in Ms. O's class made connections to bridge their world at home to the school content by using their transfronterizx funds of knowledge.

Learning About the Concept of Energy: Remedios caseros

The following example comes from a science lesson in which students were discussing the concept of energy. The students were reviewing different types of energy. Ms. O made a list on the board of words that define energy: light, sound, shock, heat, and static. Ms. O asked the students questions such as "Is the sun energy?"; "Is thunder energy?"; and "How do we know if an object has energy?" Students replied to these questions, saying that energy produces light, heat, movement, and sound. From this review of energy, Ms. O moved to the topic for that day, electricity.

MS. O: How does electricity **travel**?

MARTÍN: It **travels** through wires, cables.

ANDRÉS: También está en el **aire**. Como en el carro llega la electricidad a la antena para oír la música. (It is also in the air. Like when you are in the car, and the electricity passes through the antenna so that you can listen to music.)

MS. O: How about in addition to wires?

ESTER: Cuando se descompone, porque deja algo prendido y los cables se los ponen y se pasa la electricidad. (When something does not work because you leave it on and you put the cables on it to charge it with electricity.)

ANDRÉS: La pila se puede volver a usar. Mi papá es mecánico y agarra un motor y lo conecta a unas pinzas y prende el switch y **se pasa la electricidad**. (The battery, you can use it again. My dad is a mechanic, and he gets the motor and connects it to some cables and turns on the switch and charges it with electricity.)

SIMÓN: Como los teléfonos **se ponen en el cargador**. (Like cell phones that you put them on a charger.)

MARÍA: Yo tengo un remedio casero para volver a usar la pila. Cuando el Suavitel se acaba y se echa agua y echa la pila adentro del agua y se vuelve a **cargar** como en una hora. (I have a home remedy to be able to reuse batteries. When you finish a plastic bottle of fabric softener, you put water in the bottle and put the battery in the water, and your battery will recharge like in an hour.)

ESTER: Una señora me dijo que "si no le quieres poner pila nueva déjala [la pila] afuera en el sol y pasa una hora"; y **lo dejé, y ya empezó a servir**. (A lady told me that if I did not want to buy a new battery, I could leave it outside in the sun, so I left it for an hour and it worked.)

Ms. O created authentic activities to access funds of knowledge for academic content learning. In this event, students were able to make sense of how electricity traveled by using examples they have experienced in their everyday lives. Electricity is an abstract concept for them to understand, but by using their transfronterizx funds of knowledge, the students were able to offer concrete examples of how electricity travels. Funds of knowledge are multistranded (Moll et al. 1992). In this example, one can see how students have learned from members of their cross-border social networks and daily activities on both sides of the border. Before studying this concept at school, Andrés had acquired the notion of electricity from his father who has an auto shop in Mexico, and Ester had learned that idea when she discovered a *remedio casero* (home remedy) from a lady in her community in Ciudad Juárez. This example portrays how students draw on the labor history of the family (and neighbors) as a source of information (Moll et al. 1992) to make sense of electricity. Because his dad is a car mechanic, Andrés has learned that you can charge a battery by using cables connected to a motor. Martín, Simón, and María are drawing from their everyday activities on both sides of the border such as using cell phone chargers and car antennas.

María's proposal of using an empty bottle of Suavitel to recharge the batteries, Ester's suggestion of leaving a battery outside in the sun to recharge, and Andrés's knowledge about charging a battery are all practices learned in Mexico. They were then recontextualized, from the context of the community to the school, as well as across nations, from Mexico to the United States. These are examples of mobile resources that students tap into in order to perform academic tasks. The students incorporated their daily routines and activities from Mexico in U.S. schools. These examples show that students live simultaneously on both sides of the border and that they draw on lessons and experiences that transcend national boundaries.

Furthermore, this example also illustrates how students used their entire linguistic repertoire to make sense of science. The teacher conducted her class in English because in this particular DL program in fourth grade, science was taught in English, while language arts, social studies, and math were in Spanish. In the example presented above, the teacher asked questions in English and students answered in Spanish. This is one of the numerous examples of translanguaging practices (García 2009; García and Wei 2014) observed in the DL classrooms. We may see in the excerpt above that students built on each others' contributions in order to co-construct knowledge around the topic of energy. The words in bold in the excerpt above show the process of co-construction and scaffolding that ocurred. Ms. O encouraged the use of translanguaging, which facilitated student participation and co-construction of knowledge. Without translanguaging and students' use of funds of knowledge, the interaction would have been very different and possibly not as successful. For a fuller account of translanguaging in science lessons see chapter 6.

Bridging Knowledge of Home and School to Write a Personal Narrative: Mi abuelo

Ms. O modeled how to use diverse strategies for her fourth grade two-way DL students. The students appropriated the use of school strategies, such as "making connections" and using their funds of knowledge to make sense of texts and academic concepts. Students learned this with Ms. O's assistance and eventually were able to do it independently. Another example that demonstrates the use of transfronterizx funds of knowledge took place when students practiced written composition. In fourth grade, students were tested in writing by the State of Texas Assessment of Academic Readiness (STAAR), the Texas standardized test. Thus, during our observations, we found several writing assignments that prepared students for this test. Interestingly, encouraged by their teacher to do so, students used their funds of knowledge in their narratives.

In this assignment the students were asked to write a personal story about a day in which things did not turn out the way they had planned. The prompt asked students to write about what they wish had happened and what actually happened. The students were asked to organize their ideas in a rough draft and elaborate on them. Then they wrote a one-page personal narrative about their experience. Eva wrote about the death of her grandfather. She wrote the following (original spelling). For an edited version, see the footnote.*

---

* Un día muy soleado sonó el teléfono. ¡Rin, rin, rin! "Bueno, ¿quién es?" "Soy tu abuela. Tu abuelo se acaba de caer del camión." "¿Pero cómo?" "Se quiso subir, pero no pudo". "¿Y para dónde iba?" "Iba a ir a dejar las cosechas." "Ah, con razón, pero ¿cómo está?" ¡In, in, in!, cuelga. En menos de una hora, habló: "¿Bueno, quién es?" "Soy tu abuela. Tu abuelo está en el hospital. Le dio un derrame cerebral." "Amá,

Un día muy soleado sone [*sic*] el teléfono. *¡Rin, rin, rin!*—Bueno, quien es?—soy tu abuela, tu abuelo se acaba de caer del camion ¿pero como? Se quiso subir pero no pudo. ¿Y para dónde iba?—Iba a ir a dejar las cosechas. Ah con razon pero ¿como esta? *In, in, in* colga. En menos de una hora, ablo ¿bueno quien es? Soy tú abuela, tú abuelo esta en el hospital. Le dio un derrame serebral. Ama, ama, dice mi abuela que mi abuelo esta malo.—Ahorita que le estan haciendo—le estan haciendo una operacion.—imediatamente, mi papá mando por mi abuelo en ambulancia. Se trajeron a mi abuelo a El Paso. Entonces, llevaron a mi abuelo a la casa de mi tia Nieves. En menos de un mes, se habia mejorado mucho.—Un dia que ya se habia metido el sol, fuimos a ver a mi abuelo. Mi abuelo empezó a echar la leche. Yo me había asustado mucho. En unos minutos más tarde, nos fuimos a nuestra casa "*rin, rin, rin*"—bueno que paso tu abuelo ya se esta despidiendo de todos. Se está despidiendo de todos. En mi mente tintineaba la palabra, tu abuelo ya se esta despidiendo de todos. "No puede ser" imediatamente fuimos a la casa de mi tia Nieves y cada uno se despidio. Al dia siguiente, nos vestimos de luto para ir al velorio y enterarlo. En el velorio llegaron unos musicos y cantaron. Minutos mas tarde fuimos enterar a mi abuelo. Cavaron un hoyo que paresia como un tunel. Este fue un dia que no susedio como yo pensaba. Yo queria que mi abuelo viviera.

(One very sunny day, the phone rang. *Ring! Ring ring!* "Hello. Who is this?" "This is your grandmother. Your grandfather just fell from a truck." "How did it happen?" "He tried to get on, but couldn't." "And where was he going?" "He

---

amá, dice mi abuela que mi abuelo está malo." "Ahorita qué le están haciendo." "Le están haciendo una operación." Inmediatamente, mi papá mandó por mi abuelo en ambulancia. Se trajeron a mi abuelo a El Paso. Entonces, llevaron a mi abuelo a la casa de mi tía Nieves. En menos de un mes, se había mejorado mucho. Un día que ya se había metido el sol, fuimos a ver a mi abuelo. Mi abuelo empezó a echar la leche. Yo me había asustado mucho. En unos minutos más tarde, nos fuimos a nuestra casa. ¡Rin, rin, rin! "Bueno, ¿qué pasó?" "Tu abuelo ya se está despidiendo de todos. Se está despidiendo de todos." En mi mente tintineaba la palabra: "Tu abuelo ya se está despidiendo de todos." "No puede ser." Inmediatamente fuimos a la casa de mi tía Nieves y cada uno se despidió. Al día siguiente, nos vestimos de luto para ir al velorio y enterrarlo. En el velorio llegaron unos músicos y cantaron. Minutos más tarde fuimos a enterrar a mi abuelo. Cavaron un hoyo que parecía como un túnel. Este fue un día que no sucedió como yo pensaba. Yo quería que mi abuelo viviera.

was going to drop off the harvest" "Oh, no wonder, but how is he doing?" *Beep, beep, beep.* She hung up. In less than an hour, she called back. "Hello. Who is this?" "This is your grandmother. Your grandfather is in the hospital. He had a stroke?" "Ma, Ma, my grandma says that my grandfather is sick." "What are they doing?" "They are operating on him." My father immediately sent for my grandfather by ambulance. They brought my grandfather to El Paso. Then they took my grandfather to my Aunt Nieves's house. In less than a month, he got better. One day, when the sun had set, we went to see my grandfather. He started to throw up milk. I got very scared. A few minutes later, we went home. *Ring! Ring ring!* "Hello. What's going on? Your grandfather wants to say his last farewell to everyone." The words "he wants to say his last farewell" rang in my mind. "This can't be true." We went to my Aunt Nieves's house immediately, and we all said goodbye. The next day we dressed in mourning attire to go to the viewing and to bury him. Musicians came to the viewing and they sang. A few minutes later we went to bury my grandfather. They dug a hole that seemed like a tunnel. That was a day when something unexpected happened. I wanted my grandfather to live.)

Eva wrote a captivating story that uses many of the literary devices she was learning to prepare for the standardized test in writing. She recounts events over an extended period and includes literary devices such as onomatopoeia (ring! beep), references to multiple characters, quoted speech, similes (like a tunnel), metaphors (the words rang), and striking images (the setting sun, the musicians) that captivate her audience. The use of these literary devices learned at school coexisted with Eva's recontextualizing of her experience of the loss of her grandfather, her bringing into the text her love for her *familia*, her familial capital, her knowledge of transborder health experiences, her knowledge of agricultural activities, and so many others. By recontextualizing her funds of knowledge, she was able to marshal these resources probably first and foremost to cope with the loss of her grandfather, but also to prepare for the standardized state test in a meaningful way, relevant to her transborder identity.

Eva's story shows literal and academic border-crossings as she simultaneously draws from her experiences in Mexico and the United States. It shows how the transnational social networks come into play for Eva's family as they have the choice to transport the grandfather to El Paso to get medical attention and then go back to Mexico to bury him. The family was living simultaneously on both sides of the border, and the contact between both countries was intense and frequent as they were accessing resources on both sides (Vélez-Ibáñez and Greenberg 1992). Eva recounted the details of her experiences on both sides of the border to write an academic text and a narrative that is a compelling and poignant account of her grandfather's passing. Her border-crossing experiences serve as the subject of her writing (Medina 2010). In the process of writing her story, she is becoming an accomplished storyteller. Also, the act of writing her personal narrative potentially served to maintain personal relationships that span national boundaries (Lam and Warriner 2012). The fact that Eva can use her Spanish language, in the context of the DL program, provides Eva the opportunity to draw on her transfronterizx story.

At the same time, it is important to point out that the example also illustrates limitations of a structured writing assignment. The test practice sheet did not allow the students to write outside the box provided. Thus, we observed in her first draft that Eva brought many lived experiences and funds of knowledge to the act of writing, including intertextual resources such as the songs played at her grandfather's funeral like "La cruz de olvido," a well-known Mexican song about farewells. The context of the test preparation activities ended up limiting her writing to one page, and significant details, which included additional transfronterizx funds of knowledge initially present in her first drafts, ended up deleted from her final selection.

Bridging Knowledge of School and Home to Understand Social Studies: La economía

Ms. Ornelas knew how to draw on the students' transfronterizx funds of knowledge and considered that dialogue was important for students to understand and create academic meanings. She fostered an environment that allowed students to make connections to the text and also to connect to what the other students were sharing in the conversation. For the text to become meaningful, it was important for students to make connections between their lived experiences and the text. We must stress that Ms. O valued students' use of their funds of knowledge to mediate understanding.

The following example illustrates a recurring pattern we observed in Ms. O's classroom—using instructional conversations to create academic meanings. A free reading interaction took place shortly after the end-of-year testing was over. Ms. O spent the two previous weeks addressing ecosystems. There were several student-made webs of different ecosystems on the bulletin boards. The students had also taken a field trip to the zoo and had been expected to take pictures of animals and their ecosystems.

Ms. O was passing out the monthly magazine, *Time for Kids*, to read with the students. They were reading a section about Texas, cattle country, and the economy.

MS. O: ¿Qué es la economía? (What is the economy?)

MARÍA: El dinero que tiene un país. (The money that a country has.)

MS. O: ¿Cómo puede el ganado producir economía? (How can cattle produce an economy?)

ESTELA: Como las vacas que dan leche y carne. (Like the cows that give milk and meat.)

MARÍA: Cuando yo andaba en Chihuahua, como casi todos tienen ganado, fui a la tienda y se veían a las vacas, así, todos los huesos, vendiéndolos. (When I was in Chihuahua like almost everyone has cattle, I would see the cows and the bones being sold in the stores.)

The episode shows how students like María and Estela are both making sense of the text. María, in particular, made connections to her cross-border experiences in Chihuahua. She connected the academic concept of economy to her lived experience in the Chihuahua marketplace. She saw how family members and friends raised cattle and then sold them at the market to make money. From her visits to Mexico she learned and experienced firsthand how an economy works. She drew on her family's labor history (Moll et al. 1992) to make sense of the text. Moreover, María's example sparked further connections among other students who then started sharing experiences they had had with farm animals. For example, another transfronterizx student, Andrés, got up from his desk and went to the whiteboard and talked while simultaneously drawing a web.

ANDRÉS: La vaca se vende a Burger King y luego hacen burgers y se venden
como "La Nueva Angus." Esa es economía. [The cattle are sold to Burger
King, and they make hamburgers and sell it as "The New Angus." That is
an economy.]

Andrés also connected his experiences in Mexico with the concept of economy. Note that his use of the product is in Spanish ("La Nueva Angus").
He connects his knowledge of the world to leverage gains in the classroom.
By drawing on his knowledge of transnational economies, he positioned
himself as an expert in front of the class. He stood in front of the class and
became the teacher in that instance. Following Ms. O's model of this particular meaning-making strategy, he drew a semantic web that summarized
what he had learned in the previous weeks about ecosystems as well as making connections to his knowledge of Burger King's products in Spanish. He
used these resources, the web, and his transfronterizx knowledge to explain
to the class what an ecosystem looked like and how it created an economy,
thus answering Ms. O's question about how cattle helped create an economy.
Finally, the example also illustrates the multilayered, multi-sited character of
transfronterizx funds of knowledge.

Discussion

We found in this study that transfronterizx funds of knowledge are assets
that students tended to use in the U.S. DL classrooms. The examples presented here are just a few of the many that we found. We observed that the
role of the teacher was very important in not only allowing but encouraging
students to draw from their diverse repertoires of transfronterizx funds of
knowledge. We show how, with the guidance of the teacher, students are able
to bridge the knowledge of home/community and school, and their worlds
in two nations, in different content areas.

These examples also show how in spite of structural constraints such as
standardized testing policies, Ms. O was culturally responsive and understood the importance of working with transfronterizx students. She created

an environment that made students feel comfortable and safe, and that valued the use of translanguaging and recontextualizing in order to create meaning. She organized spaces in which students learned from each other and generated a web of meanings to understand academic text. We observed that students felt comfortable, motivated, and willing to participate. Ms. O understood how transfronterizx funds of knowledge also served to leverage academic gains. The teacher understanding their value, allowing their use, and modeling how to use them in the class are crucial for student success. As noted earlier, such teachers have the potential to challenge current school structures and transform them into a more inclusive system, one that allows all students to feel welcomed and cared for in schools and encouraged to learn.

Although the results of this study come from the particular contexts of the border and a DL program, where transfronterizxs are afforded the intense back-and-forth contacts with Mexico, the examples described here are relevant to many other contexts in which immigrant children cross the invisible and metaphorical borders of the home/community and the school.

Conclusion

Transfronterizx Practices as Generative Spaces

AS THE RENOWNED BORDER JOURNALIST Alfredo Corchado recently expressed so eloquently, our border cities are like "political piñatas, easy to hit them" (Corchado 2017). *Desde la frontera*, we are sickened about the damaging false rhetoric about the border as a lawless land and a war zone, and about border residents characterized as violent criminals. We asked ourselves what kind of discourses and thinking are those that depict the border as violent, and borderlanders as criminals, uneducated, "costly," or semilingual.* This, for sure, is not border thinking (Mignolo 2000). As scholars who live, work, and research on this U.S.-Mexico borderland we propose that perspectives of *la frontera* be not only considered but highlighted in debates on education and transnationalism.

In the first year of conducting fieldwork, a ten-year-old participant in our study told us, "Tenemos muchas cosas que contar" ("We have lots of stories to tell"), and it was true, they all did. We listened and learned from the transfronterizx experiences: their lives, their border-crossings, their funds of knowledge from both sides of the border and the in-between, their terrifying and vast understanding of violence in Ciudad Juárez, their survival strategies, and their rich repertoires of language and literacy practices. Doing

---

* See the headline of the *Houston Chronicle* article (Viren 2007).

research in these times of violence was particularly important and challenging; we questioned whether it made sense to conduct research in the middle of such turmoil and the pain the participants of our study had experienced. Learning about their stories and their practices helped us recognize not only the horrible consequences of the violence in Ciudad Juárez but also the strength and resiliency of transfronterizxs.

As the research progressed throughout the three years of ethnographic work, we realized that these repertoires of knowledges and practices were part of the community cultural wealth (Yosso 2005) that students had at their disposal, and many times used at school. Ultimately, this book documents and emphasizes the value of transfronterizx community cultural wealth. Practices analyzed here reflect the complexities of the interactive dynamics in the transborder region. In this final chapter, we discuss the implications of our study in terms of language and literacy practices' potential as border thinking (Mignolo 2000), nepantla (Anzaldúa 1999), and third spaces (Moje et al. 2004). In other words, we address these practices as generative spaces for curriculum and pedagogy in school classrooms. Even though this book tells the stories of transfronterizxs on the U.S.-Mexico border, many of the findings and examples are relevant to other transnationals who cross metaphorical boundaries every day, when they go from home to school in places far from the dividing line between the United States and Mexico.

Toward a Definition of Transfronterizx Students and Their Practices

We have paid close attention to the private sphere (Sánchez and Machado-Casas 2009) of transnationalism on the U.S.-Mexico border and its everyday practices "from below" (Smith and Guarnizo 1998). Experiences such as crossing the bridge, having two homes in two different countries, learning how to navigate an English-dominant space, bringing texts produced in Ciudad Juárez to the classroom in El Paso, and singing and using texts, such as *narcocorridos*, *telenovelas*, and Mexican film scripts, in their written work or oral presentations at school, are just some examples of the stories and experiences we have presented throughout this book. These experiences tell stories of superdiversity (Vertovec 2007) in that transfronterizxs offer particular ways to be in the spectrum of transnationalism, and their complex and mobile practices are tied to their mobile trajectories across national borders.

Transfronterizxs, as one type of the many transnational students, provide a unique opportunity to understand transnationalism when the contacts between two countries and across borders are intense and engaged in an embodied experience. An embodied border experience characterized the knowledge, languages, and literacy practices presented here. Transfronterizxs, who live both "acá y allá" use their repertoires of communicative practices and funds of knowledge as resources to navigate their diverse worlds. In chapters 5 and 6, we saw that students recontextualized both print and digital literacies from one side of the border to the other and from home to school. Through their everyday experiences with family and friends, they acquired literacy knowledge that was closely related to their identities as transfronterizxs and, at the same time, became a resource in navigating the U.S. educational system and resisting structures of inequality, such as linguistic discrimination.

When defining transfronterizxs, we should point out that they are not a homogenous group themselves. The term transfronterizx includes families who have high economic capital as well as middle-class and working-class families. In our study, most children were members of working-class transfronterizx families who experienced marginalization. However, we acknowledge the diversity within this group and argue the need for further research that considers the many diverse experiences of transfronterizx students.

We have presented in this book particular forms of knowledge of transfronterizxs, namely translanguaging, recontextualizing literacies, and transfronterizx funds of knowledge. These types of knowing are part of the toolkit that transfronterizxs draw upon in order to participate in the DL program. These forms are included in their community cultural wealth and demonstrate the integration of linguistic, navigational, resistant, familial, social, and aspirational capitals (Yosso 2002) of transfronterizxs acquired in their activities of crossing national and other kinds of borders, such as linguistic and cultural borders. Thus we contend that practices documented here produce alternative narratives about transfronterizxs, other transnationals, and their families, in line with research from a LatCrit perspective (Solórzano and Yosso 2001). The stories shared in this book produce alternative discourses and thinking. We refer, for example, to the stories of *nepantleros* and *nepantleras*, "those who live within and among multiple worlds" (Keating 2005, 1), such as those presented in chapter 4. The story of the four women of the Rendon family talks about love, sacrifice, support, and humor in the midst of the painful family separation. Isabel Rendón, who at a young age lovingly and committedly guided her sister through her traumatic transition from Ciudad Juárez to El Paso due to drug-related violence, and Maria's story, of a girl who patiently accepted this change in her life while waiting for her mother's immigration documents. Isabel and María presented the activity of crossing the bridge as what actually helped unify the family. Based on Anzaldúa's concept of *nepantla*, *nepantleras* are people who experience this space between two worlds, and who build bridges among distinct people and ways of knowing.[†] These *nepantleras* were not only physically crossing the bridge because it was part of their everyday lives as transfronterizxs but also because it was essential to their social and affective relationships; crossing the bridge was essential to be "ahora sí unidas" ("finally united"). Crossing the bridge also meant living "en los dos lados" ("on both sides"), "aquí y allá" ("here and there").

The literature tells us that *nepantlera* pedagogies (Reza-López, Huerta Charles, and Reyes 2014) are rarely found in official school curricula; hardly ever do teachers and administrators ask themselves or try to understand what transnational knowledge students possess. However, our study showed a different situation. BES was welcoming to transfronterizxs in many ways. The school leadership and teachers were understanding of the transfronterizx experience and acted as *nepantleros*, "the supreme border crossers" (Keating 2006, 9). School officials communicated values of solidarity, empathy, and acceptance. Unlike other schools where transfronterizx students felt rejected, singled out, or even "disappeared" (for example, the well-known case of Bowie High School in El Paso, Texas), BES had a history of working with transfronterizxs and their families.[‡] We think of these administrators

---

[†] ". . . the space between two worlds. It is a limited space, a space where you are not this or that but where you are changing. You haven't got into the new identity yet and haven't left the old identity behind either—you are in a kind of transition." (Anzaldúa 1999, 237)

[‡] At the same time that we conducted the fieldwork for this study, Bowie High School was involved in a cheating scandal. Administrators in this and other El Paso

and teachers as people who took risks in order to mediate between the different worlds they lived in, and who tried to work toward inclusiveness and understanding among diverse positions: "Nepantleras do not pick sides. Instead, they witness all sides. In epistemological terms, nepantleras use their views from these cracks between worlds to develop holistic, 'connectionist' approaches, enabling us to reconceive and perhaps transform the various worlds in which we exist" (Keating 2011, 144).

Recontextualizing

During this ethnography, we documented the complexities of the contexts of language and literacy learning of transfronterizx students. Their practices occurred in the local context of the DL classroom, which also was profoundly influenced by global contexts. For example, students learned the language arts discourses, concepts, and skills required by the state-mandated curriculum and assessed by the then-new test, the State of Texas Assessments of Academic Readiness (STAAR). The distant (global), disconnected, and powerful context of the Texas Education Agency, with its policies written with no bilingual transfronterizx student in mind, is nevertheless so profoundly present in the everyday local realities of the DL classrooms observed. The literacy practices and the "literacy technologies" (Brandt and Clinton 2002) promoted by these global institutional contexts in the form of standards, tests, and prescriptive curricula are very much present in the classrooms.

At the same time, in her classroom Ms. O created a local context where transfronterizx discourses, stories, and funds of knowledge were also centered. As described in chapter 6, when learning how to write the narrative school genre, students recontextualized their stories or their "content," defined as a continuum between minority and majority content as per Hornberger's continua of biliteracy model (Hornberger and Link 2012). Through their written productions, students recontextualized their lived experiences

---

ISD schools "disappeared" students or their credits were unlawfully removed from transcripts in order to meet accountability. Many affected students were Spanish speakers and students who had recently transferred from Mexico due to the drug war violence in Ciudad Juárez.

from Juárez into the context of this classroom across national borders. Students learned content that came through the school literacy artifacts, such as how to write narrative texts, how to use various graphic organizers to support the writing process, and the mechanics of writing in Spanish through the use of content that portrayed their experiences as transfronterizxs. As Pedro's example shows in chapter 6, this content was not only used for academic learning, but it was also shared and authentically discussed by teachers and classmates. Besides the formal aspects required by the language arts state curriculum, meaning-making of the content of interest to students was also a purpose of this activity. The space created by moving particular transfronterizx discourses was filled by an ideology that favors bilingualism and children's funds of knowledge (González, Moll, and Amanti 2005), including transfronterizx funds of knowledge and experiences. Through recognizing and including strategies such as "making connections," "crossing borders," or *recontextualizing* strategies, Ms. Ornelas organized a classroom ecology (Creese and Martin 2003) that offered "possibilities for teachers and learners to access academic content through the linguistic resources and communicative repertoires (students) bring to the classroom while simultaneously acquiring new ones" (Hornberger and Link 2012, 268).

Translanguaging and Multimodality

Translanguaging literature has demonstrated in the last decade that encouraging students to use their vast repertoire of language practices allows for the active participation of everyone, as well as metacognitive reflection and subject knowledge learning. Student participants of this study used both languages to learn. Both Spanish and English were not only recognized but modeled and scaffolded as well. Examples presented here show that Ms. O organized a learning environment that aided students to move from the position of an apprentice to an autonomous learner. The study shows the process in which students appropriated translanguaging practices for academic content learning.

We also found that translanguaging occurred in multiple modes of communication. Many of the literacy events described in this book show how Ms. O orchestrated multimodal resources within translanguaging practices.

The documentation of these multimodal literacies, where translanguaging was not only allowed but encouraged, contributes to the body of knowledge on literacy practices with emergent bilinguals developed in recent years. These findings challenge traditional views of literacy as isolated skills and bilingualism as solely the knowledge of two separate languages. Additionally, we contribute to the recent discussions about translanguaging practices as pedagogical practice. We present examples of what translanguaging for learning looks like in a classroom. The frequent use of translanguaging suggests that in spite of language-separation policies, students engaged in translanguaging in order to meaningfully and actively participate and make meaning in the classroom, which in turn transformed classroom discourse. Despite the fact that instruction was planned to be delivered in either Spanish (for example, in social studies) or English (as in the science class), the classroom was a space where emergent bilinguals were able to use their dynamic bilingualism flexibly to make their contributions.

Multimodal literacy practices allowed for students' agency. Even in their first weeks of enrollment in the DL program, students could meaningfully participate in the academic activities. Students drew from multiple multimodal communicative resources to engage, make meaning of, and produce texts (broadly defined). For example, the literacy event presented in chapter 5 about a multimodal presentation prepared and delivered by Ana, Mariel, Gabriela, and Patricia showed that as part of their linguistic and navigational capital, students used their print and digital transfronterizx literacies in the classroom when performing academic work. These literacies included multimodal representations that conveyed knowledge and experiences in Ciudad Juárez and El Paso. Chapter 8 provides another example, this time in the context of science class. In this particular case, multimodality played a crucial role along with the translanguaging practices observed. During the preparation of the Science Extravaganza project, emergent bilingual transfronterizxs mobilized oral language, written text, and video as diverse modes of communication in order to meaningfully participate in the academic event. Transfronterizx students were able to use a variety of linguistic and cultural resources in order to make meaning of texts broadly defined.

These findings add to the body of knowledge on sociocultural perspectives on multimodality in DL classrooms that have demonstrated that allowing students to mobilize their repertoires of language and multimodal practices enables active and meaningful participation (see review in chapter 2). In that sense, the everyday construction of "safe spaces for learning" in DL classrooms through the use of multimodality and translanguaging practices becomes a possibility for social change. Educators may work toward social change and educate all students equitably by working with students as they build on their translanguaging resources (García and Leiva 2014), particularly transnational and transfronterizx students.

Transfronterizx Funds of Knowledge

Along with translanguaging practices, we found that transfronterizx funds of knowledge are assets that students use in the U.S. DL classrooms. The study points to the importance of conducting research that resists deficit perspectives on the educational achievement of transfronterizx students. Rather than thinking of transnational students as lacking in knowledge of a new system and school knowledge, we show how transfronterizx students use what they already know to make connections and construct new knowledge. Students used their bodies of knowledge and skills based on their transfronterizx experiential reality, "rooted in daily, useful skills and information of a very broad nature . . . and expressed in a broad range of contexts" (Vélez-Ibáñez and Greenberg 1992, 318) in the classroom. Examples analyzed in chapter 9 included *remedios caseros* learned in Ciudad Juárez and knowledge of electricity learned from a mechanic dad's transnational economies. Other examples of funds of knowledge included the stories of transfronterizx activities, such as Eva's story of literal and academic border-crossings and transnational social networks when writing about her grandfather's back-and-forth trajectory to get medical attention in El Paso, and later his burial in Mexico. Transfronterizx funds of knowledge are a type of transnational funds of knowledge, keeping in mind that the transfronterizx experience is intense and engaged in mobile experiences of border-crossing and travel activity.

We show how with the guidance of a teacher, students are able to bridge the knowledge of home and school, and their worlds in two nations, in a variety of content areas. Ms. O created an environment that made students feel comfortable and safe, and which valued the use of translanguaging and recontextualizing in order to create meaning. She created spaces in which students learned from each other and generated a web of meanings to understand an academic text. Ms. O also understood how transfronterizx funds of knowledge enhanced academic gains. As noted earlier, such teachers have the potential to challenge current school structures and transform them into a more inclusive system that allows all students to feel welcomed and cared for in schools and encouraged to learn.

Transfronterizx funds of knowledge analyzed here allowed us to understand how students utilized their expertise across contexts. Furthermore, students applied these assets as well as minority knowledges learned in one situation to new situations (recontextualized), showing that the *"boundaries themselves are significant, generative spaces* where resources may be combined in new ways or for new purposes" (Barton and Hamilton 2005, 18, emphasis is ours). Throughout the book, we show many examples of transfronterizxs recontextualizing discourses, texts, knowledge, and practices from one country to another, from school to home, and vice versa, from one content subject to another. Thus, there is a flexible use of practices across contexts, which is not always free of contentions and complexities.

Generative Spaces We Learned by Working with Transfronterizxs

Contrary to deficit framings of Mexican and transfronterizx children, the literacy events which included translanguaging and recontextualizing, as well as transfronterizx funds of knowledge, are more evidence that transnational children do bring a rich array of linguistic practices and cultural resources that schools should acknowledge and use. From the subaltern perspective (Mignolo 2000) of the borderlands, we analyze the language and literacy practices that are part of the transfronterizx community cultural wealth (Yosso 2005)—that is, the "array of knowledge, skills, abilities, and contacts possessed and utilized by Communities of Color to survive and resist macro and micro-forms of oppression" (77). Practices analyzed in this book show the integration of linguistic, navigational, resistant, familial, social, and aspirational capitals (Yosso 2002) of transfronterizxs. In other words, we have presented transfronterizx students using assets and resources to leverage transcultural and transnational gains in educational contexts. Transfronterizx community cultural wealth is related to the constant and continuous border-crossings that students experience, as well as their practices, which students utilize in order to make sense of their academic experiences on a daily or weekly basis. These "third spaces" (Moje et al. 2004) or "epistemic borderlands" (Cervantes-Soon and Carrillo 2016) are alternatives for the educational experience of transnational students.

According to Mignolo (2011), colonialism has been perpetuated in today's racial, political, and social hierarchies, enacted when dominant groups are valued over others. *Border thinking* (Mignolo 2011) emerges in this space of marginalization and of coloniality; its epistemological stance moves away from the Eurocentric perspectives that dominate our educational discourses and practices. For Mignolo, epistemologies are embodied and geohistorically located in coloniality—that is, the "patrón colonial de poder" (colonial matrix of power) (Quijano 2014). Border thinking is a source of new knowledge and epistemologies created from a subaltern perspective, and critical of dominant epistemologies. New practices emerge in these borders and margins, such as translanguaging, transfronterizx literacy practices, and funds of knowledge. These practices center alternative ways of narrating language, literacy, and learning. They show alternative "world-sensing" (Mignolo 2011), which include "the effects and the realms of the sense beyond the eyes" (3). Thus, transfronterizx practices presented here stem from transfronterizxs' experiencing in their own bodies what it means to cross national and other kinds of borders. Transfronterizx practices are then compatible with the borderland ways of being and knowing introduced in chapter 1.

Borders have also been described as generative spaces by many scholars of language, identities, and education. Gloria Anzaldúa's concepts of borderlands and *nepantla* communicate that generative space. In line with Mignolo's border thinking, work by Chicana scholars of education proposes new ways of knowing and thinking about learning which disrupt colonial Eurocentric assumptions (Delgado Bernal 1998; Villenas 1996). Transfronterizx language and literacy practices are examples of these places or perspectives—"the space between two worlds" (Anzaldúa 1999, 237)—where discourses from the borders or the margins question dominant educational discourses and practices. Transfronterizx hybrid language and literacy practices occurred in between diverse discourses (such as home/community-school, Ciudad Juárez–El Paso), along a continuum of settings, fluidly and creatively recontextualizing language and literacies, similarly to findings of previous studies with emergent bilinguals (Gutiérrez, Morales, and Martínez 2009; Medina 2010). These practices occur in and are themselves continuums rather than polarized binaries. As Anzaldúa argued, "the binaries of colored/white, female/male, mind/body are collapsing. Living in Nepantla, the overlapping space between different perceptions and belief systems, you are aware of the changeability of racial, gender, sexual, and other categories rendering the conventional labeling obsolete" (2002, 541). In the words of Medina (2010), "cultural flows happen in space-time and are embedded in the reorganization of culture across localities . . . It is within these flows and movements that new cultural practices emerge" (41). Translanguaging, recontextualizing literacies, and transfronterizx funds of knowledge disrupt traditional language and literacy practices valued in schools, and in that sense, they are generative spaces or a "rich space for the reinscription of discourses as they coexist, emerge, and are reproduced and coproduced" (41).

As Marjorie Faulstich Orellana (2016) reminds us, "We are living in a time when all the borders that were built up during the age of modernity, be they linguistic, cultural, ethnic, geopolitical, and disciplinary, or those that demarcate modalities, domains, and genres, and divide body, mind, and spirit, *are* being challenged and transgressed, whether we like it or not. As a nation, and a world, we can choose to try to shore up the borders, and resist the waves of change, or flow with the forces that are breaking them down" (134). Ironically, in the very same year of Orellana's publication and after the latest elections, we find ourselves in the midst of policies that enforce borders, punish border-crossings, and build walls.

Relevance to Transnationals Beyond the U.S.-Mexico Border

Although the results of this study come from the particular contexts of the border and a DL program, where transfronterizxs are afforded intense back-and-forth movement across political and linguistic boundaries, these findings are relevant to many other settings in which transnational children cross the invisible and metaphorical borders of the home/community and the school. The lessons learned in this study are not only relevant to transfronterizxs, those border-crossers who engage in crossing national borders frequently and physically, but they are also appropriate for teachers and educational scholars who wish to respond to the growing reality of transnationalism and superdiversity in their classrooms. Transfronterizx practices allow us to move away from binaries and essentialism, and center marginalized ways of knowing, learning, living, and narrating stories.

As explained in chapter 2, we situate our study in the new turn in language and literacy scholarship, which not only defines language as a social practice but assumes that language diversity is not the "unexpected," but rather the "expected" (Pennycook 2010). Practices such as translanguaging and recontextualizing capture the multiplicity of language realities we may observe in a variety of contexts where mainstream discourses normalize monolingualism, language separation ideologies, and artificial linguistic boundaries. Many DL programs, transitional bilingual education programs, and monolingual English-only mainstream classrooms serving emergent bilinguals fall into this category.

Transfronterizx practices show what crossing national and metaphorical borders looks like in communities and classrooms. The stories and practices of transfronterizxs add to the recent scholarship concerned with offering alternative narratives to those dominant narratives and deficit framings of transnationals (García 2009; Gort 2015; Gutiérrez, Morales, and Martínez 2009; Medina 2010; Orellana 2009; Stewart 2014). Our work is relevant not only to those students who experience transnationalism on the border region but to all transnational students in U.S. classrooms and the world. By foregrounding transnational literacy practices in the school, teachers and schools not only support the language and literacy development of transnational students; they also communicate that transnationalism benefits all students as it provides opportunities to develop relationships and utilize repertoires of practice to live in an increasingly globalized world.

Appendix

Methods

THE METHODS USED in this study were participant observations, artifact collection of classroom interactions, individual formalized interviews, and student focus groups. We began the research study by going into several DL classrooms and gathering data using different methods. Following is a brief description of these methods.

Participant Observations and Artifact Collection. Participant observation helps one to describe when and where things are happening, how they are happening, and why. Participant observation provides direct access to the world of meaning of the participants (Jorgensen 1989). During the first year of the study, the team conducted participant observations (at least two times per week) at the school (in and outside the DL classrooms from grades five and six). At the beginning, our role as participant observers was to establish a place in the school on a relatively long-term basis in order to investigate, experience, and represent the life and processes that occur in that setting (Emerson, Fretz, and Shaw 1995). Each member of the research team observed a different classroom. The team conducted more than three hundred hours of participant observations over the three years of the study.

As we became familiar with each classroom, its teacher, and the students, we decided to narrow our observations and focus on one classroom only, Ms. Ornelas's. The reason why we chose this classroom was that we noted that Ms. Ornelas was translanguaging and using multimodalities in her classroom. She also had a large number of transfronterizx students in her classroom, and she was very open and interested in participating in the study. We spent the last year and a half of our research observing in her class, with more than two hundred hours of participant observations conducted in her fourth, fifth, and sixth grade classrooms over the three years.

We also participated in opportunities gathering data through casual, informal conversations, we tape-recorded interactions during classroom and other school activities, and we collected artifacts such as journal entries, notebooks, poetry, pictures, videos, and other written and creative work pertinent to the study.

Individual Interviews. The team conducted and tape-recorded in-depth, semistructured interviews with three teachers and two administrators, the school counselor, and the social worker. The interviews allowed us to hear people's ideas, memories, and interpretations in their own words, to listen to differences among people and the meanings they construct, and to forge connections over time with the interviewees (Heyl 2001). We first conducted individual interviews with the principal and the assistant principal of the school. Further into the study, we also conducted interviews with three teachers we had observed, the social worker, and the school counselor. Interviews were conducted as conversations between the researchers and the interviewees and consisted of open-ended questions (Patton 2002). The purpose of these interviews was to learn about the school, its history, and its programs. We also had a specific focus, asking about transnational students attending the school, language practices, and funds of knowledge. Many interview questions emerged from the situations and themes that came out during the analysis of data from the participant observations and related to the topic of the study. The interviewees also influenced the content of the questions. All interviews were held at the school and were between an hour and an hour and a half long.

Focus Groups. Focus groups were conducted with the purpose of gathering data on specific topics and themes that emerged from the participant observations. Focus groups are a way of learning from a group of people (Morgan 1988). A wide range of topics with a variety of individuals and settings can be examined through the use of focus groups (Stewart and

Shamdasani 1990). The group dynamics of a focus group generate a variety of ideas because of the diversity of participants and their experiences as compared to individual interviews. Analyzing data from the participant observations helped us to identify topics or themes that should be discussed in the focus groups. We conducted thirteen focus groups. The first groups were general, and students self-selected which group to be in. During the second year, focus groups were purposefully selected and were composed of different students who had commonalities observed during the participant observations. One researcher would meet with three to four students at one time. The focus groups lasted about an hour and were in the school library and the teachers' lounge. The focus groups were very flexible. As the facilitators, we encouraged all participants to hold a conversation while still making sure that participants focused on certain topics. The major topics that were discussed during focus groups were bilingual education, trips to Juárez, students' lives in El Paso and Juárez, the violence in Juárez, school involvement, and other school experiences. The sessions were relaxed, and students laughed freely as they remembered accounts in their lives.

Field Notes. The team took field notes on a regular basis, recording what we observed as well as dialogues, scenes, and researcher reflections and reactions (Emerson, Fretz, and Shaw 1995). Entries were dated and included specific information such as the lesson topic being presented, the physical setting, and student and teacher responses and actions. During all participant observation events and after all interviews and focus groups, we took notes as thoroughly as possible and included everything that we believed was worth noting that would help us to identify how transnational Mexican children transform community cultural wealth into personal and social tools for negotiating academic life in a U.S. dual immersion language program. Expanded accounts of the events or conversations were filled in after each event.

Emergent Thematic Analysis. The same process of analyzing the data and coding themes was used for participant observations, interviews, and focus groups. We analyzed the data using thematic analysis. Field notes and documents were analyzed for recurring themes (Ryan and Bernard 2000). We developed theoretical categories by using codes that were generated directly from the data through an emergent theme process (Charmaz 2000; Charmaz and Mitchell 2001). We searched for patterns, as well as connections or relationships among categories (Jorgensen 1989). During the data analysis process, the team met regularly on a biweekly or weekly basis to share observations, review field notes, and discuss emerging themes.

We used two phases of grounded theory coding: initial coding and focused coding. Coding helped to define and categorize data (Charmaz 2000). Coding enabled us to gain new perspectives and kept us studying the data. We read the data carefully and created codes. These codes were developed directly from the data through the emergent theme process that was ongoing throughout the study (Charmaz and Mitchell 2001). During our initial coding, we looked for words, sentences, and incidents. We coded the words, phrases, and concepts that recurred throughout the data into classification schemes or thematic piles. We started by dividing the data into general themes related to the literature, as well as new themes that emerged. We narrowed these after several renderings of the data (Patton 2002).

During focused coding, we continued to reread the data as we continued to consider and explore themes, concepts, and ideas, further dividing and adding new categories as we discovered other themes and categories (Rubin and Rubin 1995). We used the most frequent codes to sort and organize the data. From the codes we made comparisons between people, objects, scenes, events, experiences, actions, and inactions. We also compared incidents, data with category, and category with category, as well as data from the same people, objects, and events at different points (Charmaz 2000; Charmaz and Mitchell 2001). Our focused coding was more selective and directed to explain segments of data. This process continued as new information was gathered during the interviews and focus groups. The questions, issues, and themes that began to emerge guided the research and were the basis for some of the interview and focus group questions. We wrote memos during our analysis, which helped us compare data and further probe, clarify, analyze, and explore new questions. Our memos were spontaneous and informal. After several renderings of the data and through memo writing, some general themes that emerged included the themes addressed in this book.

References

Adelman-Reyes, S., and T. Kleyn. 2010. *Teaching in Two Languages: A Guide for K–12 Bilingual Educators*. Thousand Oaks, Calif.: Corwin.

Aguilar Barajas, I., N. Sisto, E. Ayala Gaytán, J. Chapa Cantú, and B. Hidalgo López. 2014. "Trade Flows Between the United States and Mexico: NAFTA and the Border Region." *Journal of Urban Research*. http://articulo.revues.org/2567; DOI: 10.4000/articulo.2567.

Ajayi, L. 2009. "English as a Second Language Learners' Exploration of Multimodal Texts in a Junior High School." *Journal of Adolescent and Adult Literacy* 52, no. 7 (April): 585–95.

Ajayi, L. 2016. "Mexican-American Transnational Junior/High School Students: Crossing Borders Through New Media Literacies." *Journal of Literacy and Technology* 17, no. 3 (Fall): 124–71.

Alvermann, D., K. Hinchman, D. Moore, S. Phelps, and D. Waff, eds. 2006. *Reconceptualizing the Literacies in Adolescents' Lives*. 2nd ed. Mahwah, N.J.: Lawrence Erlbaum.

Andrews, J., and W. C. Yee. 2006. "Children's 'Funds of Knowledge' and Their Real Life Activities: Two Minority Ethnic Children Learning in Out-of-School Contexts in the UK." *Educational Review* 58, no. 4: 435–49.

Andrews, M. 2013. "Mexican Students' Identities in Their Language Use at a U.S. High School." *Bilingual Research Journal* 36, no. 1: 100–120.

Anyon, J. 1997. *Ghetto Schooling: A Political Economy of Urban Educational Reform*. New York: Teachers College Press.

Anzaldúa, G. E. 1999. *Borderlands / La Frontera: The New Mestiza*. 2nd ed. San Francisco: Aunt Lute Books.

Anzaldúa, G. E. 2002. "Now Let Us Shift . . . the Path of Conocimiento . . . Inner Work, Public Acts." In *This Bridge We Call Home: Radical Visions for Transformation*, edited by G. E. Anzaldúa and A. L. Keating. New York: Routledge.

Araujo, B., and M. de la Piedra. 2013. "Violence on the US–Mexico Border and the Capital Student's Use in Response." *International Journal of Qualitative Research* 26, no. 3: 263–78.

Arnold, D., and J. de D. Yapita. 2000. *El rincón de las cabezas: Luchas textuales, educación y tierras en los Andes*. La Paz: UMSA/ILCA.

Baker, C. 2006. *Foundations of Bilingual Education and Bilingualism*. 4th ed. Clevedon, UK: Multilingual Matters.

Bakhtin, M. M. 1981. *The Dialogic Imagination: Four Essays by M. M. Bakhtin*. Austin: University of Texas Press.

Bantman-Masum, E. 2015. "Lifestyle Transmigration: Understanding a Hypermobile Minority in Merida, Mexico." *Journal of Latin American Geography* 14, no. 1: 101–17.

Barton, D., and M. Hamilton. 2000. "Literacy Practices." In *Situated Literacies: Reading and Writing in Context*, edited by D. Barton, M. Hamilton, and R. Ivanic. New York: Routledge.

Barton, D., and M. Hamilton. 2005. "Literacy, Reification and the Dynamics of Social Interaction." In *Beyond Communities of Practice: Language, Power and Social Context*, edited by D. Barton and K. Tusting, 14–35. Cambridge: Cambridge University Press.

Baynham, M. 1993. "Code Switching and Mode Switching: Community Interpreters and Mediators of Literacy." In *Cross-Cultural Approaches to Literacy*, edited by B. Street, 294–314. New York: Cambridge University Press.

Bejarano, C. 2010. "Border Rootedness as Transformative Resistance: Youth Overcoming Violence and Inspection in a US–Mexico Border Region." *Journal of Children's Geographies* 8, no. 4: 391–99.

Bernstein, B. 1996. *Pedagogy, Symbolic Control and Identity: Theory, Research, Critique*. London: Taylor and Francis.

Beyer, L., and M. Apple. 1998. *The Curriculum: Problems, Politics, and Possibilities*. Albany: State University of New York Press.

Blommaert, J. 2010. *The Sociolinguistics of Globalization*. Cambridge: Cambridge University Press.

Blommaert, J., and B. Rampton. 2011. "Language and Superdiversity." *Diversities* 13, no. 2: 1–21. http://www.unesco.org/shs/diversities/vol13/issue2/art1.

Blommaert, J., and B. Rampton. 2016. "Language and Superdiversity." In *Language and Superdiversity*, edited by K. Arnaut, J. Blommaert, B. Rampton, and M. Spotti, chapter 2. New York: Routledge.

Borjian, A., L. M. Muñoz de Cote, S. van Dijk, and P. Houde. 2016. "Transnational Children in Mexico: Context of Migration and Adaptation." *Diaspora, Indigenous, and Minority Education* 10, no. 1: 42–45.

Borunda, D. 2017. "U.S. Attorney General Calls Border 'Ground Zero.'" *El Paso Times*, April 18. http://www.elpasotimes.com/story/news/local/el-paso/2017/04/18/attorney-general-dhs-secretary-visit-el-paso/100611310/.

Boske, C., and S. McCormack. 2011. "Building an Understanding of the Role of Media Literacy for Latino/a High School Students." *High School Journal* 94, no. 4: 167–86.

Bourke, B. 2014. "Positionality: Reflecting on the Research Process." *The Qualitative Report* 19:1–9. http://www.nova.edu/ssss/QR/QR19/bourke18.pdf.

Brandt, D., and K. Clinton. 2002. "Limits of the Local: Expanding Perspectives on Literacy as a Social Practice." *Journal of Literacy Research* 34, no. 3: 337–56.

Browning-Aiken, A. 2005. "Border-Crossings: Funds of Knowledge Within an Immigrant Household." In *Funds of Knowledge: Theorizing Practices in Households, Communities, and Classrooms*, edited by N. González, L. Moll, and C. Amanti, 257–74. Mahwah, N.J.: Lawrence Erlbaum.

Bruner, J. 1991. "The Narrative Construction of Reality." *Critical Inquiry* 18:1–21.

Bruner, J. 2010. "Narrative, Culture, and Mind." In *Telling Stories: Language, Narrative, and Social Life*, edited by D. Schiffrin, A. De Fina, and A. Nylund, 45–49. Washington, D.C.: Georgetown University Press.

Budach, G. 2013. "From Language Choice to Mode Choice: How Artefacts Impact on Language Use and Meaning Making in a Bilingual Classroom." *Language and Education* 27, no. 4: 329–42. http://doi.org/10.1080/09500782.2013.788188.

Calabrese Barton, A. M., and E. Tan. 2009. "Funds of Knowledge and Discourses and Hybrid Space." *Journal of Research in Science Teaching* 46, no. 1: 50–73.

Canagarajah, [A.] S. 2011. "Codemeshing in Academic Writing: Identifying Teachable Strategies of Translanguaging." *The Modern Language Journal* 95:401–17.

Canagarajah, A. S., ed. 2013. *Literacy as Translingual Practice: Between Communities and Classrooms*. New York: Routledge.

Cavanagh, T., P. Vigil, and E. García. 2014. "A Story Legitimating the Voices of Latino/Hispanic Students and Their Parents: Creating a Restorative Justice Response to Wrongdoing and Conflict in Schools." *Equity and Excellence in Education* 47, no. 4: 565–79.

Cazden, C. 1988. *Classroom Discourse: The Language of Teaching and Learning*. Portsmouth, N.H.: Heinemann.

Cervantes-Soon, C. G., and J. F. Carrillo. 2016. "Toward a Pedagogy of Border Thinking: Building on Latin@ Students' Subaltern Knowledge." *High School Journal* 99, no. 4: 282–301.

Chapman, T., and N. Hobbel. 2010. *Social Justice Pedagogy Across the Curriculum: The Practice of Freedom*. New York: Routledge.

Charmaz, K. 2000. "Grounded Theory: Objectivist and Constructivist Methods." In *Handbook of Qualitative Research*, edited by N. Denzin and Y. Lincoln, 509–36. Thousand Oaks, Calif.: Sage.

Charmaz, K., and R. Mitchell. 2001. "Grounded Theory in Ethnography." In *Handbook of Ethnography*, edited by P. Atkinson, A. Coffey, S. Delamont, J. Lofland, and L. Lofland, 118–35. Thousand Oaks, Calif.: Sage.

Christian, D. 1994. *Two-Way Bilingual Education: Students Learning Through Two Languages*. Washington, D.C.: Center for Applied Linguistics.

City of El Paso. 2016. "Population." In *Economic and International Development*. https://www.elpasotexas.gov/economic-development/business-services/data-and -statistics/population.

Cline, Z., and J. Necochea. 2006. "Teacher Dispositions for Effective Education in the Borderlands." *The Educational Forum* 70, no. 3: 268–82.

Collier, V. P., and W. Thomas. 2004. "The Astounding Effectiveness of DL Education for All." *TABE Journal of Research and Practice* 2, no. 1: 1–20.

Conteh, J., and S. Riasat. 2014. "A Multilingual Learning Community: Researching Funds of Knowledge with Children, Families and Teachers." *Multilingua* 33, no. 5/6: 601–22.

Contreras, F. 2009. "Sin papeles y rompiendo barreras: Latino Students and the Challenges of Persisting in College." *Harvard Educational Review* 79:610–31.

Cook, V. J. 2012. "Multi-Competence." In *The Encyclopedia of Applied Linguistics*, edited by C. Chapelle. Oxford: Wiley-Blackwell.

Cope, B., and M. Kalantzis, eds. 2000. *Multiliteracies: Literacy Learning and the Design of Social Futures*. New York: Routledge.

Cope, B., and M. Kalantzis. 2009. "Multiliteracies: New Literacies, New Learning." *Pedagogies: An International Journal* 4, no. 3: 164–95.

Corchado, A. 2017 (June). "Washington and the Future of the U.S.-Mexico Border." Presentation at panel discussion organized by *Americas Quarterly* magazine, the Americas Society/Council of the Americas, the El Paso Community Foundation, and the U.S.-Mexico Border Philanthropy Partnership.

Cortéz, N., and B. Jáuregui. 2004. "Influencia del contexto social en la educación bilingüe en una zona fronteriza de Sonora y Arizona." *Revista Mexicana de Investigación Educativa* 9, no. 3: 957–73.

Coyle, D., P. Hood, and D. Marsh. 2010. *CLIL: Content and Language Integrated Learning*. Cambridge: Cambridge University Press.

Crawford, T. 2005. "What Counts as Knowing: Constructing a Communicative Repertoire for Student Demonstration of Knowledge in Science." *Journal of Research in Science Teaching* 42, no. 2: 139–65.

Creese, A., and A. Blackledge. 2010. "Translanguaging in the Bilingual Classroom: A Pedagogy for Learning and Teaching?" *The Modern Language Journal* 94, no. 1: 103–15.

Creese, A., and P. Martin. 2003. "Multilingual Classroom Ecologies: Interrelationships, Interactions and Ideologies." *International Journal of Bilingual Education and Bilingualism* 24, nos. 3–4: 161–67.

Cruz Sierra, S. 2014. "Violencia y jóvenes: Pandillas e identidad masculina en Ciudad Juárez." *Revista Mexicana de Sociología* 76, no. 4: 613–37.

Cuero, K. 2010. "Artisan with Words: Transnational Funds of Knowledge in a Bilingual Latina's Stories." *Language Arts* 87, no. 6: 427–36.

Cummins, J. 2008. "Teaching for Transfer: Challenging the Two Solitudes Assumption in Bilingual Education." In *Encyclopedia of Language and Education*, edited by N. H. Hornberger, 1528–38. Boston: Springer.

Darling-Hammond, L. 1997. *The Right to Learn*. San Francisco: Jossey-Bass.

de Guerrero, M. C. M., and O. S. Villamil. 2000. "Activating the ZPD: Mutual Scaffolding in L2 Peer Revision." *Modern Language Journal* 84, no. 1: 51–68.

de Jong, E. 2016. "Two-Way Immersion for the Next Generation: Models, Policies and Principles." *International Multilingual Research Journal* 10, no. 1: 6–16. https://doi.org/10.1080/19313152.2016.1118667.

de Jong, E., and E. Howard. 2009. "Integration in Two-Way Immersion Education: Equalising Linguistic Benefits for All Students." *International Journal of Bilingual Education and Bilingualism* 12, no. 1: 81–99.

de la Piedra, M. T. 2009. "Hybrid Literacies: The Case of a Quechua Community in the Andes." *Anthropology and Education Quarterly* 40, no. 2: 110–28.

de la Piedra, M. T. 2010. "Adolescent Worlds and Literacy Practices on the United States–Mexico Border." *Journal of Adolescent and Adult Literacy* 53, no. 7: 575–84.

de la Piedra, M. T. 2011. "'Tanto necesitamos de aquí como necesitamos de allá': Leer juntas Among Mexican Transnational Mothers and Daughters." *Language and Education* 25, no. 1: 65–78.

de la Piedra, M. T., and B. Araujo. 2012a. "Literacies Crossing Borders: The Literacy Practices of Transnational Students in a Dual Language Program on the U.S.-Mexico Border." *Language and Intercultural Communication* 12, no. 3: 214–29.

de la Piedra, M. T., and B. Araujo. 2012b. "Transfronterizo Literacies and Content in a Dual Language Program." *International Journal of Bilingual Education and Bilingualism* 15, no. 6: 1–17.

de la Piedra, M. T., and H. D. Romo. 2003. "Collaborative Literacy in a Mexican Immigrant Household: The Role of Sibling Mediators in the Socialization of Preschool Learners." In *Language Socialization in Bilingual and Multilingual Societies*, edited by R. Bayley and S. R. Schecter, 44–61. Cleveland, Ohio: Multilingual Matters.

Delgado Bernal, D. 1998. "Using a Chicana Feminist Epistemology in Educational Research." *Harvard Educational Review* 68, no. 4: 555–79.

Delgado-Gaitan, C. 1990. *Literacy for Empowerment*. New York: Falmer Press.

Delgado-Gaitan, C. 1993. "Researching Change and Changing the Researcher." *Harvard Educational Review* 63:389–411.

Díaz, M., and K. Bussert-Webb. 2013. "Reading and Language Beliefs and Practices of Latino/a Children in a Border Community." *Journal of Latinos and Education* 12, no. 1: 59–73.

Díaz, R., C. Neal, and M. Amaya-Williams. 2001. "The Social Origins of Self-Regulation." In *Vygotsky and Education: Instructional Implications of Sociohistorical Psychology*, edited by L. Moll, 127–54. New York: Cambridge University Press.

Dicks, B., R. Flewitt, L. Lancaster, and K. Pahl. 2011. "Multimodality and Ethnography: Working at the Intersection." *Qualitative Research* 11:226–37.

Díez-Palomar, J., and M. Civil. 2007. "El impacto de la migración sobre el aprendizaje de las matemáticas en el contexto de una ciudad fronteriza en el Suroeste de los Estados Unidos." *Matematicalia: Revista Digital de Divulgación Matemática de La Real Sociedad Matemática Española* 3, no. 2.

Donnellon, B., T. Kleyn, W. Pérez, and R. Vásquez. 2016. *Una vida, dos países: Children and Youth (Back) in Mexico*. Video. http://www.unavidathefilm.com/.

Duarte-Herrera, C. 2001. "Defining the U.S.-Mexico Border as Hyperreality." *Estudios Fronterizos* 2, no. 4: 139–65.

Durán, L., and D. Palmer. 2013. "Pluralist Discourses of Bilingualism and Translanguaging Talk in Classrooms." *Journal of Early Childhood Literacy* 14, no. 3: 367–88.

Durand, T. 2010. "Latina Mothers' School Preparation Activities and Their Relation to Children's Literacy Skills." *Journal of Latinos and Education* 9, no. 3: 207–22.

Dworin, J. 2006. "The Family Stories Project: Using Funds of Knowledge for Writing." *The Reading Teacher* 59, no. 6: 2–11.

Dyson, A. H. 2003. *The Brothers and Sisters Learn to Write: Popular Literacies in Childhood and School Cultures*. New York: Teachers College Press.

Emerson, R., R. Fretz, and L. Shaw. 1995. *Writing Ethnographic Fieldnotes*. Chicago: University of Chicago Press.

Escamilla, K., S. Hopewell, S. Butvilofsky, W. Sparrow, L. Soltero-González, O. Ruiz-Figueroa, and M. Escamilla. 2013. *Biliteracy from the Start: Literacy Squared in Action*. Philadelphia: Caslon Publishing.

Esquinca, A. 2011. "Bilingual College Writers' Collaborative Writing of Word Problems." *Linguistics and Education* 22, no. 2: 150–67.

Esquinca, A. 2012a. "Socializing Pre-service Teachers into Mathematical Discourse: The Interplay Between Biliteracy and Multimodality." *Multilingual Education* 2, no. 4: 1–20. DOI: 10.1186/2191-5059-2-4.

Esquinca, A. 2012b. "Transfronterizos' Socialization into Mathematical Discourse: Capitalizing on Language and Cultural Resources or Caught Between Conflicting Ideologies?" *International Journal of Bilingual Education and Bilingualism* 15, no. 6: 669–86. DOI: 10.1080/13670050.2012.699947.

Esquinca, A., B. Araujo, and M. T. de la Piedra. 2014. "Meaning Making and Translanguaging in a Two-Way Dual-Language Program on the U.S.-Mexico Border." *Bilingual Research Journal* 37, no. 2: 164–81.

Esquinca, A., E. Mein, E. Q. Villa, and A. Monárrez. 2017. "Academic Biliteracy in College: Borderland Undergraduate Engineering Students' Mobilization of Linguistic and Other Semiotic Resources." In *Academic Biliteracies: Multilingual Repertoires in Higher Education*, edited by D. Palfreyman and C. van der Walt, 41–57. Bristol, UK: Multilingual Matters.

Farruggio, P. 2010. "Latino Parent Agency Within the Restrictionist Language Policy Environment of California's Proposition 227." *Bilingual Research Journal* 33, no. 3: 292–306.

Fellows, N. 1994. "A Window into Thinking: Using Student Writing to Understand Conceptual Change in Science Learning." *Journal of Research in Science Teaching* 31, no. 9: 985–1001.

Fitts, S. 2009. "Exploring Third Space in a Dual-Language Setting: Opportunities and Challenges." *Journal of Latinos and Education* 8, no. 2: 87–104.

Flores, A. 2017. "Facts on U.S. Latinos, 2015: Statistical Portrait of Hispanics in the United States." Washington, D.C.: Pew Research Center. http://www.pewhispanic.org/2017/09/18/facts-on-u-s-latinos/.

Ford, D. Y. 2010. "Underrepresentation of Culturally Different Students in Gifted Education: Reflections About Current Problems and Recommendations for the Future." *Gifted Child Today* 33, no. 3: 31–36.

Forzani, E., and D. Leu. 2012. "New Literacies for New Learners: The Need for Digital Technologies in Primary Classrooms." *The Educational Forum* 76:421–24. http://doi.org/10.1080/00131725.2012.708623.

Francis (pope). 2016. "Homily of His Holiness Pope Francis." Apostolic Journey of His Holiness Pope Francis to Mexico, February 17, 2016, Ciudad Juárez Fair Grounds, Ciudad Juárez, Mexico. https://w2.vatican.va/content/francesco/en/homilies/2016/documents/papa-francesco_20160217_omelia-messico-ciudad-jaurez.html.

Franco, M. 2014. "Escuela de papel: Intervención educativa en una institución donde asisten niñas y niños migrantes." *Sinéctica: Revista Electrónica de Educación* 43:1–20.

Freeman, R. 1998. *Bilingual Education and Social Change*. Philadelphia: Multilingual Matters.

Fry, R. 2008. "The Role of Schools in the English Language Learner Achievement Gap." Washington, D.C.: Pew Research Center. http://www.pewhispanic.org/2008/06/26/the-role-of-schools-in-the-english-language-learner-achievement-gap/.

Fry, R., and F. Gonzales. 2008. "A Profile of Hispanic Public School Students: One-in-Five and Growing Fast." Washington, D.C.: Pew Research Center. http://www.pewhispanic.org/2008/08/26/one-in-five-and-growing-fast-a-profile-of-hispanic-public-school-students/.

Fry, R., and J. S. Passel. 2009. "Latino Children: A Majority Are U.S.-Born Offspring of Immigrants." Washington, D.C.: Pew Research Center. http://www .pewhispanic.org/2009/05/28/latino-children-a-majority-are-us-born-offspring -of-immigrants/.

Gallo, S., and H. Link. 2015. "'Diles la verdad': Deportation Policies, Politicized Funds of Knowledge, and Schooling in Middle Childhood." *Harvard Educational Review* 85, no. 3: 357–82.

Gallo, S., H. Link, E. Allard, S. Wortham, and K. Mortimer. 2014. "Conflicting Ideologies of Mexican Immigrant English Across Levels of Schooling." *International Multilingual Research Journal* 8, no. 2: 124–40.

García, O. 2009. *Bilingual Education in the 21st Century: A Global Perspective.* Malden, Mass.: Wiley-Blackwell.

García, O. 2012. "Theorizing Translanguaging for Educators." In *Translanguaging: A CUNYNYSIEB Guide for Educators*, edited by C. Celic and K. Seltzer, 1–6. New York: CUNY-NYSEIB.

García, O., S. Ibarra Johnson, and K. Seltzer. 2017. *The Translanguaging Classroom: Leveraging Student Bilingualism for Learning.* Philadelphia: Caslon.

García, O., and J. A. Kleifgen. 2010. *Educating Emergent Bilinguals: Policies, Programs, and Practices for English Language Learners.* New York: Teachers College Press.

García, O., and C. Leiva. 2014. "Theorizing and Enacting Translanguaging for Social Justice." In *Heteroglossia as Practice and Pedagogy*, edited by A. Blackledge and A. Creese, 199–216. Netherlands: Springer.

García, O., and C. Sylvan. 2011. "Pedagogies and Practices in Multilingual Classrooms: Singularities in Pluralities." *Modern Language Journal* 95, no. 3: 385–400.

García, O., and L. Wei. 2014. *Translanguaging: Language, Bilingualism and Education.* New York: Palgrave Macmillan.

García, S., and P. Guerra. 2003. "Do We Truly Believe 'All Children Can Learn?' Implications for Comprehensive School Reform." *Adelante* 4, no. 1: 1–5.

Gee, J. P. 2000. "Teenagers in New Times: A New Literacy Studies Perspective." *Journal of Adolescent and Adult Literacy* 43, no. 5: 412–20.

Gee, J. P. 2008. *What Videogames Have to Teach Us About Learning and Literacy.* New York: Palgrave Macmillan.

Gee, J. P. 2011. *An Introduction to Discourse Analysis: Theory and Method.* 3rd ed. New York: Routledge.

Geiger, A. 2017. "Many Minority Students Go to Schools Where at Least Half of Their Peers Are Their Race or Ethnicity." Washington, D.C.: Pew Research Center. http://www.pewresearch.org/fact-tank/2017/10/25/many-minority-students -go-to-schools-where-at-least-half-of-their-peers-are-their-race-or-ethnicity/.

Gibbons, P. 2009. *English Learners, Academic Literacy, and Thinking: Learning in the Challenge Zone.* Portsmouth, N.H.: Heinemann.

Gifford, B. R., and G. Valdés. 2006. "The Linguistic Isolation of Hispanic Students in California's Public Schools: The Challenge of Reintegration." *Yearbook of the National Society for the Study of Education* 105, no. 2: 125–54.

Glynn, S., and D. Muth. 1994. "Reading and Writing to Learn Science: Achieving Scientific Literacy." *Journal of Research in Science Teaching* 31, no. 9: 1057–73.

Gnam, A. 2013. "Mexico's Missed Opportunities to Protect Irregular Women Transmigrants: Applying a Gender Lens to Migration Law Reform." *Pacific Rim Law and Policy Journal* 22, no. 3: 713–49.

Gómez, L., D. Freeman, and Y. Freeman. 2005. "Dual Language Education: A Promising 50–50 Model." *Bilingual Research Journal* 29, no. 1: 145–64.

González, N., R. Andrade, M. Civil, and L. Moll. 2005. "Funds of Distributed Knowledge." In *Funds of Knowledge: Theorizing Practices in Households, Communities, and Classrooms*, edited by N. González, L. Moll, and C. Amanti, 257–74. Mahwah, N.J.: Lawrence Erlbaum.

González, N., and L. Moll. 2002. "Cruzando el Puente: Building Bridges to Funds of Knowledge." *Educational Policy* 16, no. 4: 623–41.

González, N., L. Moll, and C. Amanti, eds. 2005. *Funds of Knowledge: Theorizing Practices in Households, Communities, and Classrooms*. Mahwah, N.J.: Lawrence Erlbaum.

González, N., L. Moll, M. Floyd-Tenery, A. Rivera, P. Rendón, R. González, and C. Amanti. 2005. "Funds of Knowledge for Teaching in Latino Households." In *Funds of Knowledge: Theorizing Practices in Households, Communities, and Classrooms*, edited by N. González, L. Moll, and C. Amanti, 89–118. Mahwah, N.J.: Lawrence Erlbaum.

Gort, M. 2008. "'You Give Me Idea!': Collaborative Strides Toward Bilingualism, Biliteracy, and Cross-Cultural Understanding in a Two-Way Partial Immersion Program." *Multicultural Perspectives* 10, no. 4: 192–200.

Gort, M. 2015. "Transforming Literacy Learning and Teaching Through Translanguaging and Other Typical Practices Associated with 'Doing Being Bilingual.'" *International Multilingual Research Journal* 9:1–6.

Gort, M., and R. W. Pontier. 2013. "Exploring Bilingual Pedagogies in Dual Language Preschool Classrooms." *Language and Education* 27, no. 3: 223–45.

Gort, M., and S. F. Sembiante. 2015. "Navigating Hybridized Language Learning Spaces Through Translanguaging Pedagogy: Dual Language Preschool Teachers' Languaging Practices in Support of Emergent Bilingual Children's Performance of Academic Discourse." *International Multilingual Research Journal* 9, no. 1: 7–25.

Gregg, K., M. Rugg, and Z. Stoneman. 2011. "Building on the Hopes and Dreams of Latino Families with Young Children: Findings from Family Member Focus Groups." *Early Childhood Education* 40:87–96.

Gumble, A. 2012. "Finding a Voice: Freedom Through Digital Literacies." *Educational Forum* 76:434–37. http://doi.org/10.1080/00131725.2012.707568.

Gutiérrez, K. D., P. Baquedano-López, and C. Tejeda. 1999. "Rethinking Diversity: Hybridity and Hybrid Language Practices in the Third Space." *Mind, Culture and Activity* 6, no. 4: 286–303.

Gutiérrez, K. D., A. Bien, M. Selland, and D. Pierce. 2011. "Polylingual and Polycultural Learning: Mediating Emergent Academic Literacies for Dual Language Learners." *Journal of Early Childhood Literacy* 11:232–61.

Gutiérrez, K. D., Z. Morales, and D. C. Martínez. 2009. "Re-mediating Literacy: Culture, Difference, and Learning for Students from Nondominant Communities." *Review of Research in Education* 33:212–45.

Hall, R. E. 2016. "The Bleaching Syndrome: The Role of Educational Intervention." *Theory into Practice* 55, no. 1: 62–68.

Hamann, E., V. Zúñiga, and J. García. 2008. "From Nuevo León to the USA and Back Again: Transnational Students in Mexico." *Journal of Immigrant and Refugee Studies* 6, no. 4: 60–84.

Hamann, E., V. Zúñiga, and J. Sánchez. 2006. "Pensando en Cynthia y su hermana: Educational Implications of United States-Mexico Transnationalism for Children." *Journal of Latinos and Education* 5, no. 4: 253–74.

Hamilton, N. 2010. *Handbook of Texas Online*. http://www.tshaonline.org/handbook/online/articles/hny06.

Hand, B., L. Hohenshell, and V. Prain. 2004. "Exploring Students' Responses to Conceptual Questions When Engaged with Planned Writing Experiences: A Study with Year 10 Science Students." *Journal of Research in Science Teaching* 41, no. 2: 186–210.

Harvey, D. 1990. *The Condition of Postmodernity: An Enquiry into the Origins of Cultural Change*. Cambridge: Blackwell.

Heath, S. B. 1982. "Protean Shapes in Literacy Events: Ever-Shifting Oral and Literate Traditions." In *Spoken and Written Language: Exploring Orality and Literacy*, edited by D. Tannen, 91–117. Norwood, N.J.: Ablex.

Hedergaard, M., ed. 2001. *Learning in Classrooms*. Aarhus, Denmark: Aarhus University Press.

Hedges, H., J. Cullen, and B. Jordan. 2011. "Early Year's Curriculum: Funds of Knowledge as a Conceptual Framework for Children's Interests." *Journal of Curriculum Studies* 43, no. 2: 185–205.

Henderson, K. I., and D. Palmer. 2015. "Teacher and Student Language Practices and Ideologies in a Third-Grade Two-Way Dual Language Program Implementation." *International Multilingual Research Journal* 9:75–92.

Herrera, S. G., D. R. Pérez, and K. Escamilla. 2010. *Teaching Reading to English Language Learners: Differentiated Literacies*. Boston: Allyn and Bacon.

Heyl, B. S. 2001. "Ethnographic Interviewing." In *Handbook of Ethnography*, edited by P. Atkinson, A. Coffey, S. Delamont, J. Lofland, and L. Lofland, 369–83. London: Sage.

Heyman, J. 2013. "A Voice of the U.S. Southwestern Border: The 2012 'We the Border: Envisioning a Narrative for Our Future' Conference." *Journal on Migration and Human Security* 1, no. 2: 60–75.

Heyman, J. 2015. "Political-Ethical Dilemmas Participant Observed." In *Public Anthropology in a Borderless World*, edited by S. Beck and C. A. Maida, 118–43. New York: Berghahn.

Heyman, J., and J. Symons. 2012. "Borders." In *A Companion to Moral Anthropology*, edited by D. Fassin, 540–57. Malden, Mass.: Wiley-Blackwell.

Holguín Mendoza, C. 2011. "Dining with the Devil: Identity Formations in Juárez, México." *Identities: Global Studies in Culture and Power* 18, no. 5: 415–36.

Holliday, W., L. Yore, and D. Alvermann. 1994. "The Reading-Science Learning-Writing Connection: Breakthroughs, Barriers and Promises." *Journal of Research in Science Teaching* 31, no. 9: 877–93.

Honeyford, M. 2014. "From aquí and allá: Symbolic Convergence in the Multimodal Literacy Practices of Adolescent Immigrant Students." *Journal of Literacy Research*: 1–40.

Hornberger, N. H. 1990. "Creating Successful Learning Contexts for Bilingual Literacy." *Teachers College Record* 92, no. 2: 212–29.

Hornberger, N. H. 2003. *Continua of Biliteracy: An Ecological Framework for Educational Policy, Research and Practice in Multilingual Settings*. Clevedon, UK: Multilingual Matters.

Hornberger, N. H. 2007. "Biliteracy, Transnationalism, Multimodality, and Identity: Trajectories Across Time and Space." *Linguistics and Education* 18, no. 1: 325–34.

Hornberger, N. H., and H. Link. 2012. "Translanguaging and Transnational Literacies in Multilingual Classrooms: A Biliteracy Lens." *International Journal of Bilingual Education and Bilingualism* 15, no. 3: 261–78.

Hossain, T., and C. B. Pratt. 2008. "Language Rights: A Framework for Ensuring Social Equity in Planning and Implementing National Education Policies." *New Horizons in Education* 56, no. 3: 63–74.

Howard, E. R., T. H. Levine, and D. M. Moss. 2014. "The Urgency of Preparing Teachers for Second Language Learners." In *Preparing Classroom Teachers to Succeed with Second Language Learners: Lessons from a Faculty Learning Community*, edited by T. H. Levine, E. R. Howard, and D. M. Moss, 3–16. New York: Routledge.

Jacobo-Suárez, M. 2017. "De Regreso a 'Casa' y sin Apostilla: Estudiantes Mexicoamericanos en México." *Sinéctica: Revista Electrónica de Educación* 48:1–18. https://sinectica.iteso.mx/index.php/SINECTICA/article/view/712/674.

Jain, D. 2010. "Critical Race Theory and Community Colleges: Through the Eyes of Women Student Leaders of Color." *Community College Journal of Research and Practice* 34, no. 1: 78–91.

Jasis, P. 2013. "Latino Families Challenging Exclusion in a Middle School: A Story from the Trenches." *School Community Journal* 23, no. 1: 111–30.

Jewitt, C. 2005. "Multimodality, 'Reading,' and 'Writing' for the 21st Century." *Discourse: Studies in the Cultural Politics of Education* 26, no. 3: 315–31.

Jiménez, R., P. Smith, and B. Teague. 2009. "Transnational and Community Literacies." *Journal of Adolescent and Adult Literacy* 53, no. 1: 16–26.

Jorgensen, D. 1989. *Participant Observation: A Methodology for Human Sciences.* Thousand Oaks, Calif.: Sage.

Jørgensen, J. N. 2008. "Polylingual Languaging Around and Among Children and Adolescents." *International Journal of Multilingualism* 5, no. 3: 161–76.

Kalantzis, M., and B. Cope. 2012. *Literacies.* Cambridge: Cambridge University Press.

Kalman, J. 1996. "Joint Composition: The Collaborative Letter Writing of a Scribe and His Client in Mexico." *Written Communication* 13, no. 2: 190–220.

Kalman, J. 1999. *Writing on the Plaza: Practices Among Scribes and Clients in Mexico City.* Cresskill, N.J.: Hampton Press.

Kalman, J. 2004. "A Bakhtinian Perspective on Learning to Read and Write Late in Life." In *Bakhtinian Perspectives on Language, Literacy, and Learning,* edited by A. Ball and S. Freedman, 252–78. Cambridge: Cambridge University Press.

Kalman, J. 2005. "Mothers to Daughters, Pueblo to Ciudad: Women's Identity Shifts in the Construction of a Literate Self." In *Urban Literacy: Communication, Identity and Learning in Development Contexts,* edited by A. Rogers, 183–210. Hamburg: UNESCO Institute of Education.

Kalman, J. 2008. "Literacies in Latin America." In *Encyclopedia of Language and Education,* edited by B. V. Street and N. Hornberger, 321–34. New York: Springer.

Kalman, J., and B. Street, eds. 2009. *Lectura, escritura y matemáticas como prácticas sociales: Diálogos con América Latina.* Mexico City: CREFAL-Siglo XXI.

Kalman, J., and B. Street. 2013. *Literacy and Numeracy in Latin America: Local Perspectives and Beyond.* New York: Routledge.

Keating, A. 2005. "Shifting Worlds, una entrada." In *Entre Mundos/Among Worlds: New Perspectives on Gloria Anzaldúa,* edited by A. L. Keting, 1–12. New York: Palgrave.

Keating, A. 2006. "From Borderlands and New Mestizas to Nepantlas and Nepantleras: Anzaldúan Theories for Social Change." *Human Architecture: Journal of the Sociology of Self-Knowledge* 4:5–16.

Keating, A. 2011. "Risking the Vision, Transforming the Divides: Nepantlera Perspectives on Academic Boundaries, Identities, and Lives." In *Bridging: How Gloria Anzaldúa's Life and World Transformed Our Own,* edited by A. Keating and G. Gónzalez-López, 142–55. Austin: University of Texas Press.

Kell, C. 2000. "Teaching Letters: The Recontextualisation of Letter-Writing Practices in Literacy Classes for Unschooled Adults in South Africa." In *Letter Writing as a Social Practice,* edited by D. B. Barton and N. Hall, 209–32. Amsterdam: John Benjamin Publishers.

Kell, C. 2011. "Inequalities and Crossings: Literacy and the Spaces-in-Between." *International Journal of Educational Development* 31:606–13.

Keys, C. 1999. "Language as an Indicator of Meaning Generation: An Analysis of Middle School Students' Written Discourse About Scientific Investigation." *Journal of Research in Science Teaching* 36, no. 9: 1044–61.

Keys, C. 2000. "Investigating the Thinking Processes of Eighth Grade Writers During the Composition of a Scientific Laboratory Report." *Journal of Research in Science Teaching* 37, no. 7: 676–90.

Klein, P. D. 2004. "Constructing Scientific Explanations Through Writing." *Instructional Science* 32:191–231.

Kleyn, T. 2015. *Guía de apoyo a docentes con estudiantes transfronterizos: Alumnos de educación básica y media superior.* Oaxaca, Mexico: U.S.-Mexico Foundation. https://tatyanakleyn.commons.gc.cuny.edu/files/2013/10/Guia-Final-3-18-16.pdf.

Knight, M., and H. A. Oesterreich. 2011. "Opening Our Eyes, Changing Our Practices: Learning Through the Transnational Life Worlds of Teachers." *Intercultural Education* 22, no. 3: 203–15.

Krashen, S. D., and T. D. Terrell. 1983. *The Natural Approach: Language Acquisition in the Classroom.* Hayward, Calif.: Alemany Press.

Kress, G. 2000. "Multimodality: Challenges to Thinking About Language." *TESOL Quarterly* 34, no. 2: 337–40.

Kress, G. 2010. *Multimodality: A Social Semiotic Approach to Contemporary Communication.* New York: Routledge.

Kurth, L. A., R. Kidd, R. Gardner, and E. L. Smith. 2002. "Student Use of Narrative and Paradigmatic Forms of Talk in Elementary Science Conversations." *Journal of Research in Science Teaching* 39, no. 9: 793–818.

Lam, W. S. E. 2009. "Multiliteracies on Instant Messaging in Negotiating Local, Translocal, and Transnational Affiliations: A Case of an Adolescent Immigrant." *Reading Research Quarterly* 44, no. 4: 377–97.

Lam, W. S. E., and E. Rosario-Ramos. 2009. "Multilingual Literacies in Transnational Digitally Mediated Contexts: An Exploratory Study of Immigrant Teens in the United States." *Language and Education* 23, no. 2: 171–90.

Lam, W. S. E., and D. S. Warriner. 2012. "Transnationalism and Literacy: Investigating the Mobility of People, Language, Texts and Practices in Contexts of Migration." *Reading Research Quarterly* 47, no. 2: 191–215.

Lave, J., and E. Wenger. 1991. *Situated Learning: Legitimate Peripheral Participation.* Cambridge: Cambridge University Press.

Leco, C. 2006. "Educación binacional: Purépechas en escuelas bilingües México-Estados Unidos." *CIMEXUS* 1, no. 1: 23–38. http://cimexus.umich.mx/index.php/cim1/issue/view/3.

Lemke, J. L. 1997. "Cognition, Context, and Learning: A Social Semiotic Perspective." In *Situated Cognition Theory: Social, Neurological, and Semiotic Perspectives,* edited by D. Kirshner and J. A. Whitson, 37–55. New York: Routledge.

Lemke, J. L. 2001. "Articulating Communities: Sociocultural Perspectives on Science Education." *Journal of Research in Science Teaching* 38, no. 3: 296–316.

Levitt, P. 2001. "Transnational Migration: Taking Stock and Future Directions." *Global Networks* 1, no. 3: 195–216.

Levitt, P., and N. Glick Schiller. 2004. "Conceptualizing Simultaneity: A Transnational Social Field Perspective on Society." *International Migration Review* 38, no. 3: 1002–39.

Lewis, G., B. Jones, and C. Baker. 2012. "Translanguaging: Developing its Conceptualization and Contextualization." *Educational Research and Evaluation* 18, no. 7: 655–70.

Lindholm-Leary, K. 2001. *Dual Language Education*. Avon, UK: Multilingual Matters.

Lindholm-Leary, K., and F. Genesee. 2014. "Student Outcomes in One-Way and Two-Way Immersion and Indigenous Language Education." *Journal of Immersion and Content-Based Language Education* 2, no. 2: 165–80.

Longwell-Grice, H., and E. McIntyre. 2006. "Addressing Goals of School and Community: Lessons from a Family Literacy Program." *School Community Journal* 16, no. 2: 115–31.

Lorey, D. 1999. *The U.S.-Mexican Border in the Twentieth Century*. Wilmington, Del.: Scholarly Sources.

Lotherington, H., and J. Jenson. 2011. "Teaching Multimodal and Digital Literacy in L2 Settings: New Literacies, New Basics, New Pedagogies." *Annual Review of Applied Linguistics* 31:226–46.

Lugo, A. 2008. *Fragmented Lives, Assembled Parts: Culture, Capitalism, and Conquest at the U.S.-Mexico Border*. Austin: University of Texas Press.

Machado-Casas, M. 2009. "The Politics of Organic Phylogeny: The Art of Parenting and Surviving as Transnational Multilingual Latino Indigenous Immigrants in the U.S." *High School Journal* 92, no. 4: 82–99.

Mangual, A., S. Suh, and M. Byrnes. 2015. "Co-constructing Beliefs About Parental Involvement: Rehearsals and Reflections in a Family Literacy Program." *Linguistics and Education* 31:44–58.

Marquez Kiyama, J. 2010. "College Aspirations and Limitations: The Role of Educational Ideologies and Funds of Knowledge in Mexican American Families." *American Educational Research Journal* 47, no. 2: 330–56.

Martín-Beltrán, M. 2014. "'What Do You Want to Say?' How Adolescents Use Translanguaging to Expand Learning Opportunities." *International Journal of Multilingual Research* 8:208–30.

Martínez, R. A. 2010. "Spanglish as Literacy Tool: Toward an Understanding of the Potential Role of Spanish-English Code-Switching in the Development of Academic Literacy." *Research in the Teaching of English* 45, no. 2: 124–49.

Martínez-Montoya, J. A., and V. Garza-Almanza. 2013. "Impacto social de las narco-ejecuciones en Ciudad Juárez, México, 2008–2011 Evaluación Preliminar." *Cultura Científica y Tecnología* 51.

Martínez-Roldán, C., and P. Sayer. 2006. "Reading Through Linguistic Borderlands: Latino Students' Transactions with Narrative Texts." *Journal of Early Childhood Literacy* 6, no. 3: 293–322.

Martin-Jones, M., and K. Jones, eds. 2000. *Multilingual Literacies: Reading and Writing Different Worlds*. Philadelphia: John Benjamins.

Martin-Jones, M., and S. Saxena. 2003. "Bilingual Resources and 'Funds of Knowledge' for Teaching and Learning in Multi-ethnic Classrooms in Britain." *International Journal of Bilingual Education and Bilingualism* 6, nos. 3–4: 267–82.

Maturana, H., and F. Varela. 1998. *The Tree of Knowledge: The Biological Roots of Human Understanding*. Revised edition. Boston: Shambdala.

McLean, C. A. 2010. "A Space Called Home: An Immigrant Adolescent's Digital Literacy Practices." *Journal of Adolescent and Adult Literacy* 54:13–22. DOI: 10.1598/JAAL.54.1.2.

McGee, K. 2015. "These El Paso Students Travel Back and Forth Across the Border Daily to Attend School." Austin: National Public Radio (November 5). http://kut.org/.

Medina, C. 2010. "'Reading Across Communities' in Biliteracy Practices: Examining Translocal Discourses and Cultural Flows in Literature Discussions." *Reading Research Quarterly* 45, no. 1: 40–60.

Mein, E., and A. Esquinca. 2017. "The Role of Bilingualism in Shaping Engineering Literacies and Identities." *Theory into Practice* 56, no.4: 282–90. DOI: 10.1080/00405841.2017.1350494.

Michaelsen, S., and S. C. Shershow. 2007. "Rethinking Border Thinking." *South Atlantic Quarterly* 106, no. 1: 39–60.

Mignolo, W. D. 2000. *Local Histories/Global Designs*. Princeton, N.J.: Princeton University Press.

Mignolo, W. D. 2011. "Geopolitics of Sensing and Knowing: On (De)coloniality, Border Thinking and Epistemic Disobedience." *Postcolonial Studies* 3:273–83.

Mignolo, W. D., and M. V. Tlostanova. 2006. "Theorizing from the Borders: Shifting to Geo- and Body-Politics of Knowledge." *European Journal of Social Theory* 9, no. 2: 205–21.

Milner, R. 2007. "Race, Culture, and Researcher Positionality: Working Through Dangers Seen, Unseen, and Unforeseen." *Educational Researcher* 36, no. 7: 388–400.

Moje, E. B. 1995. "Talking About Science: An Interpretation of the Effects of Teacher Talk in a High School Science Classroom." *Journal of Research in Science Teaching* 32, no. 4: 349–71.

Moje, E. B., K. McIntosh Ciechanowski, L. Kramer, L. Ellis, R. Carrillo, and T. Collazo. 2004. "Working Toward Third Space in Content Area Literacy: An Examination of Everyday Funds of Knowledge and Discourse." *Reading Research Quarterly* 39, no. 1: 38–70.

Moje, E. B., M. Overby, N. Tysvaer, and K. Morris. 2008. "The Complex World of Adolescent Literacy: Myths, Motivations, and Mysteries." *Harvard Educational Review* 78, no. 1: 107–54.

Moll, L. 2014. *L. S. Vygotsky and Education*. New York: Routledge.

Moll, L., C. Amanti, D. Neff, and N. González. 1992. "Funds of Knowledge for Teaching: Using a Qualitative Approach to Connect Homes and Classrooms." *Theory into Practice* 31, no. 2: 132–41.

Moll, L., and J. Greenberg. 1990. "Creating Zones of Possibilities: Combining Social Contexts for Instruction." In *Vygotsky and Education: Instructional Implications and Applications of Sociohistorical Psychology*, edited by L. Moll, 319–48. Cambridge: Cambridge University Press.

Monty, R. 2015. "Everyday Borders of Transnational Students: Composing Place and Space with Mobile Technology, Social Media, and Multimodality." *Computers and Composition* 38:126–39.

Morgan, D. 1988. *Focus Groups as Qualitative Research*. Newbury Park, Calif.: Sage.

Moya, E., and M. Lusk. 2009. "Tuberculosis and Stigma. Two Case Studies in El Paso, Texas, and Ciudad Juárez, Mexico." *Professional Development: The International Journal of Continuing Social Work Education* 12, no. 3: 48–58.

National Center for Education Statistics. 2010. "Trends in High School Dropout and Completion Rates in the United States: 1972–2008." *NCES 2011–012*. Washington, D.C.: National Center for Education Statistics. http://nces.ed.gov/pubs2011/dropout08.

New London Group. 1996. "A Pedagogy of Multiliteracies: Designing Social Futures." *Harvard Educational Review* 66, no. 1: 59–92.

New London Group. 2000. "A Pedagogy of Multiliteracies: Designing Social Futures." In *Multiliteracies: Literacy Learning and the Design of Social Futures*, edited by B. Cope and M. Kalantzis, 9–37. New York: Routledge.

Noguera, P. A. 2012. "Saving Black and Latino Boys." *Phi Delta Kappan* 9, no. 5: 8.

Ochs, E., and L. Capps. 1996. "Narrating the Self." *Annual Review of Anthropology* 25:19–43.

Olmedo, I. 2003. "Language Mediation Among Emergent Bilingual Children." *Linguistics and Education* 14, no. 2: 143–62.

Orellana, M. F. 2009. *Translating Childhoods: Immigrant Youth, Language, and Culture*. New Brunswick, N.J.: Rutgers University Press.

Orellana, M. F. 2016. *Immigrant Children in Transcultural Spaces*. New York: Routledge.

Orellana, M. F., B. Thorne, A. Chee, and W. S. E. Lam. 2001. "Transnational Childhoods: The Participation of Children in Processes of Family Migration." *Social Problems* 48, no. 4: 572–91.

Oropeza, M. V., M. M. Varghese, and Y. Kanno. 2010. "Linguistic Minority Students in Higher Education: Using, Resisting, and Negotiating Multiple Labels." *Equity and Excellence in Education* 43, no. 2: 216–31.

Oughton, H. 2009. "A Willing Suspension of Disbelief? 'Contexts' and Recontextualisation in Adult Numeracy Classrooms." *Adults Learning Mathematics Journal* 4, no. 1 (February 2009). http://www.alm-online.net/images/ALM/journals/almij -volume4_1_mar2009.pdf.

Palmer, D. 2011. "The Discourse of Transition: Teachers' Language Ideologies Within Transitional Bilingual Education Programs." *International Multilingual Research Journal* 5, no. 2: 103–22.

Palmer, D. K., R. A. Martinez, S. G. Mateus, and K. Henderson. 2014. "Reframing the Debate on Language Separation: Toward a Vision for Translanguaging Pedagogies in the Dual Language Classroom." *Modern Language Journal* 98, no. 3: 757–72.

Patton, M. Q. 2002. *Qualitative Research and Evaluation Methods.* 3rd ed. Thousand Oaks, Calif.: Sage.

Pennycook, A. 2007. "The Rotation Gets Thick. The Constraints Get Thin: Creativity, Recontextualization, and Difference." *Applied Linguistics* 28, no. 4: 579–96.

Pennycook, A. 2010. *Language as a Local Practice.* London: Routledge.

Pennycook, A., and E. Otsuji. 2014. "Market Lingos and Metrolingua Francas." *International Multilingual Research Journal* 8, no. 4: 255–70.

Pennycook, A., and E. Otsuji. 2015. *Metrolingualism: Language in the City.* New York: Routledge.

Pérez Huber, L. 2009. "Challenging Racist Nativist Framing: Acknowledging the Community Cultural Wealth of Undocumented Chicana College Students to Reframe the Immigration Debate." *Harvard Educational Review* 79, no. 4: 704–30.

Petrón, M. 2003. *I'm Bien Pocha: Transnational Teachers of English in Mexico.* Unpublished dissertation, University of Texas at Austin.

Petrón, M. 2009. "Transnational Teachers of English in Mexico." *High School Journal* 92, no. 4: 115–28.

Petrón, M., and B. Greybeck. 2014. "Borderlands Epistemologies and the Transnational Experience." *Gist: Education and Learning Research Journal* 8:137–55. https://dialnet.unirioja.es/servlet/articulo?codigo=4774806.

Pirbhai-Illich, F. 2010. "Aboriginal Students Engaging and Struggling with Critical Multiliteracies." *Journal of Adolescent and Adult Literacy* 54, no. 4: 257–66.

Portes, A., L. E. Guarnizo, and P. Landolt. 1999. "The Study of Transnationalism: Pitfalls and Promise of an Emergent Research Field." *Ethnic and Racial Studies* 22, no. 2: 217–37.

Potowski, K. 2007. *Language and Identity in a Dual Language Immersion School.* Clevedon, UK: Multilingual Matters.

Poyago-Theotoky, J., and A. Tampieri. 2016. "University Competition and Transnational Education: The Choice of Branch Campus." *B.E. Journal of Theoretical Economics* 16, no. 2: 739–66. DOI: 10.1515/bejte-2015-0052.

Poza, L. 2016. "The Language of 'Ciencia': Translanguaging and Learning in a Bilingual Science Classroom." *International Journal of Bilingual Education and Bilingualism* 21, no. 1: 1–19. https://doi.org/10.1080/13670050.2015.1125849.

Prickett, J., N. Negi, and L. Gómez. 2012. "Return Migration in the Transnational Context: The Case of Male Transmigrants from Petlalcingo, Mexico." *Journal of Ethnic and Cultural Diversity in Social Work* 21, no. 1: 55–73.

Purcell-Gates, V. 2013. "Literacy Worlds of Children of Migrant Farmworker Communities Participating in a Migrant Head Start Program." *Teaching of English* 48, no. 1: 68–97.

Quijano, A. 2014. "Colonialidad del poder, eurocentrismo y América Latina." In *Cuestiones y horizontes: De la dependencia histórico-estructural a la colonialidad/descolonialidad del poder*, by Aníbal Quijano, 777–832. Ciudad Autónoma de Buenos Aires: CLACSO. http://biblioteca.clacso.edu.ar/clacso/se/20140424014720/Cuestionesyhorizontes.pdf.

Reardon, S. F., E. Grewal, D. Kalogrides, and E. Greenberg. 2012. "Brown Fades: The End of Court-Ordered School Desegregation and the Resegregation of American Public Schools." *Journal of Policy Analysis and Management* 31, no. 4: 876–904.

Relaño Pastor, A. M. 2007. "On Border Identities: Transfronterizo Students in San Diego." *Diskurs Kindheits-und Jugendforschung Heft* 2, no. 3: 263–77.

Relaño Pastor, A. M. 2008. "Competing Language Ideologies in a Bilingual/Bicultural After-School Program in Southern California." *Journal of Latinos and Education* 7, no. 1: 4–24.

Reyes, I., and P. Azuara. 2008. "Emergent Biliteracy in Young Mexican Immigrant Children." *Reading Research Quarterly* 43, no. 4: 374–98. DOI: 10.1598/RRQ.43.4.4.

Reyes S. A., and T. L. Vallone. 2007. "Toward an Expanded Understanding of Two-Way Bilingual Immersion Education: Constructing Identity Through a Critical, Additive Bilingual/Bicultural Pedagogy." *Multicultural Perspectives* 9, no. 3: 3–11.

Reza-López, E., L. Huerta Charles, and L. V. Reyes. 2014. "Nepantlera Pedagogy: An Axiological Posture for Preparing Critically Conscious Teachers in the Borderlands." *Journal of Latinos and Education* 13, no. 2: 107–19.

Richardson Bruna, K. 2007. "Traveling Tags: The Informal Literacies of Mexican Newcomers in and out of the Classroom." *Linguistics and Education* 18, nos. 3–4: 232–57.

Rincón, A. 2009. "Undocumented Immigrants and Higher Education: Si se puede." *Harvard Educational Review* 79:777–79.

Rivard, L. 1994. "A Review of Writing to Learn in Science: Implications for Practice and Research." *Journal of Research in Science Teaching* 31, no. 9: 969–83.

Rivard, L., and S. Straw. 2000. "The Effect of Talk and Writing on Learning Science: An Exploratory Study." *Science Education* 84:566–93.

Robertson, S. 2013. *Transnational Student-Migrants and the State: The Education-Migration Nexus*. New York: Palgrave Macmillan.

Rockwell, E. 2018. "Entre la vida y los libros: Prácticas de Lectura en las Escuelas de la Malintzi a Principios del Siglo XX." In *Vivir entre escuelas y relatos: Antología esencial*, by Elsie Rockwell, 601–30. Ciudad Autónoma de Buenos Aires: CLACSO. http://biblioteca.clacso.edu.ar/clacso/se/20180223024326/Antologia_Elsie_Rockwell.pdf.

Rogoff, B. 1990. *Apprenticeship in Thinking: Cognitive Development in Social Context*. New York: Oxford University Press.

Rogoff, B., C. Goodman Turkanis, and L. Bartlett. 2001. *Learning Together: Children and Adults in a School Community*. New York: Oxford University Press.

Romo, H., and B. Pérez. 2012. "Institutional and Structural Barriers to Latino/a Achievement." *Journal of the Association of Mexican American Educators* 6, no. 3: 22–29.

Rosen, J. D., and R. Z. Martinez. 2015. "La guerra contra el narcotráfico en México: Una guerra perdida." *Reflexiones* 94, no. 1: 153–68.

Rowsell, J., M. Prinsloo, and Z. Zhang. 2012. "Socializing the Digital: Taking Emic Perspectives on Digital Domains." *Language and Literacy* 14, no. 2: 1–5.

Rubin, H., and I. Rubin. 1995. *Qualitative Interviewing: The Art of Hearing Data*. Thousand Oaks, Calif.: Sage.

Rumbaut, R. G. 2009. "A Language Graveyard? The Evolution of Language Competencies, Preferences and Use Among Young Adult Children of Immigrants." In *The Education of Language Minority Immigrants in the United States*, edited by T. G. Wiley, J. S. Lee, and R. Rumberger, 35–71. Bristol, UK: Multilingual Matters.

Ryan, G., and R. Bernard. 2000. "Data Management and Analysis Methods." In *Handbook of Qualitative Research*, edited by N. Denzin and Y. Lincoln, 769–802. Thousand Oaks, Calif.: Sage.

Sánchez, P. 2007. "Cultural Authenticity and Transnational Latina Youth: Constructing a Meta-Narrative Across Borders." *Linguistics and Education* 18, nos. 3–4: 489–517.

Sánchez, P. 2008. "Transnational Students." In *Encyclopedia of Bilingual Education*, edited by J. M. González, 857–60. Thousand Oaks, Calif.: Sage.

Sánchez, P., and M. Machado-Casas. 2009. "Introduction: At the Intersection of Transnationalism, Latina/o Immigrants and Education." *High School Journal* 92, no. 4: 3–15.

Sánchez, J., and V. Zúñiga. 2010. "Trayectorias de los alumnos transnacionales en México: Propuesta intercultural de atención educativa." *Trayectorias* 12, no. 30: 5–23. http://www.redalyc.org/pdf/607/60713488002.pdf.

Sandoval, W., and K. Millwood. 2005. "The Quality of Students' Use of Evidence in Written Scientific Explanations." *Cognition and Instruction* 23, no. 1: 23–55.

Sayer, P. 2013. "Translanguaging, TexMex, and Bilingual Pedagogy: Emergent Bilinguals Learning Through the Vernacular." *TESOL Quarterly* 47, no. 1: 63–87.

Schleppegrell, M. 2004. *The Language of Schooling: A Functional Linguistics Perspective*. Mahwah, N.J.: Lawrence Erlbaum.

Schmidt, S., and C. Spector. 2015. *El crimen autorizado de México: Un paradigma para explicar la violencia*. Madrid: Fundación Baltazar Garzón.

Seiler, G. 2001. "Reversing the 'Standard' Direction: Science Emerging from the Lives of African American Students." *Journal of Research in Science Teaching* 38, no. 9: 1000–1014.

Shepardson, D., and S. Britsch. 2001. "The Role of Children's Journals in Elementary School Science Activities." *Journal of Research in Science Teaching* 38, no. 1: 43–69.

Skerrett, A. 2015. *Teaching Transnational Youth: Literacy and Education Is a Changing World*. New York: Teachers College Press.

Sleeter, C. 2005. *Un-Standardizing Curriculum: Multicultural Teaching in the Standards-Based Classroom*. New York: Teachers College Press.

Smagorinsky, P. 2011. *Vygotsky and Literacy Research: A Methodological Framework*. Boston: Sense.

Smith, M. P. 1994. "Can You Imagine? Transnational Migration and the Globalization of Grassroots Politics." *Social Text* 39:15–33.

Smith, M. P., and L. E. Guarnizo, eds. 1998. *Transnationalism from Below*. New Brunswick, N.J.: Transaction Publishers.

Smith, P., and L. Murillo. 2012. "Researching Transfronterizo Literacies in Texas Border Colonias." *International Journal of Bilingual Education and Bilingualism* 15, no. 6: 635–51.

Solórzano, D. G., and T. J. Yosso. 2001. "Critical Race and LatCrit Theory and Method: Counter-storytelling; Chicana and Chicano Graduate School Experiences." *International Journal of Qualitative Studies in Education* 14, no. 4: 471–95.

Soong, H. 2015. *Transnational Students and Mobility: Lived Experiences of Migration*. New York: Routledge.

Sparrow, T. 2015. "Mexican Children Cross Texas Border to Attend School." *BBC News Magazine*, January 31. http://www.bbc.com/news/magazine-31051630.

Spence, L. 2009. "Developing Multiple Literacies in a Website Project." *Reading Teacher* 62, no. 7: 592–97.

Staudt, K., C. M. Fuentes, and J. Monárrez Fragoso. 2010. *Cities and Citizenship at the U.S.-Mexico Border: The Paso del Norte Metropolitan Region*. New York: Palgrave Macmillan.

Stephen, L. 2007. *Transborder Lives: Indigenous Oaxacans in Mexico, California, and Oregon*. Durham, N.C.: Duke University Press.

Stewart, D., and P. Shamdasani. 1990. *Focus Groups: Theory and Practice*. Newbury Park, Calif.: Sage.

Stewart, M. A. 2014. "Social Networking, Workplace, and Entertainment Literacies: The Out-of-School Literate Lives of Newcomer Latina/o Adolescents." *Reading Research Quarterly* 49, no. 4: 365–69.

Street, B. 1984. *Literacy in Theory and Practice*. Cambridge: Cambridge University Press.

Street, B. 1993. *Cross-Cultural Approaches to Literacy*. Cambridge: Cambridge University Press.

Street, B. 1994. "What Is Meant by 'Local Literacies'?" *Language and Education* 8, nos. 1–2: 9–17.

Stromquist, N. P. 2012. "The Educational Experience of Hispanic Immigrants in the United States: Integration Through Marginalization." *Race, Ethnicity and Education* 15, no. 2: 195–221.

Swain, M. 2000. "The Output Hypothesis and Beyond: Mediating Acquisition Through Collaborative Dialogue." In *Sociocultural Theory and Second Language Learning*, edited by J. Lantolf, 97–114. Oxford: Oxford University Press.

Tackvic, C. 2012. "Digital Storytelling: Using Technology to Spark Creativity." *Educational Forum* 76: 426–29.

Tharp, R., and R. Gallimore. 1988. *Rousing Minds to Life: Teaching, Learning and Schooling in Social Context*. New York: Cambridge University Press.

Tharp, R., and R. Gallimore. 1991. *The Instructional Conversation: Teaching and Learning in Social Activity*. Washington, D.C.: National Center for Research on Cultural Diversity and Second Language Learning.

Thomas, W. P., and V. P. Collier. 2002. "A National Study of School Effectiveness for Language Minority Students' Long-Term Academic Achievement." Santa Cruz: Center for Research on Education, Diversity and Excellence, University of California, Santa Cruz. http://www.thomasandcollier.com/assets/2002_thomas -and-collier_2002-final-report.pdf.

Torrente, L. 2013. "El español y las políticas lingüísticas en Estados Unidos: El caso de los estados fronterizos con México." *Cuadernos de Lingüística Hispánica* 22:47–58.

Tudge, J. 2001. "Vygotsky, the Zone of Proximal Development, and Peer Collaboration: Implications for Classroom Practice." In *Vygotsky and Education: Instructional Implications of Sociohistorical Psychology*, edited by L. Moll, 155–74. New York: Cambridge University Press.

Trueba, E. 2004. *The New Americans: Immigrants and Transnationals at Work*. New York: Rowman and Littlefield.

Valdés, G. 1997. "Dual-Language Immersion Programs: A Cautionary Note Concerning the Education of Language-Minority Students." *Harvard Educational Review* 67, no. 3: 391–430.

Valdés, G. 2003. *Expanding Definitions of Giftedness: The Case of Young Interpreters from Immigrant Communities*. Mahwah, N.J.: Lawrence Erlbaum.

Valdez, V. E., J. A. Freire, and M. G. Delavan. 2016. "The Gentrification of Dual Language Education." *Urban Review* 48, no. 4: 601–27.

Valencia, N. 2015. "After Years of Violence and Death, 'Life Is Back' in Juárez." *CNN .com*. http://www.cnn.com/2015/04/21/americas/mexico-ciudad-juarez-tourism /index.html.

Valencia, R. 1997. *The Evolution of Deficit Thinking: Educational Thought and Practice*. Bristol, Pa.: Falmer.

Valenzuela, A. 1999. *Subtractive Schooling: U.S.-Mexican Youth and the Politics of Caring*. Albany: State University of New York Press.

Valenzuela Arce, J. M. 2009. *El futuro ya se fue: Socioantropología de los jóvenes en la modernidad*. Mexico: El Colegio de la Frontera Norte.

Vásquez, O. 2006. "Cross-National Explorations of Sociocultural Research on Learning." *Review of Research in Education* 30:33–64.

Vázquez, J., and M. de L. Hernández. 2014. "Profesores de educación básica y diseño de herramientas para alumnos transnacionales en Tlaxcala." *Región y Sociedad* 26, no. 61: 201–33. http://www.redalyc.org/pdf/102/10232573006.pdf.

Vázquez, R. 2011. "Translation as Erasure: Thoughts on Modernity's Epistemic Violence." *Journal of Historical Sociology* 24, no. 1: 27–44.

Vélez-Ibáñez, C. 1996. *Border Visions: Mexican Cultures of the Southwest*. Tucson: University of Arizona Press.

Vélez-Ibáñez, C. 2017. "Continuity and Contiguity of the Southwest North American Region. The Dynamics of a Common Political Ecology." In *The U.S.-Mexico Transborder Region: Cultural Dynamics and Historical Interactions*, edited by C. Velez-Ibañez and J. Heyman, 11–43. Tucson: University of Arizona Press.

Vélez-Ibáñez, C., and J. Greenberg. 1992. "Formation and Transformation of Funds of Knowledge Among U.S.-Mexican Households." *Anthropology and Education Quarterly* 23, no. 4: 313–35.

Vertovec, S. 2007. "Super-Diversity and Its Implications." *Ethnic and Racial Studies* 30, no. 6: 1024–54.

Vila, P. 2000. *Crossing Borders, Reinforcing Borders*. Austin: University of Texas Press.

Vila, P. 2003. *Ethnography at the Border*. Minneapolis: University of Minnesota Press.

Vila, P. 2005. *Border Identifications: Narratives of Religion, Gender, and Class on the U.S.-Mexico Border*. Austin: University of Texas Press.

Villalpando, O., and D. Solórzano. 2005. "The Role of Culture in College Preparation Programs: A Review of the Literature." In *Preparing for College: Nine Elements of Effective Outreach*, edited by W. Tierney, Z. Corwin, and J. Kolyar, 13–28. Albany: State University of New York Press.

Villenas, S. 1996. "The Colonizer/Colonized Chicana Ethnographer: Identity, Marginalization, and Co-optation in the Field." *Harvard Educational Review* 66, no. 4: 711–31.

Villenas, S., and M. Moreno. 2001. "To Valerse por si Misma Between Race, Capitalism, and Patriarchy: Latina Mother/Daughter Pedagogies in North Carolina." *International Journal of Qualitative Studies in Education* 14, no. 5: 671–87.

Viren, S. 2007. "Mexican Children Cross Border to Go to School." *Houston Chronicle*, April 29. http://www.chron.com/opinion/outlook/article/Mexican-children -cross-border-to-go-to-school-1807611.php.

Wallace, T. M. 2016. "English Spoken Here? To What Extent Are Transnational EFL Students Motivated to Speak English Outside the Classroom?" *Journal of Further and Higher Education* 40, no. 2: 227–46.

Walqui, A., and L. van Lier. 2010. *Scaffolding the Academic Success of Adolescent English Language Learners: A Pedagogy of Promise.* San Francisco: WestEd.

Warren, B., C. Ballenger, M. Ogonowski, A. S. Rosebery, and J. Hudicourt-Barnes. 2001. "Rethinking Diversity in Learning Science: The Logic of Everyday Sense-Making." *Journal of Research in Science Teaching* 38, no. 5: 529–52.

Wertsch, J. V. 1991. *Voices of the Mind: A Sociocultural Approach to Mediated Action.* Cambridge: Harvard University Press.

Whiteside, A. 2006. "Research on Transnational Yucatec Maya-Speakers Negotiating Multilingual California." *Journal of Applied Linguistics* 3, no. 1: 103–12.

Wilber, D. 2012. "Trying to Get Ahead of the Curve: Raising and Understanding Current Themes in New Literacies." *Educational Forum* 76: 406–11.

Wilkins, S., and J. Urbanovic. 2014. "English as the Lingua Franca in Transnational Higher Education: Motives and Prospects of Institutions That Teach in Languages Other Than English." *Journal of Studies in International Education* 18, no. 5: 405–25.

Wolf, D. 2002. "There's No Place Like 'Home': Emotional Transnationalism and the Struggles of Second-Generation Filipinos." In *The Changing Face of Home: The Transnational Lives of the Second Generation*, edited by P. Levitt and M. C. Waters, 255–94. New York: Russell Sage Foundation.

Wood, D., J. S. Bruner, and G. Ross. 1976. "The Role of Tutoring in Problem Solving." *Journal of Child Psychology and Psychiatry* 17:89–100.

Yosso, T. 2002. "Toward a Critical Race Curriculum." *Equity and Excellence in Education* 35, no. 2: 93–107.

Yosso, T. 2005. "Whose Culture Has Capital? A Critical Race Theory Discussion of Community Cultural Wealth." *Race Ethnicity and Education* 8, no. 1: 69–91.

Yosso, T. 2006. *Critical Race Counterstories Along the Chicana/Chicano Educational Pipeline.* New York: Taylor and Francis.

Zavala, V., M. Murcia, and P. Ames, eds. 2004. *Escritura y sociedad: Nuevas perspectivas teóricas y etnográficas*, 367–88. Lima: Red para el Desarrollo de las Ciencias Sociales en el Perú.

Zentella, A. C. 2009. *Transfronterizo Talk: Conflicting Constructions of Bilingualism Among U.S.-Mexico Border Crossing College Students*. Video. Swarthmore, Pa.: Swarthmore College. https://www.youtube.com/watch?v=VvrO1jHkcUg.

Zipin, L. 2009. "Dark Funds of Knowledge, Deep Funds of Pedagogy: Exploring Boundaries Between Lifeworlds and Schools." *Discourse: Studies in the Cultural Politics of Education* 30, no. 3: 317–31.

Zúñiga, V. 2013. "Migrantes internacionales en las escuelas mexicanas: Desafíos actuales y futuros de política educativa." *Sinéctica: Revista Electrónica de Educación* 40:1–12. http://www.redalyc.org/articulo.oa?id=99827467009.

Zúñiga, V., and E. Hamann. 2008. "Escuelas nacionales, alumnos transnacionales: La migración México/Estados Unidos como fenómeno escolar." *Estudios Sociológicos* 26, no. 76: 65–85. http://www.redalyc.org/pdf/598/59826103.pdf.

Zúñiga, V., E. Hamann, and J. Sánchez. 2008. *Alumnos transnacionales: Escuelas mexicanas frente a la globalización*. México D.F.: Secretaría de Educación Pública. http://digitalcommons.unl.edu/cgi/viewcontent.cgi?article=1095&context=teachlearnfacpub.

Index

About the Authors

María Teresa de la Piedra is an associate professor of bilingual education at the University of Texas at El Paso. Her research centers on language and literacy practices in bilingual communities on the U.S.-Mexico border and in Latin America.

Blanca Araujo is an associate professor and director of the Office of Teacher Candidate Preparation at New Mexico State University. Her most recent book is *Multicultural Education: A Renewed Paradigm of Transformation and Call to Action*.

Alberto Esquinca is an associate professor of bilingual education at the University of Texas at El Paso. His research centers on the bilingual and biliterate practices and identities of Latinxs, particularly in STEM contexts.